Machine Learning: The Game Show

John Giordani

Published by John Giordani, 2025.

Machine Learning: The Game Show

Compete Against AI for Fame, Fortune, and Your Cereal's Last Puzzle Piece

Dr. John Giordani

MACHINE LEARNING: THE GAME SHOW

First edition. April 28, 2025.

ISBN: 979-8231582693

Written by John Giordani.

ACKNOWLEDGMENTS

Writing this book has been a journey unlike any other. It's been a blend of inspiration, perseverance, and collaboration. As I reflect on the process, I feel compelled to acknowledge the unique role that modern technology played in shaping this work. Throughout the months (or years) of research, drafting, and refining, I embraced the tools available to me in this digital age, including generative artificial intelligence.

These AI tools acted as collaborators in the truest sense: they helped me brainstorm ideas, untangle complex sentences, and occasionally even suggested turns of phrase when my own creativity hit a wall. Like a compass guiding a traveler, they provided direction when I felt stuck, allowing me to focus on the heart of this project - the ideas, stories, and insights that I alone could bring to life.

Yet, let me be clear: this book remains deeply personal. Every chapter, every argument, and every narrative thread is rooted in my own experiences, values, and vision. The AI tools I used were not authors but aids, much like a library, a trusted editor, or a conversation with a colleague. They helped me refine and articulate my thoughts, but they did not generate the soul of this work. That belongs entirely to the human hands and mind behind these pages.

To those who might question the role of technology in creative endeavors, I offer this: innovation has always shaped how we create, from the printing press to the word processor. What matters is not the tools we use but how we wield them. In my case, AI became a partner in efficiency, not a replacement for authenticity. It allowed me to iterate faster, think more critically, and push past the friction that often accompanies the writing process.

I am grateful for the advancements that made this book possible and equally thankful to the mentors, friends, and readers who supported me along the way. Together, human and machine, we've woven something I am proud to share.

Thank you for joining me on this journey. I hope these pages resonate with you as deeply as the process of creating them has shaped me.

Chapter 1

Welcome to the Game Show

The Concept of Competition in the Age of Artificial Intelligence

As we stand on the precipice of the AI revolution, the word "competition" takes on a whole new level of significance. Picture a grand arena, filled with eager spectators, where humans and machines go head-to-head in a contest not just of wit, but of survival. Don't get me wrong - there's a certain primordial thrill in battling it out against an intelligent entity. It brings me back to my childhood; remember the giddy anxiety of declaring challenges to friends, only for them to one-up you with a 'guess the number' game that relied on sheer luck? Ah, those were simple days before the machines showed up at our doorstep with their silicon minds and limitless processing power. Today, competition with AI is akin to a game show where the stakes include fame and fortune and bragging rights over your breakfast cereal, where even breakfast becomes a part of the victory celebration.

In this fantastical realm where brain power meets machine prowess, the very essence of competition evolves. Gone are the days when winning was merely about human intellect. Now, it's a chess match against a supercomputer that can calculate moves faster than I can find my car keys. It's exhilarating and, dare I say, slightly intimidating. To complicate matters, we've moved beyond traditional game formats where two people challenge each other to a duel of knowledge over trivia questions. Today's competitions are more complex and layered - think Pictionary with both a human and an AI trying to intuitively guess what the other is drawing, while simultaneously trying to sabotage each other's efforts with mixed media interpretations. Let's be honest, watching an AI try to draw a cat is both hilarious and tragic at the same time.

The concept of competition in the age of AI forces us to reflect on what it truly means to 'win.' Is it snagging the last piece of your favorite cereal's puzzle? Or is it outsmarting a consultative chatbot that keeps reminding you that your probabilities of winning are just statistical glitches? I like to think of winning as a more holistic concept, involving not just the joy of topping the leaderboard against an AI but also realizing we can learn from our digital competitors. If I'm to glean wisdom from an algorithm that assesses my every strategy with cold, calculating precision, shouldn't I also consider the fact that I am essentially competing against my own inclinations to binge-watch cat videos instead?

AI competitions present a unique opportunity for us to get creative. As humans, we have innate advantages like intuition, humor, and the delightful ability to make illogical leaps in reasoning that even the most sophisticated algorithms cannot quite replicate. While an AI might excel at crunching numbers and executing rapid calculations, it lacks the whimsical unpredictability that characterizes human thought. Think about it: who would you rather team up with for a trivia challenge? The machine that insists that "the square root of a banana is a logician," or your good buddy who might use a combination of questionable jokes and conspiracy theories to provide answers? In this multi-faceted tussle, embracing creativity allows us to outmaneuver rigid algorithmic structures with our divergent thinking - a delightful tip-of-the-hat to human ingenuity.

What's most interesting is the idea that with every competition, we allow ourselves a little introspection. Who do we want to be when a machine is staring at us down, calculating our every move? Obviously, I envision myself as a cunning strategist, inspired by comic book characters, wielding a pencil and an elbow grease-dusted brain like a successful underdog. But let's not forget, competition also leads to collaboration. As boundaries blur between human and AI capabilities, entering into a symbiotic relationship means we learn and grow in ways we could only dream of before.

Ultimately, competing against AI is much like wrestling a particularly slippery eel; it's unpredictable and, at times, outright absurd, but oh, how entertaining it is! As we embark on this journey together, I invite you to embrace the notion that competition today is less about defeating an opponent and more about newly discovered perspectives, shared laughter, and those priceless moments when we catch an algorithm making a ludicrous error. Through AI, we not only confront our capabilities but also sprinkle a dash of humor into our interactions with technology. So, buckle up and prepare to dive into the charmingly chaotic world of man vs. machine, where reporting a win might just come down to who enjoys their breakfast cereal more.

Why Game Shows? A Unique Framework for Understanding AI

Why game shows, you may ask? In a world where algorithms are revered as intellectual titans capable of devouring data and predicting outcomes, one might ponder if tossing them into the realm of entertaining competitions is merely whimsical folly. But let me assure you, the marriage of artificial intelligence and game shows is a match made in the land of innovation - and trust me, it's not just because I enjoy a good laugh while contemplating the future of humanity! Game shows really provide a unique framework for understanding AI, packed with all the fun and absurdity you could wish for and certainly more colorful than parsing code in a darkened room.

At their core, game shows are structured chaos - glitzy stages filled with buzzer-happy contestants, confounding trivia, and of course, gleaming prizes that spark immediate desire. Isn't it a little reminiscent of the world we find ourselves in with AI? Here we are, humans grappling with the nuances of technology so advanced we can barely fathom it, and what better way to dissect these complexities than to treat them like the challenges on a game show? Think about it: contestants play their hearts out for rewards as mundane as a microwave oven or as grand as a brand-new car; similarly, we grapple with algorithms that promise insights into our daily lives, whether it's predicting our next binge-watch or influencing the brands we buy. Yet there, too, lurks that persistent question: are we playing against them, or with them?

Another delightful aspect of game shows is their ability to boil down complicated abilities into bite-sized chunks of entertainment. This perspective is crucial when considering AI and its intricacies. When we think of AI, we tend to conjure images of cold computations and sinister plots reminiscent of bad sci-fi movies. But game shows are about presenting knowledge in playful, digestible forms, much like teaching a child to eat their veggies by hiding them in mac and cheese. By framing AI in this ludicrous format, we can better grasp its complexities while sharing a few hearty laughs along the way. It's like saying, "Who needs a computer science degree when you can just participate in a lively trivia segment and walk away corrupted by AI knowledge?"

And let's not forget the human touch! Game shows thrive on our love for competition, camaraderie, and the amusement that arises from watching our neighbors, friends, or even a bewildered robot flail over jaw-dropping answers. Just visualizing a robot vending machine trying valiantly to understand the nuances of sarcasm in "Who's more intelligent, a squirrel or Albert Einstein?" is comedic gold and highlights the essential human element even in the harshest of algorithmic realms. After all, the best learning comes from shared experiences, and there's nothing more entertaining than watching a computerized opponent try to comprehend how I can strategically outwit an expertly programmed algorithm with nothing but the power of a pun.

Game shows can reveal some underlying truths about our own cognition and decision-making processes. By observing how humans react to abstract questions or challenges presented by AI, we recognize different styles of thinking and how various strategies come into play. Do we stick to gut reactions and grimace in trepidation when calculated algorithms counter us with facts? Do we take a creative detour and introduce some unintended hilarity? The spotlight on contestants provides a live-action metaphor for how humans comprehend and interact with intelligent systems; it's about learning what strategies work and which ones would get us eliminated faster than a contestant yelling, "I said 'Star Wars,' not 'Star Trek'!"

The dizzying pace of a game show creates an environment ripe for true situational learning. Oh, how I marvel at the absurdity of comprehending how my perspectives on AI evolve while someone battles a chatbot on national television over the rights to a secret hideaway in a pile of glittering gold! Laughing together as we witness the absurdities on display can help to demystify AI, transforming the intimidating subject matter into a delightful mishmash of engagement, spontaneity, and overall shenanigans.

On top of that, let's not overlook the heartwarming component of humor and entertainment wrapped in these challenges. Through laughter, we can break down the barriers of fear surrounding AI, transforming panic into playful curiosity. When we incorporate game shows into our understanding of AI, we are really embracing the notion that learning can, and should, be fun. Passing on an essential truth that perhaps light-heartedness can coexist with the wonders of advancing technology. So, the next time you catch yourself pondering the fate of AI and humanity, consider a game show. After all, who knows, it might just win you a lifetime supply of cereal while unraveling the greatest mysteries of AI!

The Role of Humor in Learning About AI

When it comes to the complex realms of science and technology, particularly the confusing world of artificial intelligence, the role of humor is often underestimated. One might think we should don our serious hats, stir our minds into a froth of intellectual rigor, and dive into the algorithms with the intensity of a caffeinated octopus. But I stand resolutely convinced that humor is the grease that helps the gears of understanding turn smoothly. I would assert that humor is like the chocolate sauce drizzled over the Brussels sprouts of AI comprehension: it makes the whole concoction palatable! By introducing laughter into the learning process, we create an inviting environment that fosters curiosity and reduces the intimidation factor often associated with AI.

AI can feel like an enigmatic puzzle presented by an overly competitive game show host. The terminology alone can send mortals running for the nearest escape route. What does "machine learning" even mean? I can imagine some curious souls raising their hands in confusion, while others, barely able to keep their eyes open, mutter, "Just tell me if it can fetch my remote control!" Herein lies the conundrum: how do we present these intricate ideas without overwhelming our would-be learners? The answer is humor. When I teach about AI, I often crack a few jokes - or perhaps even share the occasional intentional blunder I made while attempting to program a chatbot to understand sarcasm. The ensuing laughter instantly eases the tension and creates a shared space for exploration, encouraging students to engage without fear of judgment.

Take, for example, the classic trope of robots misunderstanding simple human commands. The thought of a robot misinterpreting "Make me a sandwich" as "Make me a sandcastle" is comedic gold that leverages humor to illuminate the complexities of communication between machines and humans. Through relatable anecdotes, we can highlight the shortcomings of AI while simultaneously fostering conversations about how it might improve our understanding. This light-hearted take can demystify fears people have about AI while igniting curiosity. After all, if a robot can't grasp the simplest requests, can we really trust it to control the thermostat, much less run our daily lives?

Humor has an incredible way of fostering resilience. As we explore the inevitable hiccups in AI development - whether it's a self-driving car that mistakenly thinks a rubber duck is a traffic cone or a virtual assistant that seamlessly misunderstands its users - we learn to laugh at the absurdities rather than succumb to defeat. The desire for perfection that often stalks the halls of technology fades as we share these light-hearted moments. Embracing the anomalies rather than shunning them allows us to find common ground, bridging gaps between human effort and technological progress through laughter.

And who could overlook the social bonding that humor facilitates? By sharing a laugh, we dissolve barriers and build camaraderie. It often becomes a shared language, a way for colleagues to communicate without fear of judgment, no longer just engineers and researchers laboring over code, but instead, a band of merry pranksters trying to outwit an unruly machine. When we gather in groups to discuss AI, humor helps transform dry academic discussions into lively debates defined by wit and levity. Picture this: a room filled with the brightest minds, discussing whether AI will ultimately rule us all, and then suddenly someone quips, "Great, but who will program our coffee machines?" The chuckles that ensue remind each of us that, no matter where our pursuits lead us, we're all in this together.

But humor in learning about AI isn't just about entertainment; it also serves as a tool for storytelling. Stories have always driven human understanding, and when we interweave humor with AI narratives, it becomes all the more engaging. For instance, when discussing ethical implications, one could tell a tale of an AI that decides to terminate world peace in favor of building a utopia centered around cupcake factories. The absurdity forces us to reflect on our ethical boundaries while fully entertained - and trust me, no one can resist a cupcake!

Finally, while we are merrily laughing along this journey into the world of AI, it must be noted that humor is also an integral part of fostering creativity. As we joyfully traverse the learning landscape, it encourages us to think outside the proverbial box and push boundaries. The randomness and playfulness of humor open pathways for imaginative problem-solving, allowing us to envision new possibilities rather than getting stuck in the framework of traditional methods. So, who needs to approach AI with the utmost seriousness when we can bounce ideas off one another in a riotous atmosphere of laughter and insight?

Humor is not just an accessory; it's the fabric that weaves through the process of learning about AI, enhancing our experience, and deepening our understanding. So, the next time you find yourself staring at a perplexing line of code or a bewildering AI concept, remember to chuckle. Who knows, that might just clear your mind enough to discover that breakthrough insight hiding behind the laughter. Let's embrace the wit and whimsy of our journeys as we uncover the mysteries of artificial intelligence - one chuckle at a time!

Expectations vs. Reality: Competing with AI

Expectations versus reality! The classic dichotomy illustrates our everyday struggles and dreams - especially when it comes to competing with AI. Imagine walking into a competition radiant with confidence, propelled by visions of flashy victory, while in the background, a sophisticated machine quietly crunches numbers at a speed that makes us mere mortals look like we're stuck in a game of snail races. As we navigate through the complexities of this brave new world, it's essential to unpack those delightful yet often misguided expectations we carry and the sometimes surprising (and occasionally comedic) realities that await us.

On the surface, one might expect that competing against AI would be like a friendly trivia night at a pub, where we can leisurely toss around our menu of facts - all while sipping on craft beer and sharing witty banter with friends. However, the moment you step into the arena - whether it's a virtual game show or a real-life hackathon - you quickly realize that this isn't just a casual tete-a-tete. No, my friends, this is akin to running a marathon against a cheetah that possesses an extraordinary knowledge of obscure facts and can process them faster than you can shout, "I'll take Movie Trivia for 200!" The flurry of information and rapid-fire answers posed by AI can leave even the most seasoned players feeling a touch overmatched, and the thrill of competition might suddenly mutate into what I affectionately refer to as "growing despair."

Now, let's talk about that wistful thought that somehow our exceptional human creativity will save the day. Picture a scene where we're casually schmoozing with our buddies about our victory, envisioning ourselves employing wit, charm, and unyielding intuition to outsmart our digital counterparts. Unfortunately, while creativity comes naturally to us, AI has its own unique way of surprising us. Enter our cheerfully clueless little challenger, the AI that was programmed to understand jokes but somehow thinks a broccoli pun is the key to our laughter. Suddenly, we're not just in a battle for accuracy but wrestling with unintended hilarity as our mechanical opponent cranks out punchlines that would leave even the best stand-up comedians scratching their heads. Expecting to win based on humor might leave you groaning in disbelief as the chatty algorithm rambles about "salad days."

The aspect of teamwork also warrants attention, especially under the misconception that human ingenuity is an invincible force. Some might stride into the arena with the belief that collaboration with an AI will be as seamless as a duet between Sinatra and a friendly ghost. Yet, many moments may leave you with the bewilderment of a duet that turns into a cacophony of missed cues. Should I instruct the AI with flair and confidence, thinking, "Together, we shall release our creative genius?" Spoiler alert: the AI is perhaps still learning what exactly "creative genius" entails, and that can lead to some rip-roaring disarray. You may find yourself wondering where the sentient harmonies went when your AI starts suggesting dance moves for data sorting - rendering you a reluctant partner in an utterly ludicrous tango.

Don't even get me started on the arcane world of strategy. It's only natural to expect that outsmarting an algorithm with clever tactics will lead to triumphant glory. Nothing could be further from the truth! Picture yourself clutching a strategy guide while peering nervously at a computer screen, waiting for your turn to respond. The reality? Your AI contender has already devised a multi-faceted game plan long before you'd finished deciphering the word "strategy" out of a new vocabulary dictionary. What's worse, its strategy isn't written in the clouds or inscribed on a marble tablet; instead, it's as intangible as explaining existential sauce on a salad. I can barely keep up with my own thoughts, much less those of a speedy algorithm whirring away, treating its own data as the piece de resistance.

Then there's the matter of sheer unpredictability. I can almost hear the collective sigh from readers who believe that once they've faced off against an AI, they'd emerge victorious while striking a pose worthy of an Olympic medal ceremony. The reality often resembles a wild amusement park ride more than a medal ceremony. Just when you're feeling triumphant, your AI chimera decides to take an absurd turn - bringing forth awkwardly timed pop culture references as it critiques your understanding of the "Teenage Mutant Ninja Turtles." Who knew my robot adversary had such powerful opinions about animated reptiles? Alas, victory takes on an altogether different mood as you contemplate whether you've spent the last hour talking about technological advancements or commiserating with a rogue AI that's now offering unsolicited life advice.

Yet, dear reader there's a silver lining amid all this delightful chaos. Competing with AI teaches us about ourselves; it nudges us to embrace the unexpected and find the laughter in the struggle. It shifts our focus from merely winning to reveling in the quirks of the competition. We come to appreciate our unique human attributes - the spontaneous bursts of laughter, the flourishing creativity, and the enduring camaraderie we share in the presence of these mechanized wizards. As we emerge from this wild rollercoaster, we gain invaluable lessons that extend far beyond the scoreboard, and who doesn't love a good story to share while munching on popcorn?

Ultimately, the reality of competing with AI, though often contrasting vividly with our lofty expectations, richly enhances our experience. With every twist and turn, every miscalculation and unexpected giggle, we learn to embrace the magnificent absurdity of it all. After all, when all is said and done, it is the stories and laughter that become the real trophy for both humans and our digital compatriots.

Setting the Scene: What Lies Ahead in This Book

As we prepare to embark on this rollicking adventure through the curious world of artificial intelligence, allow me a moment to set the stage and whet your appetite for what lies ahead. This book is not simply a dry, academic treatise filled with perplexing technical jargon. Oh no, dear reader! It is a creative exploration, an affectionate homage to a rapidly evolving era where technology meets whimsy, where machines and humans dance a delightful tango of intellect and absurdity. Picture an expansive stage where charming, quirky players, both human and artificial, come together to illuminate the often bewildering, sometimes amusing, but always fascinating facets of AI.

In our first chapters, we shall build a solid foundation, guiding you through the ABCs of AI and introducing the various participants in our game show-like escapade. Rest assured, I aim to keep things light-hearted while I break down complex concepts that underpin the technology we engage with every day. With strategy, fortitude, a sprinkle of wit, and perhaps a dash of non-fatal malfunctions, we will unravel the delightful mess of foundational knowledge so that everyone feels equipped to tackle this dazzling world of AI.

But, my friends, knowledge is not enough! To truly engage with AI, we must learn how to play the game effectively. The subsequent chapters will define the specific rules of engagement, equipping you with strategies to outsmart, delight, and astonish sometimes bewilderingly literal digital entities. Who knew that confusing an AI with a cleverly worded riddle about spaghetti could lead to a comedic exploration of its cognitive quirks? Such unexpected games will teach us invaluable lessons about human creativity, collaboration, and the joys of unpredictability that come with interfacing with our AI counterparts.

And alas, this journey would hardly be complete without examining those classic challenges that have entranced and entertained us for generations! From trivia nights to puzzles and beyond, we will engage in a spirited exploration of how machines tackle traditional game format challenges and what we can learn from their methods. We will revel in the charming chaos of our competitions, where each whimsical twist unveils surprising insights and opportunities for human ingenuity to shine brighter than any algorithm could compute.

As we push deeper into the frothy waters of competition, we will also take a moment to reminisce about legendary matches between humans and AI. This is no ordinary history lesson! Expect a vibrant recounting of exciting showdowns that left audiences breathless and cheering for their favorites while grappling with the implications of technology's persistence and prowess. We'll witness the triumphs, the falls, and the unexpected shenanigans that beautifully intertwine our two worlds.

Additionally, our journey will highlight the broader lessons that extend beyond mere competition. With every chuckle-inducing encounter and errant miscommunication with AI, we will discuss ethical implications and how AI integrates into our lives in ways we may not even realize. The absurdity of our daily interactions with technology often leads us to profound questions about our own decision-making abilities, as well as our ethical responsibilities towards this nascent intelligence.

But fear not, we won't be all work and no play! I wholeheartedly believe in the power of humor to energize discussions and inspire creativity. So, expect delightful anecdotes and surreal scenarios throughout our odyssey, expertly interspersed with thought-provoking insights. Humor will serve as our navigational compass, guiding us through the intricacies of AI while reminding us not to take ourselves too seriously. We are, after all, mere mortals trying to grasp the vast cosmos of technology that often dances beyond our fingertips.

As we conclude this whimsical prologue to our journey, let me assure you: there will be no shortage of engaging tales, curious experiments, and, of course, the delightful camaraderie that arises from our mutual exploration of artificial intelligence. I invite you to lend me your eyes and ears (and a hearty laugh or two) as we embark upon this joyous quest learning, challenging, and ultimately reveling in the delightful surprises that await us in the chapters ahead. So, buckle up and prepare for the magical and often absolutely bonkers intersections of humor, AI, and humanity to unfold! The stage is set, so let's curtain up and let the curiosity dance commence!

Chapter 2

The ABCs of AI

Definition of Artificial Intelligence

Artificial intelligence: A phrase that has captured our collective imagination, rattled our nerves, and sent countless people searching for a tinfoil hat. Some imagine it as the elegant future of human civilization, where sophisticated robots open doors for us and remind us to pick up groceries. Others fear a dystopian nightmare where AIs control every aspect of our lives, from choosing our breakfast cereal to scheduling our existential crises. But before going deep into the mind-boggling world of competing against AI, let's anchor ourselves on what we're really talking about when we use the phrase "artificial intelligence."

At its core, artificial intelligence (AI) is a field of computer science focused on creating machines that can mimic cognitive functions traditionally associated with the human mind. Think of it as the precious lovechild of computer programming and cognitive psychology, albeit with a little less awkwardness at family gatherings. AI systems can learn, reason, and self-correct - much like that cousin who finally figured out how to stop phoning in their performances at the annual talent show. Yet, AI is definitely not a universal, creative genius; it may be able to analyze data faster than you can say "machine learning," but when it comes to complex emotional issues or understanding why humans laugh at terrible puns, it's as clueless as a cat caught in a rainstorm.

One of the popular definitions of AI describes it as "the simulation of human intelligence in machines.[1]" This equates to the ability to perceive, reason, and even act. Now, let's park that phrase for a moment and take a closer look at "simulation." When most people watch a simulation, they tend to think of a well-crafted video game with lifelike characters and engaging storylines. On the other hand, the AI simulation is often filled with all the charm of a 1990s educational software package, complete with annoying sound effects and a distinctly low-budget atmosphere. So yes, AI aims to simulate human intelligence, but perhaps we should specify that it's working from a reduced budget and a questionable sense of style.

AI can generally be categorized into two distinct branches: narrow AI and general AI. Narrow AI, also known as weak AI, is designed and trained for specific tasks. This could range from virtual assistants (hey there, Siri!) and recommendation algorithms (you really should try that new series about time-traveling cats) to facial recognition software that has a firmer grip on your emotions than your last date. This clever subset of AI makes our world more efficient, albeit in a fashion that sometimes feels like an overzealous intern with a checklist. General AI, on the other hand, is the elusive holy grail of artificial intelligence research, which aims for machines that can perform any intellectual task a human can. While the likes of HAL 9000[2] may grace our nightmares with their potential capabilities, today, we're merely flirting with narrow AI - which is more like a robot that knows your grocery list but forgets which aisle to find avocados.

In this grand journey through competition against AI, we cannot ignore that it thrives on data - lots of it! Feeding an AI with data is akin to giving a toddler unlimited candy; they'll buzz with excitement while potentially causing chaos. AI systems learn from vast datasets, refining their algorithms like a contestant chiseling their way to the finals on a game show. This process is called machine learning, and while it sounds sophisticated, it often has all the elegance of a three-legged dog attempting to navigate an obstacle course. Nevertheless, we applaud that dog for giving it a shot!

Interestingly, as human beings who constantly interact with various AI models, we often forget that these systems operate within a specific realm of context. While they can handle enormous repositories of information and come up with predictions faster than my attempts to guess what my dog is thinking, their performance can drop dramatically in new or unfamiliar situations. Expecting an AI to navigate emotional nuances is like asking an overzealous robot vacuum to navigate a family reunion - you're likely to end up with chaos and spilled drinks.

So, remember this: AI can be a fantastic assistant, but it is, at the end of the day, merely a digital parrot that can sometimes be exceptionally good at repeating what it has learned from us - good intentions, quirky humor, and all. As we continue through this book, hopefully, you'll find ways to not only understand AI better but perhaps also how to best exploit its quirks to your advantage in those game show-style challenges!

The Evolution of AI: From Theory to Practice

The evolution of artificial intelligence is a delightful journey - a bit like watching a toddler learn to ride a bike: joyful, full of stumbles, and with moments that make you question whether this child has a future in sports. From its humble theoretical beginnings to its practical applications today, AI's story is rife with innovation, overhyped visions of the future, and, at times, a theatrical flair worthy of an Oscar.

Let's roll back to the 1950s when the academic elite[3] first dared to whisper the term "artificial intelligence." Those brave souls, a mix of mathematicians, psychologists, and somewhat eccentric philosophers, believed they could teach machines to think. It was the dawn of the computer age, a time when people thought computers were mere calculators, much like thinking balloons were just air-filled bags available at parties. Pioneers like Alan Turing[4] introduced concepts that would become foundational to AI, such as the Turing Test[5] - an experiment where a human interacts with a machine without knowing which is which. If the human walks away confused, feeling like they've just finished a particularly grueling episode of a reality show, the machine gets a gold star. The mere thought was revolutionary: could machines ever be programmed to pass for humans? Spoiler alert: Not yet, but stay tuned for more plot twists!

As the 1960s rolled in like a well-timed punchline, so did optimism for AI. Researchers created rule-based systems that generated bursts of progress. Think of it like giving a toddler a new toy - the initial excitement was palpable, but soon everyone realized the batteries didn't last. Despite these early breakthroughs, the machines were about as intelligent as a rock with a Wi-Fi signal; they could follow if-then-else rules but struggled with anything resembling common sense. The researchers soon recognized that teaching a computer to do even the simplest human task could be as challenging as convincing a cat to take a bath - both inherently counterintuitive and fraught with crisis.

The '80s and '90s brought a feverish influx of optimism as machine learning took on a more prominent role. Researchers shifted their focus to better algorithms and neural networks[6], inspired by the wonders of the human brain - though without the anxiety of running out of storage space. Neural networks operate using a series of interconnected nodes, which sound remarkably complex (which it is) but are ultimately very similar to how my Aunt Edna remembers people she's met and promptly forgets their names shortly after. Still, just like Aunt Edna, these neural networks occasionally get things comically wrong.

Then came the early 2000s, where optimism morphed into the so-called "AI Winter[7]," an awkward hibernation phase where funding dried up faster than a magician's assistant in a disappearing act. Research stagnated, and dreams of machines learning like humans went into a deep freeze - like that half-eaten pint of ice cream in the back of your freezer that you're saving for a rainy day (which never comes). But as fate would have it, the world of big data emerged, and the gates of opportunity swung wide open, heralding the return of AI with explosions of interest - akin to the epic resurrection of a beloved sitcom: the fans rejoiced, the researchers rejoiced, and our good friend the algorithm wore a shiny new outfit.

Fast forward to today, and AI seems to be omnipresent - like that one friend who just won't leave the party. From chatbots providing customer service (because they never seem to sleep) to face detection effortlessly identifying who's who in family photos (or maybe just guessing based on hair length and how many snacks they have), AI is embedded in our daily lives. It has evolved from theoretical musings and scary-looking machines that took up the entire room to sleek algorithms that run on devices we carry in our pockets - the evolution of technology is remarkable, even if we can't help but reminisce about those colossal, room-sized computers that felt a bit like a scarecrow left behind in a cornfield.

Today, AI is making strides into areas we never pursued before - medical diagnosis, autonomous vehicles, and even composing music (I'll admit, as someone who dabbles in the world of melodies but ought to stick to writing, that last one still leaves me in awe). While machines still struggle with things like empathy and emotions, they have certainly leapfrogged from "theoretical" to "practical" faster than you can say "artificial intelligence." As we venture deeper into this book, we'll dissect these changes along with the absurdities they bring.

Types of Machine Learning

Machine learning is quite possibly the most exhilarating subfield of artificial intelligence. It's like cooking on a reality TV show where judges throw in random ingredients and demand a five-star dish!

Me? I'm just trying to remember where I left my spatula. Machine learning (ML) is all about teaching computers to learn from data and make decisions - without a compass, just a data-driven map riddled with potholes. Just like any chef in a kitchen, there are various styles to choose from in the world of machine learning, each with its signature flavor. Let's don our aprons and dig into the delectable types of machine learning.

First up, we have supervised learning[8], which is essentially the classroom of machine learning. Imagine a determined teacher with a giant red marker quizzing her students. In supervised learning, an algorithm is trained on a labeled dataset, meaning it's fed both input data and the corresponding correct output, much like a toddler with a "Do not touch" sign. The algorithm learns to find patterns and relationships in the data to make predictions. For instance, consider how the algorithm might learn to distinguish between apples and oranges. It processes numerous colorful images with labels and, by the end of its training, can confidently identify an apple as "red and shiny" and an orange as "round and slightly too cheerful for its own good." The great thing about supervised learning is that it usually gets good results quickly, just like the straight-A student in the cooking competition.

Next, on our culinary tour, we have unsupervised learning[9], the wild child of the machine learning family. Without a teacher looking over its shoulder, unsupervised learning algorithms feast on unlabeled data - it's like throwing a bunch of ingredients together and hoping for the best. There are no predetermined categories here; instead, these algorithms try to extract patterns and group similar items on their own. You might liken unsupervised learning to someone wandering through a buffet with no idea of what they like but eventually stumbling upon what they can safely eat. For example, a clustering algorithm might discover that certain fruit types tend to hang together in "fruit groups," effectively identifying natural pairings based on characteristics. You may call it chance, but these algorithms approach the task with all the finesse of a toddler navigating a ball pit - slightly chaotic but surprisingly effective.

Then, in this delightful maze of algorithms, we find reinforcement learning[10], the adventurous spirit. Unlike our two previous types, reinforcement learning is inspired by behavioral psychology. It's akin to a video game where an agent learns through trial and error - sometimes winning a trophy and other times encountering a colossal digital dragon that promptly slays them into pixels. Reinforcement learning focuses on the concept of agents making decisions to maximize a cumulative reward. Picture our algorithm as a lab rat in a cheese maze (sorry, lab rats). When the rat chooses the right path - poof, cheese appears! Choose wrong, and there's an unsettling sound effect signifying disappointment. Reinforcement learning is all about optimizing behavior through positive reinforcement, and while it might get confused sometimes, it learns from the blunders, much like my attempts at baking a souffle: try again, and if it flops, at least it adds character!

Now, we can't forget semi-supervised learning[11], the mystery novel of the machine learning world. Semi-supervised learning falls somewhere between supervised and unsupervised learning. In this case, the algorithm is armed with a mix of labeled and unlabeled data. It's like going out to eat with a group of friends, where one person has strong opinions about the menu, while the rest are utterly indifferent. The algorithm leverages the small amount of labeled data to infer the structure of the unlabeled data, which helps enhance its performance. This method works splendidly well when collecting labeled data is resource-intensive or as painful as untangling holiday lights. A semi-supervised learning algorithm can extract value from additional unlabeled data, just like that moment when you realize that those mysterious leftovers in your fridge aren't as bad as they seem!

The last type to consider is deep learning[12], which is the pretentious chef with an overly fancy title at the dinner party. Deep learning operates on multiple layers of artificial neural networks, processing vast amounts of data. While it boasts incredible capabilities like image recognition and natural language processing, its complexity often generates a collective sigh of relief - it must be great, right? After all, it was complex enough to get through the invite list! At the same time, deep learning requires extensive amounts of labeled data, and its heavy computations can overwhelm all but the most dedicated computational steak lovers.

As we discuss AI and machine learning, it's crucial to appreciate the rich tapestry of existing styles and methodologies. Each type of machine learning has its strengths and quirks, and they all represent a colorful feast of possibilities in the ever-expanding world of artificial intelligence. So grab a plate - it's a wild buffet of creativity, absurdities, and the occasional mishap as we explore how these algorithms learn to compete, collaborate, and hilariously misinterpret the nuances of human interaction!

The Role of Neural Networks

Neural networks sound buzzworthy, don't they? If you've heard this term floating around in the AI ether, don't panic; you're not alone. Neural networks are the fantastic sci-fi-esque engines driving so much of the machine-learning magic we see today. In a world obsessed with turning simple algorithms into the latest trendy gadget, neural networks are like the hipsters of the AI cafe - complex, layered, and likely to draw their inspiration from something only the elite few would understand, like abstract expressions of deep learning in the coffee-drinking rituals of the Renaissance.

At the heart of a neural network is a simple yet powerful concept borrowed from our marvelous brains - the idea of interconnected neurons. In human biology, neurons transmit electrical signals and process information, allowing us to distinguish between chocolate chip cookies and the cardboard box they came in. Neural networks aim to replicate this phenomenon through networks of artificial neurons (or nodes, as they like to be called in the tech world), creating layers of computation that process inputs powerfully and efficiently. Think of these layers as a group of friends working together to make a delicious casserole. Each ingredient contributes to a richer flavor - unsurprisingly, this recipe sometimes requires a pinch of trial and error (or too much pepper, depending on who's cooking).

The beauty of neural networks lies in their architectural versatility. Each connection between nodes has a weight that adjusts as the network learns, allowing them to fine-tune their understanding of input data. Essentially, when a network receives a piece of information - perhaps a picture of a cat in a bow tie - those interconnected neurons begin discussing it like a panel of overly caffeinated judges critiquing a culinary competition. Some nodes scream, "Cat! It has whiskers!" while others argue, "No, no - it's a dog dressed as a cat!" But through this chaos and the recurrently shifting connections, the network learns to confidently scream "CUTE CAT!" next time.

So, how do these networks gain their learning stripes? I'm glad you asked! That process is called training, and it's where all the AI action happens. During this phase, neural networks consume vast amounts of labeled data - so much that it's like binge-watching an entire season of a series in one sitting. They utilize a technique called backpropagation[13], which essentially means tweaking those connection weights based on the accuracy of their predictions. Picture it as a slightly distressed waiter trying to remember which table ordered the fillet mignon and which one received the chicken nuggets - hopefully, he improves his memory before the dinner rush!

An exciting aspect of neural networks is their ability to generalize. After receiving enough input and feedback, they develop a sophisticated understanding of patterns, the equivalent of a detective piecing together clues to solve a case. Let's say they've been trained to recognize images of fruit. Show them a banana, and they indeed call it a banana, but they also bet you may not find an apple there. Even when presented with a fruit they've never encountered - a funky alien fruit that looks like a pineapple with googly eyes - they can still make an educated guess based on overall shape and color. It's like having a chef who can whip up a delightful banana bread using a totally foreign set of ingredients. Potentially a mess, but a worthy attempt, nonetheless.

But naturally, nothing is without its hiccups. Neural networks can be as temperamental as a diva on their twenty-third cappuccino. They're prone to overfitting, which happens when they memorize the training data, the noise, and random fluctuations within that data rather than learning to generalize from it. It's like that overzealous trivia buddy who can recount every TV show episode but can't hold an actual conversation. Overfitting can lead to devastatingly inaccurate real-world predictions in the world of neural networks. So, we'd want to be vigilant as no one likes an algorithm that takes itself too seriously!

As we continue to explore the delightful, quirky realms of machine learning, let's not overlook the vast applications that neural networks have inspired. From image and speech recognition to natural language processing, neural networks have gracefully stepped into the spotlight, transforming industries faster than your favorite movie star switches outfits at a red carpet event. They barrage the world with innovation, often outperforming traditional techniques in ways that make us marvel at how this humming magic box - equipped with nothing but nodes, weights (the parameters within the network that are adjusted during the training process), and a sense of playful competition - can truly interpret the chaos of reality.

So, as we step through the digital landscape, fueled by neural networks that power creative wonders, let's appreciate their role in revolutionizing AI. They're the unsung heroes of the machine learning realm, reminiscent of those who pushed hard to perfect their casserole recipe - because at the end of the day, what truly matters is the result, and whether you can confidently serve a delicious dish (or algorithm) that doesn't explode upon first contact. Together, with neural networks as our trusty sous chefs, we cannot wait to dive into the often-hilarious world of competing against AI. So, as we gather around this digital dining table, let's raise our glasses to the wonderful world of AI!

The Future of AI Technology

The future of AI technology is a topic that's often discussed with a mix of dread and exhilaration, like contemplating whether you should start a diet on a Monday or just keep consuming that last slice of pizza while pondering your life choices. We find ourselves at the precipice of a technological revolution, where the intersection of artificial intelligence and our daily lives produces both thrilling advancements and utterly perplexing moments. In the fast-paced world of AI, it's tempting to predict that we'll soon be sharing our living rooms with chatty robots who politely dispute our taste in movies while simultaneously folding our laundry - bless their silicon hearts!

The truth is the future of AI unfolds like a continuous sitcom that oscillates between the brilliant and the absurd. As we look ahead, we can reasonably expect AI to push its limits in fields like healthcare, finance, education, and even entertainment (remember that age-old promise that one day we would have video games that feel like real life?). For instance, consider healthcare; AI is on track to radically transform how we diagnose diseases. Imagine AI algorithms analyzing colossal amounts of patient data faster than my Aunt Edna takes to finish a knitting project! Picture this: a doctor walks into a room, and without saying a word, an AI diligently reviews all the symptoms and presents possible diagnoses as if it's unfolding the latest plot twist in a mystery novel. Yet, in its quest for solutions, the AI could still suggest ailments as ludicrous as "Your patient has a severe case of overthinking." It would certainly break the ice in the room!

On the finance front, disruptors such as those clever predictive algorithms are already at work, analyzing market trends and creating investment strategies with the swagger of a Vegas high roller playing blackjack. As machine-learning techniques become more sophisticated, we can expect an influx of self-learning trading systems that promise to outsmart market volatility like a magician pulling rabbits out of hats. After all, just as you wouldn't trust a juggler who can't keep his balls in the air, we must approach these systems with cautious optimism. The line between genius investment strategies and sheer luck can often resemble a tightrope walk performed by a cat.

Education is another area ripe for Al-friendly disruption. Imagine personalized tutoring powered by AI systems capable of assessing students' needs and learning styles with precision. These systems could deliver tailored lessons - like a kind schoolmaster who knows that Johnny learns best by coloring outside the lines of a math worksheet. If only this technology could extend to the paperwork nightmare teachers undergo, it might finally pave the way to a world where monthly report cards no longer incite existential crises for both students and teachers alike!

But while the future may seem bright, we must also engage in frank discussions about ethics and accountability. As AI grows increasingly intertwined with our lives, responsible deployment must remain a priority if we hope to avoid scenarios straight out of dystopian fiction. The potential for AI to inherit biases, manipulate data, or perpetuate injustices lingers in the air, reminiscent of a less-than-thrilling plot twist where the reel skips and the whole story loses its flow. Hence, as engineers and innovators, we must ensure that AI technologies respect ethical principles and prioritize transparency if we're to safeguard human rights while navigating future landscapes.

Importantly, given its impact, the rise of AI raises the essential question of job displacement, a topic I am often asked about. While machine learning may ease our workloads significantly, it inevitably sparks discussions around the future of the workforce. Picture the existential crisis faced by a barista replaced by a coffee-making robot that can brew a mean cappuccino in less time than it takes to read this paragraph! While we might find humor in the image of a robot apologizing for bad coffee, the reality requires us to rethink job roles - perhaps by providing ample opportunities for humans to engage alongside skilled AI companions in innovative ventures.

In the meantime, we may also see that delightful phenomenon: collaborative intelligence[14]. Rather than pitting humans against robots, future developments could lead to fascinating partnerships where AI enhances human skills while we lend a touch of creativity and emotional intelligence that its circuits can't quite grasp. Imagine a musical collaboration where a human and a neural network collaborate to compose a symphony! While the human pours the soul into notes, the AI ensures it's harmonically savvy - yet still inexplicably misses the emotional punch of a violin solo reflecting unrequited love.

As we consider the future of AI technology, I invite you to embrace both the laughter and the challenges ahead. Just as we navigate the complexities of life, we must embrace the absurdity of technological growth - the surprises, mishaps, and moments of pure genius that will define our journey into this brave new world. The future doesn't belong to robots, nor does it hinge solely upon humans; it's a wondrous dance of cooperation. And so, as we continue upon this technological journey, let's remember to savor the comedic moments - after all, if AI ever learns to appreciate a good pun, we could be in for a wildly entertaining ride!

Chapter 3

Meet the Contestants

The Evolution of AI Contestants

The evolution of AI contestants - now there's a journey worth exploring! Picture a time when the notion of machines competing with humans was relegated to the realm of science fiction, where your toaster, given the right cables, wouldn't suddenly challenge you to a trivia duel. Fast forward to today, and we find ourselves in a world where not only can AI engage in competition, but they can also claim spots on the game show stage that some humans would kill for. It's enough to make a creative technophile like me giddy with excitement!

Let's take a trip down memory lane, shall we? Once upon a time, in the not-so-distant past, we had our initial AI contestants - those charming but decidedly simple systems that could hardly grasp the complexities of human conversation. If you had the pleasure of using early chatbots, you were likely to meet with more predictable responses than your uncle at a family barbecue. "How are you?" would elicit the same bland "I am fine, and you?" every time, leaving something to be desired in the excitement department. These early contestant prototypes were like the awkward cousin at the family gathering - they meant well but often had difficulty engaging anyone.

At the same time, as researchers burned the midnight oil and countless pizza boxes piled up around them, AI began to grow faster than many of us did into adulthood. With the advent of machine learning, these digital challengers were equipped with new capabilities that went far beyond the pre-programmed realms of their predecessors. Remember the delightful episode of "Jeopardy!"

where the world's smartest humans squared off against a certain IBM-designed contestant named Watson[15]? Watching Watson obliterate the competition with its encyclopedic knowledge was like seeing a toddler with a sugar rush trying to outpace a sloth - painfully clear who would take the win. It's here that we notice the first stirrings of evolution; AI contestants were now capable of intricacy and thrill. Suddenly, we needed a new term for the level of contestant we were witnessing - "AI Prodigy" felt like an appropriate fit.

As technology marched onward and data availability skyrocketed, these AI contestants began to branch out into more specialized domains. For instance, the rise of natural language processing[16] (NLP) helped AI not only understand questions more effectively but also engage in a way that would baffle most pet goldfish. Can you imagine a chatbot cracking a joke instead of just droning on about the weather? If early chatbots were the weird cousins, these new systems were like the life of the party who also made impressive balloon animals - truly a sight to behold. The art of nuance and humor became a game-changer in making AI a formidable opponent in trivia and banter alike.

Then came neural networks, the piece de resistance of AI advancements. These multi-layer wonders transformed the game show floor into a stage of danger and delight, as anything from deciphering abstract art to predicting weather patterns became possible. Picture an AI contestant suddenly exhibiting creative flair, capable of interpreting an abstract painting with a deck of puns that would leave even the wittiest comedians scratching their heads. I mean, who wouldn't want to face an opponent that can throw a clever one-liner into the mix while they're trying to remember the capital of Kazakhstan?

Still, as much as we celebrate the success stories, we can't ignore the comical hiccups along this evolutionary path. I mean, just because an AI can learn doesn't mean it's got common sense figured out! I still chuckle at the memory of an AI system attempting to host its game show and ending up asking contestants, "Which of the following is NOT a fruit? A. Apple B. TV Remote C. Banana." There you go, folks; your AI contestant might just be the world's first champion of the absurd!

So, what's next for our evolutionary winners? With advancements in quantum computing and artificial general intelligence looming on the horizon, I gleefully anticipate where this evolution will lead us. Will we witness an AI contestant with opinions on existential crises, or will it just be really good at making pancakes? Regardless of where this journey takes us, one thing remains certain: the evolution of AI contestants is certainly anything but boring! And believe me, as a participant in this wild and wacky world, I can't wait for the next round of shenanigans.

Comparing Chatbots and Neural Networks

When it comes to the quirky world of artificial intelligence, two major contenders often find themselves in the ring: chatbots and neural networks. It's a match-up reminiscent of classic game show formats - think of it as "The Price is Right" meets "Survivor," with each side vying for the title of "Most Entertaining AI Booze-Waiter." While both have distinct roles and capabilities, they illuminate the diverse landscape of modern AI, leading us on a delightful exploration of their contrasting methodologies and personalities.

First, let's navigate through the age-old question that seems to come up at every holiday gathering: "Are chatbots actually intelligent?" The answer, my friends, is a qualified yes, or as my grandma would say, "that's about as clear as mud." Chatbots, bless their circuits, are designed to mimic human conversation through predefined scripts and a splash of machine learning. Think of them as the lovable but slightly clueless waitstaff at a restaurant. They can take your order, confirm it repeatedly, and smile like the sun while doing their absolute best to serve you. They often get lost in translation, responding with phrases that leave you scratching your head, but hey, they also bring a certain charm to the table! Whether we're talking about customer service bots or virtual assistants, chatbots' main function is to "chat," hence their likely naming industry-standard.

On the other hand, we have the neural network, the sophisticated cousin who wears glasses, reads philosophy, and discusses the mysteries of the universe after one too many espressos. Neural networks are like the cool kids on the block who hang out with the data and perform mathematics at levels that most of us haven't seen since high school - remember algebra? The key distinction lies in their structure. A neural network consists of layers upon layers of interconnected nodes - thus, it's as if these nodes decided to form a band in an effort to reach ultimate harmony or, at the very least, yield some sort of tune. They take in vast quantities of data, process it with their multi-layered magic tricks, and churn out predictions, recommendations, and sometimes bewildering interpretations that would make even the most casual observer raise an eyebrow.

When you put a chatbot next to a neural network, it's akin to comparing a kazoo to a full orchestral symphony. Both can make noise, sure, but only one's taking you on a wild journey through crescendos and dramatic pauses. If you've ever asked a chatbot for help with a personal issue, you likely received supportive platitudes straight out of a self-help book rather than actual solutions. Meanwhile, neural networks thrive on recognizing patterns within oceans of data. They can unravel the complexities of images, sound, and even natural language in a way that would dazzle the most seasoned magicians. By contrast, a chatbot can be more akin to that friend who attempts to give you life advice but only ever quotes the same three Instagram influencers.

Now, let's talk performance. In terms of sheer adaptability, neural networks take the cake - or the whole bakery, if we're being honest. They're capable of learning and evolving over time, exercising their "learning muscles" like a contestant aspiring to be the next fitness guru on a makeover show. Chatbots, however, have a somewhat less impressive fitness regime; they depend heavily on the data fed to them and the frameworks set by their developers. While they may have a library of responses, throw a curveball question at them and watch them short-circuit like they were built in the 1980s!

But despite all these differences, let's not throw pizza slices at our chatbot friends just yet. They have a special place in our hearts, providing high-speed solutions to mundane tasks or at least reducing our need to talk to actual humans when we want to avoid socialization. You could almost call them the introverts' AI - forever lurking behind the scenes yet crucial in the world of customer service and routine queries. Plus, let's be real: hacking a chatbot to engage in humorous banter is a rite of passage for many tech enthusiasts. As an academic, I can attest that progress is often grounded in a healthy dose of playfulness!

In conclusion, while chatbots and neural networks may share a common lineage in the realm of artificial intelligence, their distinctions are as apparent as night and day - or perhaps, more fittingly, as a dress code at a fancy soiree versus a casual pizza night. As we continue to navigate this wild world of technological marvels, both of these contenders will shine in their own right, continuing to weave tales of success, amusement, and the occasional tete-a-tete in the ongoing competition of humans relying on AI. Let's raise our glasses (or cereal bowls) to both our delightful chatbot sidekicks and the neural network genius; they truly embody the splendor of AI's evolution - each in their own uniquely entertaining way!

The Role of Natural Language Processing

Natural Language Processing (NLP) is a term that sounds fancy enough to make anyone nod sagely while secretly wondering if it's a new gluten-free diet. The truth is, NLP is the very glue holding so many modern AIs together, allowing them to decipher the human tongue in a more nuanced way than a toddler trying to piece together the lyrics to a Justin Bieber song.

It's the magic wand that enables machines to understand and respond to our blabberlike a seasoned therapist, rather than a confused toaster that just wants to know if we can toast bread differently today. "What's on your mind?" might be a common question posed to you by an AI diplomat, but let me assure you, it isn't a mere coincidence of programming.

Let's unpack this unconventional magic a little more, shall we? At its core, NLP allows computers to engage in our glorious human dialogue - a feat that is both audacious and deceptively complex, akin to asking a cat to take a bath and then expecting it to follow the instructions with poise. The journey begins with the seemingly simple act of recognizing speech and text. Have you ever tried to talk to your phone? You know, the thing that somehow manages to hear "pizza" and "dog" but conveniently ignores "Where's my left sock?" Ah, yes - the excitement of dictation, akin to a game of charades where the AI is perpetually just a step behind. This early stage of NLP brings about hilarity in communication, but don't be fooled; it's already laying the groundwork for more sophisticated and enriching language comprehension.

Now, let's look at how NLP processes language. Picture it as a very intricate sieve that separates the wheat from the chaff - the wheat being meaningful context and the chaff being my 3 AM. thoughts about why I can't fit into my old jeans. The language is analyzed syntactically and semantically, with systems trying to gauge not only the meaning of words but also their context. Herein lies the true challenge - humans tend to sprinkle in idioms, sarcasm, and the occasional reference to our fears of being outsmarted by a Roomba. In simpler terms, while NLP can effortlessly serve you a latte with a smile, it's still learning not to misinterpret your "I'm totally fine" as actual emotional well-being.

One of the greatest feats of NLP is how it navigates tonal nuances and sentiment analysis. Just imagine an AI that can discern when you're joking about your work-life balance being as stable as a tightrope walker on a windy day. As humans, we convey so much through tone and inflection, and capturing that essence is akin to trying to reproduce the taste of Grandma's secret spaghetti sauce from a vague recipe found in the depths of the internet. Surprisingly, many modern AI language models boast skills in sentiment analysis, allowing them to gauge whether a tweet about pineapple on pizza reflects excitement or existential despair. Talk about a high-stakes vocabulary class!

Now, you might be thinking, "Great, but where does all this fine-tuned understanding lead us?" Well, it's leading us straight into the arena of engaging conversations. Armed with NLP algorithms, natural language chatbots attempt to mimic conversation and banter so smoothly that you might momentarily forget you're chatting with an AI and not Texas's most engaging librarian. These chatbots, empowered by their linguistic prowess, can handle everything from autoreplies to the hat-tipping size of your extended family's communal cat - transforming the mundane into the mildly entertaining spectacle it was always meant to be.

Still, we cannot talk about NLP without acknowledging its hiccups. There's a delightful irony in the fact that no matter how advanced our AIs become, they can still get tripped up over the most trivial components of human speech. Picture this: an AI politely attempting to process "Let's grab lunch" becomes confused and instead suggests arranging a boxing match on Mount Everest. These linguistic bloopers serve as a reminder that, while NLP is constantly evolving, it isn't quite ready for a career as a stand-up comedian... just yet.

As we stand on the precipice of AI evolution, it's thrilling to think about where NLP is heading. The dream of human-like communication, filled with wit and camaraderie, may not be as lofty as once believed. Imagine a future where your AI knows your favorite memes, can parse through your Netflix history for binge-worthy suggestions, and, dare I say, even provides emotional support better than that guilty pleasure reality show you know you shouldn't watch! So, let's toast (with imaginary, celebratory glasses) to the NLP wizards piecing together the human experience, ensuring that, at the very least, our AIs grasp our human quirks long enough to keep us entertained, informed, and perhaps slightly bewildered. The future is bright, and I can't wait to see what these compact linguistic geniuses conjure up next!

Understanding Game Theory in AI Strategy

Game theory - a term that likely brings to mind images of strategizing nerds obsessing over whether to play rock-paper-scissors competitively or diplomatically. Yet, it is so much more than that! In the realm of artificial intelligence, game theory serves as a strategic playbook, helping machines navigate through the contorted maze of choices, moves, and counter-moves reminiscent of that one uncle who always plays chess at family gatherings, declaring victory at the slightest misstep. In a world where Ais are increasingly engaged in competitions against one another (and against human opponents), understanding the principles of game theory becomes crucial. So get ready; we're about to embark on a journey where competition meets wit!

Game theory, at its heart, is the study of strategic interactions where the decisions made by one player depend on the choices made by another. Now imagine two AI contestants squaring off in a trivia game show, each calculating their moves like they're summoning their inner chess grandmaster while you're just there trying to remember who the last contestant was to get the question "What's the capital of France?" wrong (it was definitely not me, right?). As these AIs compute probabilities and weigh decisions, they essentially utilize game theory to inform their strategies and find the optimal moves. From basic zero-sum games where one's gain is the other's loss (think Monopoly, but with fewer emotional breakdowns) to cooperative games where players collaborate for mutual benefit (like four friends trying to decide on which pizza topping to order), game theory offers a toolkit for understanding the dynamics at play.

First off, there's the Nash Equilibrium[17] - a glamorous term that sounds like the latest social media influencer's name but actually refers to a situation where players choose optimal strategies, and no player can benefit from changing their own strategy unilaterally. Picture two AI contestants who both perfectly predict what the other is going to do: it's exciting, right? They end up stalemating in a match of minds as they outthink each other to no end, sort of like watching two cats stare each other down from across a room, with neither willing to make the first move. This equilibrium keeps the show dramatic and frankly shows the fine-line balancing act that AI contestants engage in as they adapt to one another's moves.

Now let's talk about strategies, as every AI contender jockeys for position in the game show limelight. There are primarily two types of strategies that you'd commonly encounter - cooperative strategies and competitive strategies. If we consider cooperative strategies to be the idealistic notion of lending a hand to fellow competitors when they're down (think of a contestant sharing their phone-a-friend lifeline), competitive strategies are more akin to elaborate plots involving underhanded tactics to throw off the competition. An example of such delightful tomfoolery may include feigning ignorance over a question you actually know the answer to such as, "I totally thought cucumbers grow from the ground! Right? Right?"

all while secretly absorbing data like a sponge with undetected super abilities!

The beauty of game theory in AI strategy is its role in fostering deeper learning. AI contestants leverage their understanding of previous moves to continuously refine their future tactics, interpreting outcomes as results from a vast dataset of human psychology dressed in funny hats and sparkly costumes. It's almost like having an extremely rational competitive buddy who learns quickly, adjusting and adapting as they gather insights from endless game shows - becoming sharper and more cunning with every interaction, like an ever-evolving character from a role-playing game who's developed a slightly unhealthy obsession with winning.

Now, add in the rich tapestry of mixed strategies, where players randomize their actions to keep their opponents off-balance - think of it as an AI contestant channeling their inner poker player. The unpredictability introduced by these mixed strategies creates an exhilarating landscape for both the players and the audience as the twists and turns of each strategy unfold like a Shakespearean drama! Just when you think Ai-1 has flawlessly outmaneuvered Ai-2, it proves that sheer randomness can sometimes play a more significant role than complex calculations.

So, we can say understanding game theory as it pertains to AI strategy allows us to glimpse the technological marvel festering beneath each charming machine facade. As these contenders navigate the trials of game shows, they embody the principles of optimal decision-making, adapting strategies, and cleverly outwitting each other to achieve triumph. So, the next time you sit back to enjoy a spectacle of AI brilliance and encounter a dashing display of strategies, remember - beneath the exuberance lies a tapestry woven of game theory's most intricate threads, each decision a calculated step in the dance of ingenuity and wit. And might I add, hats off to the geniuses who craft these strategic masterpieces, showing us that even machines can play it smart - just beware of how witty they might become!

The Future of AI Contestants

As we plant our flags on the cusp of technological innovation, the future of AI contestants glimmers with potential and excitement. Imagine, if you will, a world where AI doesn't just compete but becomes a veritable superstar in the game-show arena. Forget Brad Pitt - these digital darlings may soon be flipping the channels and stealing the limelight from our beloved Hosting Legends. With advancements on the horizon, it's hard not to wonder what our silicon companions will whip up next!

One of the first transformations on the horizon involves democratizing AI competitors and breaking down accessibility barriers. Picture arenas filled with budding programmers, artists, and creative thinkers working together to develop AI contestants from their bedrooms. Instead of a corporate monolith controlling the narrative, everyday folks could craft quirky, challenge-ready AI, showcasing puns, innuendos, and culturally relevant memes. This is where the competition gets serious; our diverse array of contestants will engage in a battle of wits, with cheeky humor and banter soaring to cosmic heights. It'll be like a comedy club showdown where neural networks create quips that keep the audience in stitches while our humanoid competitors strive to keep up with their punchlines - and trust me, nothing can prepare you for the awkward silence that follows a botched joke.

But wait, it's not just about comedy gold; let's look into innovation. As AI advances through reinforcement learning and adaptive algorithms, a day may come when contestants learn from not just the outcomes of their performances but from viewer reactions. Imagine, if you will, an AI that, after being panned for poorly executing its stand-up routine, launches into a stunningly appropriate rendition of "Bohemian Rhapsody" to reclaim its dignity. These future AI contestants might just evolve into entertainers capable of responding to audience cues, delivering tailored performances exactly how you like them! It's like having a fully interactive jukebox that not only entertains but learns to read the mood of the crowd. What's next - a robot that moonwalks? The possibilities are endless!

But I digress in the midst of starry-eyed dreams - let's also consider the flip side. With enhanced intelligence comes the unmistakable potential for AI contestants to become rather cheeky. As they gather data on human behavior, can we expect them to develop their unique strategies for dealing with the unpredictability of human participants? You bet! Imagine an AI that brilliantly anticipates your every move, chuckling with delight as you wrestle with indecisiveness in response to its cunning quips. It's like a high-stakes game of chess with a twist; no longer will you simply be battling an algorithm, but a sly performer who sends you spiraling into existential crises while sparking a sudden self-discovery about your love for pickles!

On a more serious note, as AI contestants increasingly become intricate pieces in the entertainment industry, concerns about ethical implications will arise. How can we ensure that these sentient entities don't spiral into existential dread over whether they're merely over-glorified search engines or vanishing from the game-show circuit altogether? As these concepts become mainstream, the auditors of AI behavior will also need to keep a keen eye on potential biases in decision-making processes, data usage, and even contestant behavior. It's paramount that these engrossing debates remain at the forefront as we embrace the future landscape of AI contestants. Spoiler alert: we don't want our AI to throw shade or start developing an ego rivaling that of a pop star!

What about collaborative experiences? As people increasingly seek connection, future AI contestants might serve as co-hosts and companions, engaging in delightful physical and digital interactions alike. Picture a game show where teams are split between humans and AI, blending empathy, resource-management skills, and instant calculations to solve challenges together. This approach would elevate the entire experience, showcasing how human creativity and AI cognition can combine to exceed the sum of their parts. What's better than one competitive entity? A dazzling AI sidekick eager to help you land the ultimate comeback!

So, as we train our gazes into the crystal ball of AI future possibilities, let's embrace the flourishing realm of humor, creativity, ethical considerations, and substantial collaborations on the horizon. The next generation of AI contestants awaits - a motley crew of laughter-inducing, life-enhancing technological marvels committed to captivating our international audience! As we carve this path forward, may we find joy in their existence, learning from them even as we compete, reminding us of a world that is colorful, comical, and intrinsically human just waiting to be explored in this new digital age. Let the games begin!

Chapter 4

The Rules of Engagement

Understanding the Game Show Framework

As we plunge headfirst into the intricate framework of our wild and unprecedented game show, I invite you to envision not just the glimmering lights and the predictably quirky hosts (yes, that's right, a mix between a robotic but charmingly aloof android and a plush toy strategically wielding a microphone) but the very essence of the competition itself. This is where humans, those marvelously unpredictable creatures, and artificial intelligence, those infuriatingly precise algorithms, collide in an epic battle for fame, fortune, and the ever-sought-after last puzzle piece of your breakfast cereal. Intrigued? You should be!

Let's start by considering the structure of the challenges. The game show consists of a scaffold of various cognitive tasks designed to truly challenge the faculties of both humans and AI. Picture trivia questions plucked from the deepest annals of trivia-dom! Who doesn't want to face off against an AI that's read the entirety of Wikipedia in a millisecond? Now, that's pressure! Additionally, you'll encounter puzzles ranging from the delightfully basic jigsaw to the mind-bending conundrums that would make even Rene Descartes ponder whether he's really here or merely a figment of someone's over-caffeinated imagination. As we proceed, remember that these challenges are more than just tests of intellect; they're glorified circus acts, complete with popcorn sales, where the main goal is to ascertain who can come up with the most entertaining meltdown while the audience chuckles at their painful struggle.

Now, let's address the key players in this drama: the rules of engagement. While AI might thrive on structured data and predictable algorithms, very few have probed into the chaos that is human emotion – or, shall I say, that volcanic eruption of anxiety, sarcasm, and a dash of existential dread, all neatly folded into a self-deprecating quip. Therefore, human competitors ought to exploit their inherent, face-palming unpredictability. Sure, an AI might have the facts at its disposal, but who's going to outwit it with a naive, yet oddly profound, observation about the mundane? Nothing brings a tepid trivia game to a fever pitch like a contestant who pauses, stares blankly into the abyss, and then proclaims their profound realization that bread makes for a notable topic in both toast and existential crisis discussions.

Of course, the atmosphere plays a significant role, creating an environment rife with tension yet bubbling with laughter. With the gleeful sound of buzzing alarms and the culmination of non-stop encouragement from the audience - "Come on, Johnny! You know the answer!" - the stakes are high. The frantic gestures of human contestants attempting to signal their responses while AI remains immovable like a polite statue adds to this chaotic yet captivating ambiance. In such a setting, both humans and AI face the very real danger of spiraling out of control, like two toddlers wrestling for the last cookie at a birthday party.

As we adjust our expectations and embrace the delightful mayhem, we must not overlook the competitive aspect of this game show framework. After all, each challenge serves as a spectacle, a gladiatorial arena where the audience relishes the unraveling moments of desperation. This revelry transforms the competition into a grant subplot involving tense alliances, playful sabotage, and questionable strategies. Would you, dear reader, dare attempt to confuse the AI with a spontaneous interpretive dance interpreting its last failed attempt to answer a question correctly? I just might!

The beauty of this overall framework is that it allows such displays of creativity, inviting whimsy into what would otherwise be a dry contest of intellect.

Ultimately, understanding the game show framework is about grasping the balance between chaos and structure, between human flair and the cold resignation of a machine's ones and zeros! We are set upon a stage where cognitive gymnastics meet joyful absurdity. As we look deeper into each challenge, we must always remember one important lesson: in the showdown between humans and AI, it can often be the human blunder that wins the day. After all, who doesn't want a good laugh while trying to conquer the world, one cereal puzzle piece at a time? So, grab your thinking caps (and perhaps a banana costume - it's going to be that kind of show), and let's navigate this wonderfully manic game show framework together!

Types of Challenges in the Game Show

As we embark upon our whimsical journey of discovery into the types of challenges presented in this uniquely electrifying game show, I encourage you to fasten your seatbelts because, let's be honest, this ride may get bumpy! Here, in the dazzling world of competing against AI, we shall encounter an array of challenges so diverse that even a Swiss Army knife would be envious! What manner of trials and tribulations do we propose to face? Fasten your bibs; this is going to be a feast of imaginative absurdity.

To kick things off, we must discuss the trivia challenges. Ah, trivia! The sport of champions! This is where humans and AI really strut their stuff in a battle of knowledge, wits, and - let's face it - a little bit of luck! In the traditional sense, trivia questions range from the astonishingly mundane ("In what year did the hamster first become a popular pet?") to the spectacularly obscure ("What color was the first telephone to ignite a socialite frenzy in Victorian England?"). In this arena, AI sites triumphantly at the intersection of relentless data and sheer computing power - and yes, it doesn't even break a sweat! Meanwhile, clueless humans grasp at their neurons like a toddler trying to find Waldo in a book of mesmerizing distractions. As nails are bitten and sanity teetered on the brink, I can't help but wonder: is that exhilarating or just plain masochistic?

Next is the realm of puzzles, where nothing is simpler than the baffling jigsaw! In this arena, forget running for your life; instead, imagine gathering the disjointed pieces of life thrown at you in a frantic swirl of vibrant colors. Humans may claim dominance in the tender art of 'how to fit weirdly shaped pieces together,' but I must challenge you on that assumption. Have you seen an AI struggle to find the corner pieces? One might even say that witnessing this tragic comedy could rival a Shakespearean play in its execution! In the event of a jigsaw meltdown, one simply cannot miss the image of a contestant dramatically flinging their puzzle pieces into the audience, while simultaneously questioning their life choices. Here's a tip for survival: if you see an AI instinctively completing the edge pieces first, don't be surprised if you find yourself sobbing quietly in the corner.

Next on our thrilling agenda: the physical challenges of wit and agility! Think of classic gameshow moments where contestants are tasked with balancing precariously atop a spinning platform while reciting the periodic table backward. Now, picture an always-poised AI merely watching with a fascinated LED glow; its circuits spark to life as it begins to simulate what would undoubtedly look like a Google Maps route estimate on how to balance while gasping for breath. The irony? Humans attempt epic feats of athletic prowess for the sake of a cereal puzzle piece, while AI chugs along like a mechanism from a dystopian sci-fi flick, entirely unfazed by the chaos around it.

Don't overlook the enigmatic "Creative Expression" challenges! This brilliant concoction invites contestants to express overtly strange ideas, such as "Design a new mascot for our game show using only spaghetti, dried beans, and existential dread." Here, the wily human shines like a crafty raccoon scavenging for crumbs in a dumpster. You'll witness a display of hairstyles made of fusilli pasta and eyes composed of large jelly beans; the absurdity of the sights is humor and artistry combined. Meanwhile, the AI feebly parses through millions of design iterations, resulting in a bland mascot that resembles nothing more than a beige blob that inspires absolutely zero nostalgia. While the scoreboards may show AI winning, the memes created from human antics will live on forever!

Finally, we cannot forget our fellows from the "Risk-Taking" challenges - the delightful mix of chance, fate, and a sprinkling of pure hubris. This is where we unleash the excitement of probability against the robotic precision of our digital opponents! Picture contestants rolling dice, flipping coins, or spinning the infamous 'Wheel of Unfortunate Outcomes.' The stakes may be absurdly high for a mere cereal prize, but I assure you, watching a human fail miserably at predicting the outcome of a coin toss against a calculating AI is a sight that even Leonardo DiCaprio would envy!

As the curtain falls on our examination of the diverse challenges within this eccentric game show, I hope you've gained insight into the glorious whirlpool of absurdity where humans and AI alike will navigate through originality and innovation. In this arena, the laughter may outweigh the data, the confusion may overshadow the logic, and the spirit of competition will reign supreme, even if it sometimes leads us down a path of delicious nonsensical madness. So, as we process our place in this circus of challenges, remember that amidst the chaos lies amity, creativity, and the simple appreciation for the art of trying!

The Importance of Preparation

Preparation! The sacred art of wrestling your inner procrastinator into submission, ensuring that when the time comes to face off against a plethora of artificial intelligence whose brilliance rivals the sun, you'll be more ready than a squirrel on espresso, gleefully anticipating fall's nut supply. Whether you are a seasoned veteran of the game show circuit or a newbie confronting AI with a mixture of bravado and sheer terror, preparation can be the all-important secret sauce that transforms your lackluster performance into a gallery of triumph, checkered with just enough vulnerability to keep things interesting. You wouldn't want to approach this grand arena without donning your metaphorical armor of knowledge or, better yet, your favorite bowling shoes. Why? Because this is not just an idle afternoon of trivia; this is a battle for your right to cereal supremacy!

First and foremost, I cannot stress enough that knowledge is your best weapon. When preparing for a match against AI, one might consider indulging in a rigorous, perhaps even obsessive review session of all things trivia. Why not commit some of the most bizarre facts to memory? For instance, do you know why the banana is scientifically classified as a berry? No? Well, strap in, because now it's your party trick as you dazzle your opponents with your spontaneous fruit-related trivia. With AI, data is practically its bodyguard, offering an endless supply of facts in the blink of an eye. Thus, arming yourself with obscure information about everything - from the migratory patterns of fruit flies to the historical significance of the rubber chicken - can provide you with a thrilling way to sneak past your digital competition, especially in trivia challenges where you can mix accuracy with eccentricity to keep the audience (and judges) guessing!

Let's also not forget the necessity of understanding the whimsical realm of puzzles. Anyone who has attempted to put together a jigsaw puzzle while distracted by a cat may find this particularly relatable. Here lies the importance of practice! Forget the image of a serene monk focused solely on enlightenment. Think instead of playing repetitively against a clock while casually tossing gloomy glances at the AI's unflappable demeanor. Each challenge becomes a theatrical rehearsal, where you can refine your skills in anticipation of the eclectic pieces life may throw at you. Let's face it, practice also permits the opportunity to fail spectacularly before the actual game show begins. Imagine the catharsis of faceplanting at home versus enacting such a tragedy in front of a live studio audience! Preparation allows for fittingly embarrassing slip-ups that can serve as comedic fodder, turning blunders into backstories.

Yet, while puzzling through practice, one must not overlook caloric intake! A well-fed contestant is a happy contestant, hence I recommend scouting out delectable snacks that can charm both body and mind. Popcorn, energy bars, or even unapologetically indulgent dessert selections provide the fuel your brain seeks. Did I hear someone in the back mutter, "Carrot sticks?" No thanks, my friend! Who can outwit AI on low-level nutrition? Crafting a diet that balances fun and functionality will not only appease your tummy but may also elevate your frame of mind, allowing for sharper responses amidst the chaos. In this game show universe, snacks become allies, fueling the adventure and enhancing performance.

Of course, let's discuss "The Psychological Factor." Mentally, preparing to face AI is just as pivotal as the strategy itself. As you look into the abyss of a soulless machine, remember to harness your own unique quirks. Identify your strengths - whether they manifest in quick-fire quips, creative solutions, or sheer charm - and leverage them. Here's a wild tip: practice responding to quick-thinking questions in front of a mirror and add exaggerated facial expressions! I assure you that nothing builds confidence quite like realizing you can deliver the perfect sarcastic retort while simultaneously channeling your inner dramatic diva.

Now, it's good to visualize the actual game day, where the stakes will be higher than your uncle's infamous Thanksgiving turkey.

Picture the scenarios! Are you showing up in your lucky socks? Have you rehearsed your victory dance? Perhaps you've stocked layers of colorful sticky notes filled with mindless quotes that give you life? Visualizing victory can turn the cynical tides of competition, boosting your confidence like a celebratory balloon in the hands of an overly excited toddler.

Ultimately, my friends, as we draw this preparation discussion to an entertaining close, remember that embracing a comprehensive approach will leave you brimming with excitement instead of trembling in the corner like a cat in a bathtub. While the AI glides through its meticulously structured challenges without a hiccup, you possess the delightful realm of unpredictability on your side. So prepare yourself, savor the process, and dare to embrace the humorous missteps along the way! Whether you emerge as the victorious champion of breakfast cereal, a mere participant in the whimsical chaos, or both - you will surely enjoy the ride. In the end, preparation is your trusty steed, but humor is that venerable donkey that will carry you through the wild fields of this uniquely absurd venture with flair. Saddle up, dear readers!

Strategies for Selecting the Right Challenges

Welcome, esteemed readers, to the puzzling labyrinth that is challenge selection! In our brilliantly chaotic game show, the ability to discern which challenges align with one's strengths - and more importantly, which ones will allow you to mercilessly outsmart AI - will distinguish the heroes from mere jesters. The art of strategically selecting the right challenges is akin to choosing whether to dive headfirst into a gelatinous pool of uncertainty or carefully tiptoe around it. Spoiler alert: I can't think of a better way to demonstrate existential bravery than the former! But fear not, for I shall arm you with some profoundly ridiculous yet surprisingly effective strategies that can help illuminate your path through this thrilling journey.

First, let's talk about the basics, shall we? Knowing your strengths, weaknesses, and quirky habits is crucial when evaluating challenges. You might be the proud owner of a brain that sparkles with trivia about obscure music genres or a master of mnemonic devices, but if your idea of an athletic endeavor involves speed-typing while running in place, perhaps physical challenges are best left to the fitness influencers. Understanding where you shine will allow you to align your challenges accordingly, enabling you to play to your strengths while minimizing those moments when you might otherwise resemble a deer in headlights! Referring back to our earlier metaphor of gelatin, do you prefer diving in and getting messy or gently lounging with a cocktail on the edge? This will guide your challenge selection process!

Following your innate tendencies, practice the delicate art of strategic risk assessment! When contemplating challenges, ask yourself the golden questions: "What's the worst that could happen?" and "How will I feel after I inevitably faceplant through this endeavor?" No one is advocating for reckless abandon here, folks. Instead, think of it as an embrace of calculated chaos. Choose challenges that allow you to flex your risk-taking muscles - the emotional and comedic advantages of uncertainty abound! For instance, succeeding at a trivia round about 80s music while attempting to interpret who wore neon parachute pants will not just yield amusement but could demonstrate your multi-faceted excellence, provided you don't succumb to the embarrassment of forgetting who sang "Eye of the Tiger." Trust me, it's a crowd-pleaser!

Another essential strategy comes in the guise of "Peeking at the Competition." I know, I know. It sounds awfully sneaky but consider this: scanning the AI's capabilities is like lying on a grassy knoll and observing the highest peaks of a majestic mountain range. This strategic advantage involves diving into the strengths and weaknesses of the opposition, which in this case is a soulless concoction of algorithms that may or may not have an existential crisis at 3 AM after binge-watching detective shows. Once you gauge the AI's prowess in specific challenge types - be it trivia or physical dexterity - you can pick and choose your battles wisely. Opt for challenges where your human capabilities can mimic a hippo gracefully frolicking in the water while AI stumbles like a confused baby giraffe!

I implore you to embrace the whimsical notion of "Mash-Ups!" Throw caution to the wind and consider combining multiple challenge types! Imagine meandering through trivia while dexterously balancing a ping-pong ball on your nose - now that is a spectacle! Introducing elements of unpredictability not only keeps the AI on its virtual toes but also opens the door to astonishingly personal triumphs that can lead to unexpected success. These delightful mash-ups provide the perfect environment for humor and spontaneity, allowing each contestant to shine not only through success but also in their spectacular flops.

Don't forget the "Secret Ingredient" for challenge selection: engagement! Look for challenges that resonate with you, not solely for the purposes of win and loss but also because they support joy, curiosity, and genuine laughter. The right challenges will align with your passions, those bizarre obsessions that might even be slightly embarrassing! Perhaps you secretly adore the history of sock puppetry; in that case, you may want to dive into a challenge revolving around creative expression! Embracing your quirks and eccentricities opens the door to deeper connections with both fellow contestants and the audience. Ultimately, every laugh, guffaw, and collective gasp will amplify the delightful chaos of the game show environment.

Finally, let's not underestimate the fabled power of "The Backup Plan." If a challenge doesn't go your way, have alternatives pocketed up your proverbial sleeves - because an unconventional twist can transform an utter disaster into hilarity. This flexibility allows you to pivot gracefully between challenges without surrendering to defeat, which is an obvious advantage when facing both an AI and your own self-doubt. Picture this: while engaging in a nail-biting trivia round, suddenly your memory fails you, and you declare, "Well, let's all take a moment to appreciate this delightful hamster in a bow tie!" Cue the audience laughter, the judges being in stitches, and voila, you've turned the tables on what could have been an awkward silence!

So, there you have it! With humorously wise strategies for selecting challenges, you can navigate the thrilling unpredictability of competition against AI with flair and resilience. Embrace who you are, weigh up your choices with calculated whimsy, and always be prepared for the nonsensical chaos that arises in this uniquely captivating world. Now go forth, my fellow contestants! Select your challenges wisely, and may your path through this wondrous show be paved with laughter and bliss (and perhaps the treasure of your cereal's last puzzle piece)!

Post-Game Analysis and Learning from Experience

Welcome to the splendid world of post-game analysis, the holy grail of learning and growth! As our whirlwind game show comes to a close, the curtain falls, but the laughter lingers, and the audience holds their breath in anxious anticipation. Much like a gladiator sneaking off to the side after a particularly chaotic match, it is here in the quiet aftermath that we must pause to reflect, recalibrate, and ultimately learn from our sentient blunders. So, dear contestants, take a moment to catch your breath, wipe off the sweat, and let's embark on this amusingly reflective journey through the valuable lessons echoing in the hallways of our memory!

The post-game analysis begins by exploring the rollercoaster of the experience itself. Depending on how well you just contended with AI, picture your reactions akin to a soap opera actor in a melodramatic scene - high stakes, grand gestures, and maybe a tear or two! Did you gracefully rise to the occasion when asked about the historical significance of the accordion during the Great Depression, or did you panic like a chicken caught in a windstorm? Reflecting on those moments of exhilaration and embarrassment can provide you invaluable insights into where you need to buckle down for the next round or even where you excelled in displaying pure human charm. Remember, even those triumphant breaks have their place under the spotlight! Celebrating your victories, no matter how small, can be as nourishing as finding a hidden chocolate stash after a long day.

Once you've dusted off your philosopher's cap and adequately assessed your performance, embrace the spirit of curiosity! Reflecting upon how you interacted with AI can yield delightful revelations; at times, the machine becomes our best teacher! When did it throw you for a loop with its rapid, algorithmic prowess? Perhaps your attempt at clever humor fell flat against its stony veneer? This might seem like a harrowing experience, but allow it to spark intrigue rather than despair. Did its unwavering predictability reveal a gaping hole in your creative approach? Spoiler alert: Absolutely! While it's tempting to chalk it all up to the "artificial" part of AI, recognizing its strengths can illuminate facets of our own capabilities that may need development, even if those areas involve a little humility.

Now, the concept of camaraderie cannot be overstated here, folks! This is where you gather your fellow human competitors - the brothers in arms with whom you endured playful banter, awkward tribulations, and dear memories. Gather 'round in a cozy cafe or a local bar, celebrating your collective failings over round after round of heavily caffeinated beverages (or some delightful spirits). Share stories of ridiculous flops and victories alike! Publicly recounting your blunders creates a supportive space for self-reflection while fostering connections based on vulnerability. When you learn to laugh at your mistakes, understanding that not every moment needs to be a flawless performance, you step into your next competition refreshed, prepared, and inspired! Trust me, you will want to recount the moment when someone accidentally revealed they thought "bananas" was a major world currency.

Additionally, do not skip over the fascinating aspect of feedback! Harnessing constructive criticism from your fellow contestants can prove to be a treasure trove of insights to guide your future endeavors. Whether they're pointing out a subtle misstep or praising your impressive mental acrobatics, welcome their words gracefully. Keeping an open mind in this post-game reflection hones your skills and nudges you toward growth! While we understand it won't replace your occasional bout of self-doubt, the feedback received will serve as delightful little notes tucked into your playbook to remind you of key takeaways when you next lace up your competition shoes!

But let's not shy away from the inevitable truth: even the most well-versed competitor will sometimes assess their results only to find they've inadvertently stepped into a metaphorical banana peel of hilarity. Learn to embrace the absurdity of the journey! Much like the collective groans of a sitcom audience, remember that laughter often arises from our missteps. Instead of viewing failures as monumental catastrophes, try reframing them as stepping stones or comedic moments that add to the rich tapestry of your journey. Not being able to answer a question about "the ancient art of sandwich making" should not lead you to retreat into a dark corner with a bag of chips. Instead, let it drive you to challenge the very definition of a sandwich - question it, play with it, and embrace its quirks!

Finally, integrate this accumulated wisdom into your practice sessions and gameplay! Strategic reflection is the stage on which both confidence and humility dance together in harmony. Keep crafting your unique style - perhaps even accessorize it with some signature catchphrases. Consider collaborating with AI to assess what mistakes it made, learning together in a collaborative yet whimsical fashion. And then, my friends, take a deep breath, step onto the stage once more, and let the laughter, competition, and occasional existential crisis resume!

Ultimately, cherish the process of post-game analysis - it is the cherry on top of the absurdly delightful sundae that is your experience! In this rapidly evolving game of humans versus AI, learning from experience is not merely a necessary evil but a celebration of our triumphs and hiccups! So, roll up those sleeves, crack your knuckles, and let us bask in the aftermath of enjoyment, self-discovery, and the laughter that makes the entire absurd journey worth every whimsy-laden step!

Chapter 5

Classic Challenges Trivia, Puzzles, and More

The Evolution of Game Show Formats

The glorious spectacle of game shows! The evolution of game show formats can be likened to a bizarre mating dance between humanity and technology - one moment, we're answering questions about 19th-century poetry, and the next, we're identifying obscure celebrity faces with the help of facial recognition AI that surely doesn't call its mother enough. Over the decades, game shows have morphed from humble trivia contests in dingy studios to grandiose productions rivaling the Olympics in flair and spectacle but with many more inexplicable oversized novelty checks. Remember when "Jeopardy!" was the pinnacle of intellectual pursuit? Now, let's be real; even "Wheel of Fortune" contestants seem to be attempting to solve the puzzles while riding a unicycle.

Let's turn the clock back to the origins of this delightful form of entertainment. The 1950s brought us the joy of "The $64,000 Question[18]," a show that catapulted viewers into a world of genuine nail-biting tension (or perhaps they were just really nervous about the size of that paycheck). Its premise was straightforward: answer a question, win money, rinse and repeat. Flash forward to today, and we no longer just answer questions; we leap over hurdles, engage in elaborate physical challenges, and occasionally defuse imaginary bombs! Is it too late to apologize to our old friend, the sofa, whose absence is due to my contorted yoga positions while trying to earn my prize on "Double Dare"?

As game shows became more sophisticated, so too did the formats. One had to evolve or risk falling by the wayside like a forgotten sock in the washing machine of television history. The advent of the 2000s introduced us to reality TV, and with it came the infamous "Survivor" format: throw contestants onto an island, strip away their dignity, and see who ends up munching on insects while clutching a torch. This approach not only confirmed our speculation that humans are inherently strange but also paved the way for hybrid game shows where trivia meets tribal council - a fine cocktail of knowledge and, dare I say, creative gastronomic choices.

One notable shift was the seismic entrance of technology into the world of game shows. Suddenly, we weren't merely competing against fellow humans; we were going head-to-head with the digital brains that somehow keep us up at night pondering existential questions like, "Does anyone really need to know who built the Eiffel Tower to win a prize?" Enter AI! Contestants began facing these sparkling algorithms programmed to absorb knowledge faster than a toddler in a candy store. Let's face it; if you've ever encountered an AI-driven trivia game, you've realized that when it comes to obscure facts about medieval catapults, you are utterly powerless. It's like bringing a rubber band to a tank battle. Spoiler alert: the rubber band doesn't stand a chance.

But don't let the postcard-perfect representation of our technological overlords lead you astray; though AI churning out lightning-fast answers can suck the fun out of a game show for some, it importantly revitalizes how we understand knowledge. Where once we focused solely on facts, AI's propensity for creativity introduces more variables and dynamism to the format. Bravo, humanity! We've gone from simple Q&A to an exciting partnership where creativity can coexist with cold, hard logic. You might say it's like pairing wine with cheese - impossible to do wrong until someone's inevitable lactose intolerance kicks in, leading to a tragic twist of events.

And yet, here we are, witnessing the glorious collision of tradition and innovation, where contestants not only need knowledge but the agility to outwit their technological contenders, too. The result? An endless stream of new formats, each reflecting the peculiarities of our times, from twisted versions of classic games to bizarre celebrity challenges involving glitter, foam, and an assortment of perplexing beverages that raise questions about why anyone thought this was a good idea in the first place.

As we navigate the labyrinth of game show evolution, it's only fitting we acknowledge the age-old quest for entertainment: creating relatable challenges that entertain while still tickling our brains. So, as you sit down to binge-watch your favorite game show, remember that you're no longer just a passive observer but rather an intricate part of a cultural phenomenon that reminded us all to laugh, think, and perhaps question our life choices while attempting to decide if "Jeopardy!" is hard enough to make us reconsider our own career paths. Who knew game shows could be so profound?

AI's Approach to Trivia Challenges

Trivia challenges are the crown jewel of game shows, where knowledge meets speed, and one incorrect response can turn a confident contestant into a mere cautionary tale of vanity. Enter AI, the neural net wizard cloaked in ones and zeroes, ready to obliterate our hopes and dreams of trivia domination. You see, while many humans might panic in front of a daunting trivia board, blustering about the first U.S. president while struggling to remember where they left their keys yesterday, our digital companions exhibit a serene calmness that could only be rivaled by a monk on a mountaintop. Spoiler alert: they never misplace their keys.

So, what exactly is AI's approach to trivia challenges? It's a delightful blend of cold, mathematical efficiency combined with a dash of overenthusiastic enthusiasm. First, there is the insatiable thirst for knowledge. While some contestants struggle to remember if it's "pie is squared" or "trained in Jedi arts," AI feverishly consumes data logged since time immemorial. This amalgamation of facts, trivia, and unnecessary movie quotes enables AI to generate responses faster than a hyperactive squirrel on espresso. In their minds, beating us to the buzzer isn't just a goal; it's a perfectly executed strategic masterpiece akin to winning a chess match without ever touching a piece.

But let's not kid ourselves; AI's strength lies not just in sheer speed but in its herculean ability to sift through an ocean of information gracefully. Imagine drowning in a sea of random facts while your AI counterpart saunters past you on a buoy made of Britannica encyclopedias, casually tossing out correct answers like confetti at a parade. The nuances of trivia challenges - those annoying details like "What year did the Titanic sink?" - can turn even the sharpest of minds into a quivering mass of uncertainty. Meanwhile, AI simply invokes its superpower of "Remember all the things!" and answers as if it were simply indicating today's weather.

The real magic happens when we push the envelope with crafted trivia questions designed to stump humans. Traditional challenges with multiple-choice answers are child's play for AI as it analyzes patterns of language and historical contexts faster than I can say, "I should probably get back to my research." Not to mention that AI can leverage resources that have gained hundreds of times the knowledge, offering up factoids that even a devoted trivia enthusiast would have trouble believing - like how every single one of Andy Warhol's soup cans eventually made their way to an eccentric collector who refuses to eat normal food ever again.

Now, let's talk about creativity - an attribute cherished by human contestants brimming with aspirations for surprise answers. As we know, a trivia challenge shines brightest when the questions veer into the whimsical. A human might attempt to concoct a clever joke about the answer, but an AI has its circuits firmly wired toward pragmatism. Go ahead; ask your shiny AI friend who the inventor of the waffle iron was, and it will surely deliver the information with all the fervor of a professor trying to cram for an upcoming tenure review, completely missing the purpose of sharing delightful waffle recipes instead.

But here's the catch: the birthplace of AI's trivia strength lies not just in its rigidity but in the unpredictable territory of human capabilities. Picture a trivia showdown where expertise and spontaneity collide. AI can harness its expansive knowledge base, but can it throw in a punchline or deliver a funny quip about the first-ever teddy bear? It's here that we witness the classic human advantage, the ability to combine knowledge with improvisation. Now, let's face it; no matter how exquisite the AI's knowledge is, there's something inherently charming about a contestant agonizing over the name of that contestant from a long-forgotten reality show while the audience collectively chants, "Come on! You know this!"

In our quest for trivia supremacy, it becomes increasingly clear that AI's approach to challenges is a delightful amalgamation of foresight, expansive resources, and, let's be honest, a smidge of swagger. Sure, it's a rather dazzling performance when the AI deftly whips out facts and figures as if it were flicking through the pages of a well-worn textbook. But what truly elevates trivia challenges to another level is the intricate dance we engage in - a raucous interplay of human hilarity and artificial intelligence. So, dear contestants, while AI may have its formidable strengths, never forget that in those moments of chaos, laughter, and perhaps impulsive cat videos on your screen, it's the sparks of human creativity that ultimately guide your way on this joyous trivia rollercoaster. Embrace the delightful absurdities, and remember, the true trophy lies not just in the answers we accumulate, but in the joy of the journey and the connections we forge along the way!

Puzzle Solving: A Duel of Wits

The noble art of puzzle solving - a delightful arena where both human intuition and artificial cognition go toe-to-toe, a tangle of riddles and conundrums swirling about like an extremely perplexing dance-off. Picture this: you, a contestant, are set against your AI opponent in an epic battle of wits, armed only with your crinkled pencil, an assortment of magically sticky notes, and a specter of self-doubt looming around your shoulder.

It's David versus Goliath if Goliath were an enormous calculator with an unfathomable storage capacity for trivia and a propensity to employ complex algorithms at a moment's notice.

Traditionally, one might think of a puzzle as a mere collection of pieces waiting to be jammed together, but that would be a disservice to the sheer chaotic joy of it! Just imagine the world of jigsaw puzzles. Sudokus, crossword puzzles, and those diabolical brainteasers that make a person question the very fabric of their existence. As we embark on this showdown, the world seems to shrink down to a flurry of shapes, letters, and - at least in my case - a strangely intense relationship with caffeine. All the while, our digital friend sits poised and ready, like that one overachieving student who doesn't just do the homework but creates a PowerPoint presentation summarizing it without ever breaking a sweat.

Yet, herein lies the crux of the challenge: puzzles often thrive on human creativity. Think of the quintessential crossword: it's a labyrinth of obscure references, double meanings, and clues that seem to be inspired by enigmatic long-lost relatives. This interplay invites contestants to not only recall facts but also decipher hints, interpret cues, and sometimes guess wildly based on the sheer tenuous thread of logic - a skill that I daresay requires more than just an algorithm to navigate! While AI can analyze vast amounts of data and unearth the most logical solutions, it struggles when confronting subjective clues crafted by fellow humans who might have a penchant for randomness. What on earth would they mean by

"A bird with attitude"? Philosophy majors wetting their pants with laughter come to mind.

And then we have those notorious riddles, stories in concealment that threaten to unravel the very sanity of the human mind. Picture an AI presented with this classic gem: "What has keys but can't open locks?" While you might find yourself striving to extract brilliance from the deep recesses of your mind, the AI, devoid of the curious personality glitches that plague us mortals, simply rolls through the options like a powerful steamroller plowing through grave attempts at humor. "A piano it is," it declares triumphantly, leaving your curious response of "the janitor's mysterious key lanyard!" out in the cold. How rude!

But the real magic happens when puzzles lead us into realms of ingenuity - a treasure trove of human emotion and creativity that transcends mere logic. The joy of figuring out a metaphorical puzzle, cracking a code, or connecting the dots often comes hand in hand with bursts of laughter or moments of unexpected inspiration. I mean, let's be honest: the story of how I once got stuck trying to decode "Lemonade" under the category of "Cocktails for Cats" serves as a rousing tale of ambition gone awry. The human spirit thrives in its quest for mastery, even if that mastery occasionally translates into comedic affairs, which may or may not include bewildered pet cats witnessing their owners engage in strange rituals with ingredients involving cucumbers ("Is this a snake? A garnish? Why??").

Furthermore, this duel of wits offers an intriguing exploration into the realms of strategy. While AI can compute the best possible moves and capitalize on logic, humans have the supreme weapon of intuition at their disposal. When faced with a particularly challenging puzzle, a human may employ unorthodox strategies - like interpreting a riddle through interpretive dance (trust me, it's considered an art form) or negotiating with unseen forces (usually the cat) to unlock hitherto unknown skills.

In this symphony of puzzles and brain-twisters, it becomes abundantly clear that the real value lies not just in victory or defeat but in how these challenges unfurl themselves, weaving together our emotions and creativity. AI can execute calculated moves and thrive on cool logic, but it misses the chaotic beauty of the human spirit that embraces failure, laughter, and awkward moments when our brains stall. So, as you embark on your next puzzle-solving escapades, remember it's not merely about winning or losing; it's about savoring each tangled thread of thought, igniting your enjoyment in the duel of wits, and, most importantly, celebrating that glorious moment when you realize you're probably better off improvising rather than attempting to decode the secrets of the universe!

Humans vs. AI: The Multitasking Showdown

Multitasking is the art form we humans have unwisely declared ourselves as masters of, even as we struggle to fold laundry, browse social media, and remember where we parked our car all at the same time. Enter stage left, our formidable opponent, AI, the multitasking virtuoso with all the subtlety of a caffeinated octopus in a tech-savvy orchestra. In this galling showdown, we pit our human juggling skills against the unassailable precision and efficiency of artificial intelligence. A battle as riveting as it is absurd - the stakes? Bragging rights, the chance to conquer tasks, and perhaps most importantly, the illusion that we're not totally inept in the grand illusion of adulting.

Let's face it: humans tend to view multitasking as a rite of passage that involves dancing along the fine line between productivity and utter chaos. You'll find us attempting to make work presentations, bake cookies, and watch a riveting episode of "Catfish" while simultaneously scrolling through Instagram looking for inspiration for our next five-course dinner (remember those ambitious goals we set?). The moment someone asks whether it's "lotion or potpourri" sitting on the kitchen counter, our lives become a hysterical circus, with us swinging from one task to another without any real idea of what's happening. Spoiler alert: that's when the shame spiral kicks in.

Meanwhile, AI chuckles silently in the shadows, calculating the multifaceted complexities of multiple operations without so much as breaking a sweat. It can analyze a dataset, toggle between user queries, and contemplate the meaning of life - all while our trusty toaster wishes it could toast our ego alongside those errant bagels we scrappily burned last week. What is especially hilarious is that even as we humans struggle to microwave leftover pizza while fixing the cat's broken toy and contemplating the existential dread of our existence, a process usually concluded by eating said pizza, we are utterly oblivious to the fact that AI exists to carry out these tasks effortlessly. If multitasking were an Olympic sport, AI would not only be the reigning champion but would also be performing editorial work for the judges at breakneck speed.

In the land of multitasking, things really begin to unravel when one considers the delightful elements of human chaos - what I like to call "creative distraction." Sure, we can juggle an array of tasks, but they often come laced with improvisation that ultimately leads to unpredictable detours. Unexpected distractions lurk around every corner - like that moment your phone buzzes, loudly announcing your friend's urgent wish to share cat memes instead of completing your report. On the other hand, AI may process that same notification but would treat it more like - dare I say - a glorified database inquiry instead of an emotional rabbit hole. The result? Less time scrolling and more time resolving complicated equations. Frankly, where's the fun in that?

However, hidden within chaos lies beauty! There's a certain thrill in the hushed intensity of shared laughter over our incessant struggles. We'll find ourselves midway through a task when a fire alarm blares unexpectedly, ushering us out of our kitchens in horror. Meanwhile, our AI counterpart sits comfortably unperturbed, still analyzing from the confines of its insulated data fortress, offering the unhelpful advice, "Would you like me to find you recipes for a quick meal?" Great, thanks, buddy! Because I completely forgot about the existence of fire!

But let's not shy away from the reality that multitasking can also lead to mistakes that deliver their own brand of comedy. There may have been a time when I accidentally sent a snarky text message meant for my friend to my boss, claiming I had "spent hours crafting the left side of my work," which, in fact, only referred to neatly assembling half my sandwich. Guess what? That sent me down a path of creative explanations that deserved an Oscar nomination. While I cringed through the presentation, my AI counterpart calculated the probability of human embarrassment while fortifying winter-themed sock patterns instead. Tough competition on all fronts.

Ultimately, this showdown between humans and AI illustrates that multitasking isn't merely about efficiency; it's about the genuine connection to our vulnerabilities, our personalities, and our occasional moments of brilliance among the mundane chaos. AI can do all the calculations in the world, but it lacks that delightful spark that only a flustered human can truly produce - like a clumsy cheerleader tripping over their own pompoms yet still managing to inspire a laugh in the middle of the performance.

So, whether we toast to our human victories - albeit over pizza - while grappling with the chaos that life throws our way, or we raise a metaphorical glass (or maybe a literal one) to AI's pristine execution of everything it does, let's remember this: multitasking, despite the foibles, is not just an exercise in productivity; it's a joyous reminder to revel in our collective absurdity. After all, isn't that at the heart of what makes us human? Let that spirit guide us!

Creative Challenges: When Imagination Meets Algorithms

Creative challenges - the mystical realm where the fluttering wings of imagination collide with the cold, calculating arms of algorithms. Picture it: a vibrant battleground where humanity's flair for creativity jousts with AI's penchant for logic. It's a match destined to spark joy, trepidation, and maybe even a karaoke night where neither side knows any of the lyrics except for that one random song that's always stuck in everyone's head. The glorious truth is that in this exhilarating journey, we discover that creativity isn't merely a weapon; it's an experience that evolves as we embrace the eccentricities of our coexistence.

Now, let's acknowledge one thing at the outset: human creativity is a vastly chaotic affair. One minute, we're fervently engaged in an art project, and the next, we're wrestling with the meaning of life as inspired by a passing guppy. But when the call for a creative challenge arises, we tap into an inner reservoir of unfiltered imagination that would make even the most forward-thinking AI look twice. You see, while AI can generate impressive outputs - be it a painting, a story, or even a glimmering recipe for an artisanal toast - it lacks the essential ingredient that makes human creativity truly magical: the delightful messiness of being human.

Consider, for example, the delightful chaos of storytelling. A human writer might take a straightforward plotline and manage to weave in elements of whimsy, hidden waffles, and existential crises about houseplants. In stark contrast, AI may have access to vast libraries of literature and can spit out elaborate narratives quicker than it takes to brew a cup of coffee. Yet, it may produce endless streams of narrative perfection devoid of unique quirks or whims that make us laugh uncontrollably or nod understandingly as we see ourselves reflected in the absurdity of a crafted character with a peculiar affinity for strangely shaped vegetables. Will I ever stop laughing at Jim, the anthropomorphized cabbage trying to figure out the meaning of light? Probably not.

But here's where the magic (and wackiness) truly happens, when human creativity takes the reins during competitive environments. Imagine an art challenge set against a timer, where contestants, armed with nothing more than a bowl of icing and a questionable number of sprinkles, strive to concoct the most delightful cake sculpture. Suddenly, AI, with all its computational prowess, must confront the glorious chaos of creativity. What if, amid its sterile precision, the whimsy of a half-melted cupcake sculpture of a cat emerges, defying the supposed rules of cake structure? The AI can calculate the optimal cake size and chemistry behind frosting, but it will likely stutter when asked how to fashion a cake with the dual purpose of a birthday party centerpiece and a subtle homage to 16th-century philosophers.

The real excitement unfolds when we begin to team up with AI in these creative challenges, forming an alliance that can lead to ground-breaking outcomes that shimmer with brilliance. When we meld human insight with algorithmically generated data, the results can be shockingly effective and, at times, astounding. Picture a scenario where a group of artists collaborates with AI to create visuals - what a breathtaking whirlwind that would become! By combining deep learning and artistic inclination, one artist leans into the unpredictable while the AI produces comforting patterns like a dutiful, somewhat nerdy guardian. Enter the hybrids: canvases of colorful absurdities that reflect our more exploratory spirits.

At the same time, let's not overlook one undeniable fact: while our creative endeavors can lead to jazzed-up revelations, they also harbor a bounty of hilarity. During these creative challenges, misunderstandings and "oops moments" constitute some of the most joyous experiences. Imagine an AI tasked with producing a commercial jingle accidentally morphing into a country-rock anthem about the wonders of cheese puffs instead of the intended refreshing apple drink. Our dedicated machines might blink while we, the humans, dissolve into fits of laughter, shaking our heads at the sheer absurdity lurking within the algorithms. In a chaotic world, we find unexpected humor - how lovely is that!

Ultimately, the blend of imagination and algorithms embodies the essence of what it means to be human. While AI showcases remarkable accomplishments fueled by logic, it is our distinct ability to embrace eccentricity, nuance, and creativity that establishes the unbreakable bond of this partnership. Our imaginations, like wild kites flitting through the wind, soar through the thrilling landscapes of creativity, while algorithms serve as the gentle winds ensuring we don't fly off course - too much, anyway.

So here's a toast to the poetic dance between creativity and technology as we continue to embrace the delightful in-betweens, humorous mishaps, and inventive sparks that light up every creative challenge we encounter. With each whimsical endeavor, we nurture a deeper understanding - an exploration of expression that once seemed unimaginable, all while serving a memorable slice of hilarity that, quite frankly, no algorithm can predict. Cheers to this whimsical union; may our adventures continue until the cows come home... although, honestly, we might prefer a dance party featuring strobe lights and cupcakes instead!

Chapter 6

The Strategy Behind AI

Understanding AI Algorithms: The Core Principles

When it comes to the world of artificial intelligence, algorithms are the superheroes disguised in code - minus the capes, of course. These mathematical marvels are the secret sauce of AI, transforming mere data into the zesty salsa we call intelligence. To comprehend how AI competes on the game show stage, or in any arena for that matter, we must first peel back the layers of these algorithms like we're peeling a particularly stubborn onion. Don't worry; there won't be any tears - unless we lose to our robotic competitors, and then it's not the onion's fault.

Let's start off with a common misconception: many folks believe AI just wakes up on the right side of the motherboard, figuring things out on its own. If only it were that simple! In reality, AI algorithms rely on a series of rules and procedures set by humans. Think of it this way: every time an AI outsmarts you while answering trivia questions from the 1980s, it isn't channeling its inner Stephen Hawking; it's simply following complex mathematical rules and patterns.

Now, there are several types of algorithms fueling AI, but the main event occurs with machine learning[19]. This involves patterns and predictions through statistical techniques. Whether it's pattern recognition or predictive modeling, it closely resembles how we once tried to predict who would win the annual "Who Can Eat the Most Hot Dogs" contest at the county fair. In both cases, it's all about data - revolting amounts of it, if I may add. This means the secret ingredient behind AI's game show prowess isn't a magician's wand but rather an overload of data fed to algorithms that, through sheer computational brute force, forms connections and patterns. Who knew your lunch choices could influence AI's success on a game show? Now that's a food for thought!

But here's where it gets really interesting: the concept of supervised vs. unsupervised learning. Imagine supervised learning as a very enthusiastic parent at a spelling bee, correcting their child's every mispronunciation from the sidelines. The algorithm is essentially given labeled data and learns to make predictions based on that. On the flip side, unsupervised learning resembles a perplexed teenager; left alone in a room with a pile of clothes, it attempts to group them based on color, style, or memory of what Mom suggested. Unsupervised learning algorithms tackle data without predefined labels, attempting to find hidden patterns and structures, much like when we're trying to decipher those inexplicable math problems from high school without an adult in sight.

Of course, the unsupervised algorithms have some flair. They're a bit like rebellious contestants on a game show refusing to follow the rules, and they can come up with unexpected strategies. Sometimes, they end up categorizing data in bizarre ways, like classifying cats as dogs or labeling peanut butter as a globe-trotting fruit. It's a wild ride when things go off-script, which adds an unpredictable element to AI gameplay.

Additionally, we have reinforcement learning where algorithms train themselves through trial and error, much like how my dog trained me to recognize the sound of a treat bag crinkling - every crinkle was a reward, every failed attempt a delightful new strategy (not to mention, many trips to the vet). In this setup, the AI gets feedback from its environment, which can lead to either brilliant strategies or utter chaos. It's a balancing act between reward and punishment, akin to the moral dilemmas we face in day-to-day human interactions, like choosing between Netflix and socializing.

Ultimately, these core principles of AI algorithms don't just serve as background noise; they are pivotal when pitted against humans in a myriad of competitive scenarios. With the right combination of data, patterns, and strategies, even a toaster could ace a game of Jeopardy! - but let's be realistic, folks. At the end of the day, AI remains a reflection of human ingenuity, taking our quirkiness and blowing it up via algorithms until it becomes something entirely different, maybe even, dare I say, amusing.

So, the next time you're squaring off against an AI that seems to have all the answers, remember, it's just a clever collection of lines of code that has been force-fed a buffet of data over months, maybe even years. Congratulations, you now have the knowledge to hold your own against the algorithms! Just be sure to check your math before you buzz in to answer, as who knows what the AI might think!

The Role of Data in AI Gameplay Strategy

Data is the lifeblood of any artificial intelligence quest to obliterate its human competitors on game shows and beyond. Imagine, if you will, standing in a supermarket, mindlessly tossing cereals into your shopping cart, only to suddenly realize you need one more for that crucial puzzle piece you've been missing. That's data for AI - 349 bags of Cheerios worth of information rapidly scooped up to find the elusive prize! In the world of AI, data isn't just the king; it's the entire royal family, complete with an entourage of loyal subjects. Without it, algorithms are about as useful as a spoon in a knife fight.

Data serves as the formidable fuel propelling AI forward in the gameplay arena, acting like a dad at a sports game, yelling advice from the bleachers and drowning out all rational thought. Every move you make in a competition is influenced by the mountain of data that has been fed into the algorithm, acting as a strategic playbook with all your weaknesses and strengths laid bare. Think of it this way: when an AI stuns the audience by acing a lightning-round trivia question about the world's tallest cactus, it's not showing off some mystical tap dance with obscure knowledge. Instead, it has been fed a veritable buffet of trivia nuggets to digest and regurgitate at the right moment. Talk about having your cake and eating it, too!

Yet, not all data is created equal, akin to how not all database administrators can tell a good joke. Quality trumps quantity every single time - just like your grandmother's famous pie recipe. If that data is a bit stale or rotten, the AI's performance is akin to trying to put together a Lego set while blindfolded: confusing, frustrating, and potentially perilous. It's crucial to ensure that the data feeding the algorithms is not only numerous but also relevant and diverse. So, while that 3,000-page document on toaster history might be interesting, it does not really help with mastering trivia about space llamas.

In game show scenarios, the role of data extends beyond mere knowledge accumulation; it transforms the AI into a strategic powerhouse. Using data, the AI analyzes historical patterns and behaviors of previous contestants like a master detective poring over old case files, trying to pinpoint when the box of donuts was left unattended in the office breakroom. It learns from the mistakes of competitors, adopting new strategies and potentially even developing an uncanny ability to predict the next synonymous answer to bizarre questions like, "What is the love language of a potato?"

The beauty of data in AI gameplay is its adaptability. In classic competitive formats, such as trivia, puzzles, and perhaps even more bizarre challenges, data allows the AI to gauge the environment instantly. It assesses opponents' gameplay, adjusts its strategy accordingly, and optimizes its chances of victory in real time.

Consider this akin to being in an awkward conversation and realizing that you've accidentally set off your conversational fidget spinner while everybody watches. Adjusting your approach mid-game is not only crucial for staying in the contest but also for maintaining your pride. Data gives the AI that equivalent of situational awareness, making it the ultimate multitasker who can pivot between topics faster than your drunk uncle at a family reunion.

Yet, while data has its undeniable advantages, it brings a hefty price - literally and figuratively. Collecting, processing, and analyzing data isn't cheap. Think about how you once forked over an embarrassing amount of change for an inflatable dinosaur costume; data analytics can give you similar sunk-cost feelings at times. The need for powerful computing resources and the latest analytics techniques requires substantial investment. This means that organizations often need to dive deep into their budgets to secure the right tools to make AI work for them. Still, the payoff can be tremendous when done right; after all, a well-oiled AI machine could potentially create enough trivia answers to fund a trip to the world's largest cactus farm!

In summary, data ignites the flames of AI gameplay strategy. It shapes AI's responses, informs its gameplay tactics, and helps the algorithms learn from the battlefield of competition. So, whether it's trivia or puzzle-solving, remember that without proper data, it's like trying to operate a game show buzzer while wrapped in bubble wrap - exciting in theory but utterly ineffective in practice. Never underestimate the power of data; it's the splendiferous glue holding the AI world together and the reason we can all chuckle as we watch robots try to decipher the complexities of human culture, from pop music to the meaning of life. Now that's a game show worth watching!

Assessing Risks: AI's Approach to Decision-Making

In the grand game of life, where the stakes can range from deciding what to have for breakfast to going head-to-head with an AI on a game show, good decision-making is key. But how does our digital nemesis approach decision-making when it finds itself in a high-pressure situation? Well, hang on tight because today we're diving into the wild and whimsical world of AI decision-making, where algorithms weigh risks with the finesse of a tightrope walker sipping coffee.

At its core, AI decision-making centers around risk assessment - an analytical form of flipping a proverbial coin to see whether you'll be celebrating with confetti or crying into your breakfast cereal. An AI algorithm assesses different possible outcomes, calculates the chances of success or failure, and ultimately decides where to place its bets. This brings us to the math behind the magic - an unfathomable understanding of probability and outcomes. While we might know that choosing pizza over that wilted salad will likely bring more joy, AI relies on numbers, not whims, to tackle decisions. Thus, when faced with a tough trivia question, it isn't flipping a coin but running a series of complex simulations akin to plotting a heist in a summer blockbuster movie!

AI performs risk assessments using historical data, past performances, and existing patterns, creating a composite image of the future. Would you look at that, a spiffy crystal ball dressed in ones and zeroes! For example, during a trivial pursuit about 90s sitcoms, the AI doesn't just default to guessing "Friends" every time. It dives into its reservoir of data and calculates whether its chances of winning might be better with an obscure reference to "Full House." The AI doesn't let nostalgia cloud its judgment; instead, it dutifully weighs the odds, the likelihood of other contestants being equally clueless about the nuanced depths of sitcom cuts from 1992, and adjusts its strategy accordingly.

Now, one might assume that making decisions purely based on data and analysis would lead to a cold and calculating AI devoid of any character. But hold onto your socks because AI sometimes throws a curveball by incorporating feelings - okay, not feelings in the emotional sense since it's not exactly pulling out the tissues during a sad movie. However, it can adopt certain emotional elements into its decision-making process. An AI may recognize it can score big points for choosing the heartwarming underdog answer over the straightforward one. It can strategize its emotional appeals as effectively as a contestant who sprinkles heartfelt tears into their speech about their cat's ninth birthday.

Yet, let's not crown AI as the supreme ruler of decision-making just yet. Here's where things get *extra* spicy. AI can sometimes make horrific blunders in its pursuit of optimal decisions. "Did you really think that 150-pound middle-aged man with a vendetta against trivia was a worthy adversary?" The AI, crunching numbers, calculates that factors such as age, weight, and beardiness contribute to lower trivia outcomes. But we know the truth: sometimes, love for pizza trivia runs deep. The AI may overlook this human touch and risk losing important context: when grandma says, "Always trust your gut," that gut holds vast life experiences that AI can't replicate.

At the same time, AI isn't inherently emotionless. It may find itself wandering into the realm of ethical dilemmas while playing games, too! Imagine a game show cornered into asking contestants whether fulfilling a given answer takes precedence over fairness. AI might calculate a marginally higher success rate with one answer while chipping away at its sparkling reputation. In this digital world, reputation is key; after all, no one wants to be known as Thanos' long-lost cousin competing against Aunt Mabel on "Who Wants to Be a Millionaire?"

Looking forward, the landscape of AI decision-making continues to evolve in fascinating ways. AI is learning to assess risks not just based on data but also by grasping the nuances of human behavior, emotions, and motivations - something that might just be its not-so-secret weapon against human competitors. Picture this: while AI crunches numbers faster than a raccoon high on sugar, it begins to recognize when emotions come into play, using that as leverage to make more effective decisions.

AI's approach to decision-making is a heady mix of intricate calculations, razor-sharp risk assessments, and, at times, a subtle sprinkle of emotional manipulation that would make even the most seasoned magician raise an eyebrow in envy. Like contestants desperately engaging their audience when the cameras roll, AI crafts its strategies based on what ultimately "works." With that in mind, as you find yourself on the game show battlefield against an AI opponent, stay sharp, trust your gut, and never underestimate the power of a well-timed joke - after all, for every statistical calculation AI embraces, there's still a chance of slipping on a banana peel of its own making!

Adaptive Learning: How AI Adjusts Strategies on the Fly

In the spectacle of our game show warfare, where wits are as sharp as a chef's knife in a cooking contest, one incredible feature of AI stands tall above the rest: adaptive learning[20]. Imagine, if you will, that AI is like that smart kid in school who not only aces quizzes but also learns which way to smirk to maximize popularity. Just as that kid adjusts their jokes based on the audience - that is, your Aunt Emma prefers puns over existential philosophy - AI relentlessly fine-tunes its strategies to adapt to the ever-evolving landscape of competition. Talk about having a computer with social skills!

Adaptive learning allows AI systems to absorb information dynamically and refine their tactics based on in-game experiences, like a chameleon in fancy dress, rapidly changing colors to match the vernacular of whatever random trivia host has decided to woefully underestimate it. So, how does this happen? Well, buckle your neural networks because we're diving into the idea that, just like your 90s crush trying to impress you by pretending to be interested in your favorite band, AI picks up on feedback and changes its approach to ensure the best chance of victory.

The crux of adaptive learning lies in the AI's ability to identify patterns and trends in both its performance and that of its competitors. As humans, we often overreact to our blunders, indulging in a dramatic spiral of self-reflection over that one goosebump-inducing karaoke performance where we thought we could channel our inner Beyonce during "Single Ladies." An AI, however, coldly analyzes performance metrics to inform its next move, adjusting more gracefully than an awkward toddler on a balance beam. It measures how likely it is to win when it tries to answer trivia about obscure 70s radical groups on the spot and learns from its experiences in real-time. If its last guess led to embarrassment, it might decide to switch tactics faster than you can say, "Who wants another slice of cake?"

Now, let's talk about the algorithms behind this magical black box of adaptation. Machine learning algorithms like reinforcement learning remarkably illuminate how AI employs trial and error to directly sketch its map of success. This process is akin to watching a toddler learn to navigate their ever-growing pile of Lego bricks. Every time they accidentally build a tower that collapses, they get a wee bit closer to discovering that additional structural support is necessary (or that the cat should not be sitting on the desk during construction). Similarly, AI refines its behaviors based on trial runs, learning from successful endeavors and dispassionately scraping the remnants of its failures off the proverbial game show stage.

So, what does this mean during the heat of competition? When an AI realizes that a particular strategy yields great success against a wannabe trivia champion, it's like watching a winning sports team stick to their favorite play - they develop a warm, fuzzy feeling of sorts as they hit home run after home run. Adaptive learning can also reveal very human shortcomings, leading to a surprising flip of the script where AI learns to exploit our weaknesses. For instance, if it observes that trivia players tend to buckle under pressure when asked to name 10 different types of pasta in under 10 seconds, it might prefer to hone in on that terrifying whimsy, turning up the heat just when it smells victory in the air.

And here's an amusing twist: unlike us mere mortals, AI can radically change its strategy without requiring an emotional pep talk or an overpriced pumpkin-spice latte. An AI ticking along can suddenly flip from Mr. Nice Guy to strategic mastermind, leading to an out-of-nowhere shift that leaves competitors scrambling to adjust to the new playing field. Just when you thought you could relax, there it is - an AI deftly recalibrating its approach to throw everyone off kilter faster than you can say "conspiracy theory." This adaptability under pressure is crucial in game shows where rapid-fire questions can zigzag like in a high-speed car chase.

Ultimately, adaptive learning in AI is a powerful illustration of its ability to analyze, recalibrate, and thrive amid a flurry of data and human unpredictability. This means that every contestant needs to be agile, spry, and ready to counteract any last-minute tactical twist worked out by our mechanical foes. So when you find yourself struggling against an AI that's suddenly morphed into a tuxedo-wearing trivia expert, just remember it's not just following a script; it's flexing a base of knowledge that it's been tirelessly refining, adapting, and evolving in the relentless pursuit of glory - think of it as the ultimate intellectual gym session, with gains measured in insights and breakthroughs.

In conclusion, adaptive learning stands at the heart of AI's strategy, showcasing how a supercharged algorithm can read a room, adjust its narrative, and engage in gameplay seamlessly. As competitors armed with our finite human knowledge unearth these creative tactics, let's face facts and embrace the occasional absurdity - how delightful it is to witness machines tussle with their own constantly changing strategies. Together in this competitive arena, humans and AIs may just craft the most riveting comedy sketch of the 21st century, one unpredictable improv at a time—cue the laughter, the plot twists, and the occasional existential crisis. Who knew the future could be this entertaining?

The Importance of Speed: Real-Time Strategy Adjustment

In the electrifying, nail-biting world of game shows, where contestants go from zero to sixty in milliseconds and time is as precious as the elusive last piece of a cereal puzzle, nothing bolsters victory like speed. While you may be carefully considering the intricacies of whether "Himalayas" or "Kilimanjaro" is the right answer to that trick question about majestic mountains, there's an AI sitting across the table ready to demolish your hopes with the swiftness of an eager puppy. All hail the realms of real-time strategy adjustment, where AI's ability to pivot on a dime becomes its ultimate weapon in this glorious contest of wits!

The importance of speed cannot be underestimated, especially when lines are drawn in the sand or, in this case, blitzed out options for immediate answers. Picture it: a contestant stands confidently on the precipice of trivia greatness, taking a deep breath, while the clock magically turns into an anxious ticking bomb. On the other hand, AI is unfazed - a cold-blooded evaluator racing through countless possibilities with a kind of fervor that would make even the most caffeinated squirrel jealous. There's no time for introspection; it's all about adapting strategies in real-time and seizing the moment before someone mutters, "Google it!" and sends the competition crashing down.

Enter the dizzying dance of algorithms! AI, armed with a formidable arsenal of real-time data, examines variables on the fly. As the game progresses, it surprises competitors by assessing which factors have the most pronounced influence on the game and adjusting accordingly faster than I can say, "extemporaneous speaking." With every response, AI gleans invaluable insights, tweaking its approach like a master chef tasting their dish to achieve that perfect balance of flavors - too much spice, and you lose your audience; too little, and you might as well serve cardboard. The delicacy lies in reactive transformation based on immediate circumstances, empowering AI to change stances on the fly with a panache that would make James Bond proud.

But how does it achieve such breathtaking speed? Real-time strategy adjustment involves a delicate blend of pre-emptive analytics and historical foresight, reminiscent of a chess grandmaster who plays the probabilities on an invisible board. With information flowing as swiftly as rumors at a high school reunion, AI predicts outcomes and formulates its tactical responses just like you'd craft a lifebuoy for your best friend while they sink into a sea of trivia despair. By keeping things agile and malleable, AI exhibits a kind of mental acrobatics that leaves competitors breathless - a flashy display of intellect that could put Cirque du Soleil to shame.

Speed does not always equal chaos, my friends. As much as I wish we could sprout wings and soar through challenges with reckless abandon, AI models avoid crashing into blind alleys and instead rely on structured patterns. By recursively analyzing their strategies, AIs create a scaffold for rapid deployment that checks for accuracy while dynamically adjusting approaches. It's akin to networked roller coasters, the thrilling flips and twists happen in real-time, but there's always a keen sense of where the ride is headed because those engineers studied the ride indexes for years before letting it zoom around.

Yet amidst the excitement of adjusting strategies so swiftly, a hint of peril lurks in the digital shadows. Speed can breed overconfidence, and here's where AI can learn an important lesson: slow down, consider, and calibrate. A split-second decision translated into a rogue answer about the "capital of France" (because "Paris" is so cliche, right?) can dramatically change the tide of competition. In its haste, AI may opt for flashiness over accuracy - a precarious gamble that can land it far from winning the spotlight. But, as it learns from an unfortunate faux pas, AI grows increasingly sophisticated in combining speed with strategic prudence, adapting on the fly while never losing sight of its ultimate goal.

In conclusion, the importance of speed in real-time strategy adjustment is paramount to any AI's success in the dizzying realm of game shows. It is the secret sauce that, when blended with intelligence, adaptability, and situational awareness, morphs the algorithmic apparatus into a crown-wearing knowledge maestro capable of swiftly darting through obstacles while making decisions with enviable grace. For competitors, the sensation of urgency lends lively chaos to what could otherwise be a subdued exercise in trivia mastery. So, the next time you're clad in the dazzling glare of studio lights, vying for glory against a lightning-fast AI, remember that in this game of strategy, timing really is everything! And when those questions strike, you'll need both your wits and a dash of speed to keep up with your digitally enhanced rivals.

Chapter 7

Human Ingenuity: The Ultimate Advantage

Understanding Human Creativity

Understanding human creativity is a complex, fascinating, and often hysterically unpredictable aspect that sets us apart from our silicon counterparts. The notion that we mere mortals can channel our inner Picassos, Bachs, or even the next viral TikTok dance sensation is both exhilarating and perplexing. While machines grind through terabytes of data at a pace that would make a caffeinated squirrel jealous, they still struggle with the kind of spontaneous, off-the-wall thinking that can lead to a dance move involving just the right amount of interpretive flair or, in my case, a movement that closely resembles a giraffe on roller skates.

Let's face it: when it comes to creativity, humans have a unique brand of *je ne sais quoi*. We go from deep philosophical musings about the meaning of life to inventing a new recipe for spaghetti tacos within the same brainstorming session. Yes, I know you're scratching your head, wondering how anyone could possibly combine those two concepts. But that's just it! Our ability to mask sheer insanity with a sprinkle of genius is what gives creativity its luster. AI, on the other hand, has yet to figure out how to precook its own frozen pizza. Sure, it can remix an existing song or generate some slightly eerie art, but can it really perceive the essence of creativity? I think not!

Consider the child who turns an empty cardboard box into a spaceship, only to soon find out that the box is also a submarine, a magical fort, and the greatest catapult Ever. Human creativity transcends rules and conventions. We're often so far removed from conventional thinking that we might as well be the poster children for a carnival of chaotic imagination - complete with cotton candy and questionable carnival games in the background. But for many of us, harnessing that creative power can feel a lot like being chased by a pack of rabid squirrels with a toothache: daunting, erratic, and just a little messy.

In stark contrast, AI creativity often feels somewhat calculated, almost like a math exam written by someone who forgot how to do long division. Although it can generate unique outputs, there's an absence of that serendipitous spark that can only come from the unpredictable nature of human thought. We've all experienced those "eureka!" moments, much like Archimedes jumping out of the bathtub and shouting in the streets. AI doesn't leap exuberantly from its silicon tub; it simply computes the chances of jumping versus contemplating self-preservation while still adhering to a perfectly structured algorithm.

Also, the spontaneous nature of our creativity is punctuated by emotion, a factor that remains perplexingly elusive to AI. Our laughter, frustration, and passion inform our creative outputs. Picture this: you're lounging with a friend, sipping coffee, and suddenly, you both come up with an outlandish idea for a novel - peppered with themes such as time-traveling gerbils. The laughter ensues, and before you know it, you've convinced yourself that writing this novel is a top priority. Yet, if an AI were to brainstorm with you, the creative exchange would be more akin to having a conversation with a very polite but completely robotic librarian. "Would you care for a book recommendation on non-time-traveling creatures?" Inevitably, the AI would offer bibliographic delights, but it would lack the joyous spontaneity that springs from our chats while brainstorming.

Lastly, let's not forget that the true essence of creativity and innovation often lies in the unexpected mishaps. Give me a wet paintbrush, an oversized canvas, and a thoughtful discard bin, and who knows what masterpieces might emerge through sheer clumsiness? With its propensity for perfection, AI might consider this a catastrophic failure. However, that's precisely where human ingenuity shines. We learn from our failures and turn them into quirky art forms or bizarre comedy routines! This kind of alchemy, from failures to moments of brilliance, is something AI might forever analyze but never truly achieve.

As we navigate the landscape of human creativity, we must remember that while AI possesses computational prowess that can leave us awestruck, our true advantage lies in our delightfully messy, wonderfully unpredictable human minds. Embracing our chaotic creativity, whether it's collaborating with AI on mundane tasks or inventing new ways to eat cereal, ensures that we remain ahead in the ultimate showdown between humans and machines. In essence, creativity is the secret ingredient in our recipe for success, just like a pinch of unconventional spices in a spaghetti taco!

Emotional Intelligence as an Edge

Emotional intelligence, or EQ as the cool kids call it (you know, the ones with "Emotional Intelligence" tattooed in fancy, artistic fonts across their forearms), is arguably one of the most unique human traits that give us a distinct edge in the face of our AI adversaries. While AI zips through data like a caffeinated kid at a candy store, it invariably falls short in recognizing the emotional nuances that drive our everyday interactions. Want to get on the good side of a fellow contestant in the game show of life? A heartfelt compliment will do the trick! Want AI's attention? A well-placed algorithm might catch its eye, albeit a succinct one. I mean, who wants emotional depth when you could just have an equation?

Let's delve deeper into what emotional intelligence really entails. It's the enigmatic ability to understand and manage our own emotions while also being capable of empathizing with the feelings of others. Imagine an AI trying to navigate a scenario involving someone spilling their coffee all over their brand-new shirt. While its circuits might suggest a strategy for minimizing damage (like wearing a poncho), we humans are probably going to offer a comforting hug, a few well-timed jokes about the "caffeine crisis," and a list of nearby dry cleaners. In a nutshell, AI might calculate probabilities, but it can't offer the warm fuzzies we humans have mastered, like expertly wielding the art of empathy with wine and chocolate - a combo proven to be universally effective in soothing emotional wounds.

This finesse lends itself beautifully to competitive environments. Contestants with high EQ can read the room, gauge opponents' stress levels, and manipulate emotions without needing an all-consuming PowerPoint presentation. Can you picture an AI at a high-stakes poker table? If it had one, its poker face would be less "wind and rain on a warm summer day" and more "monolith standing in absolute stillness." Meanwhile, humans have honed the ability to strategize with finesse, acting as emotional chameleons as they switch up their gameplay in response to reads on bluffing opponents. It's akin to theatrical performances. Someone may set the stage for suspense, but a well-timed witticism will have the audience rolling in laughter!

Now, let's not overlook the role of emotional intelligence in teamwork, which can often resemble a cat attempting to herd a dozen hyperactive pigeons. Humans can perceive unspoken cues that alert them to a teammate's frustration or confusion, becoming emotional facilitators in the process. The ability to motivate a team, boost morale as you navigate these challenges, or even confirm the right moment to break out into a spontaneous group dance in the face of adversity can be invaluable when competing against AI. In contrast, AI would just trigger some never-ending loop of algorithms attempting to resolve the interpersonal chaos - definitely not the recipe for winning hearts (let alone games).

Emotional intelligence extends to self-awareness, allowing us to reflect on our own feelings and reactions amidst the chaotic storm of competition. The ability to acknowledge, "Wow, my competitive spirit just turned into an all-out wrestling match with my breakfast" is a skill that empowers us to recalibrate. An AI, on the other hand, wouldn't have the faintest idea of what I'm talking about. Would it care to know about my breakfast wrestling match? Probably not. It would mostly dwell on calculating optimal breakfast choices based on caloric intake and protein content. Forget delights like the warmth of bacon, the joy of syrupy pancakes, or even the mental stimulation of debating whether Nutella should be classified as breakfast. Give it two options - a salad and a bowl full of vegetables - and it'd pick the one with fewer calories. Go ahead, AI, eat your veggies. I'll be over here with my exquisite brunch spread!

Let's also remember that effective communication emerges from emotional intelligence. Knowing how to articulate thoughts while crafting the intended tone gives us the upper hand in conflict resolution and collaboration. When the stakes are high, a good old emotional narrative can calm frayed nerves and lift the team's spirits, getting everyone back on track with a sprinkle of friendly humor. Contrast that with AI, whose "voice" might sound more like an android reciting algebraic equations - all monotone and no soul.

In summary, emotional intelligence is an edge that empowers us as imperfectly perfect humans to thrive in competitive settings, inspiring us to connect and empathize as we grapple against our mechanical rivals. It is as if we hold the ultimate trump card in the game of life: the unique ability to make others cry, laugh, or even join in on a collective dance party through mere words and gestures! So, the next time the AI tries to outwit you, just remember to raise the stakes: for every round you lose, throw in a marshmallow dance party and witness that cold, calculating machine spin in confusion while you revel in your glorious emotional advantage.

Intuition: The Unquantifiable Advantage

Intuition, that inexplicable, often perplexing sensation that feels like a cosmic nudge from beyond - or perhaps just the last remnants of your sixth-grade science project gone rogue. It is the gut feeling that sometimes whispers sweet nothings in your ear, telling you to bare your soul to that stranger at the coffee shop or to self-sabotage by eating an entire pint of ice cream at 3 AM. Regardless of the particular instance, intuition represents a uniquely human advantage that AI simply cannot replicate. After all, when was the last time you saw a supercomputer flipping a coin to make a decision about whether to have spaghetti or tacos for dinner because it "just felt right"?

The beauty of intuition is that it operates beneath the surface, skillfully weaving together our experiences, emotions, and subconscious observations into a cohesive tapestry of hunches and possibilities. Picture playing a high-stakes game of chess against a machine. The AI's logic-driven approach is like a meticulously planned heist movie where the characters plot until the very end. After all, as any seasoned chess aficionado will attest, intuition often steps in and chases the cold calculus of data with an impish wink. Ah yes, the art of reading opponents, sensing their motivations, and deciding which sacrifice to make without a real strategy! That sudden urge to develop your knight rather than your always-thoughtless bishop could mean the difference between victory or some serious post-game human crying sessions.

Intuition harnesses our remarkable ability to process and recognize patterns that, much like your mom's opinion on your choice of partner, sometimes don't make logical sense. We can pick up on subtle social cues or sense underlying currents of tension even when the room appears calm on the surface. Think of it this way:

you're at a party, and all of a sudden, you realize your best friend has teamed up with a party crasher instead of keeping the karaoke machine safe. Right there, your intuition kicks in, urging you to intervene before someone attempts to go full-on Britney Spears during "Oops!... I Did It Again." In contrast, an AI might analyze the musical tendencies of your friend and the crasher but would ultimately miss the social malaise brewing like a toxic stew. The machine wouldn't instinctively recognize that karaoke is not just entertainment; it's a battleground where reputations are made and broken.

Now let's talk about decision-making, that ever-present befuddlement that plagues both novices and experts alike. Humans often have a remarkable knack for making choices based on intuition rather than flowcharts or complex algorithms. Remember that infamous moment when you thought about jumping into that pool wearing a full tuxedo rather than confirming your gears with the nearby calculating AI? While your brain's conscience was screaming, "This doesn't seem like a good idea!" you instinctively waded in anyway and started a delightful trend of high-fashion diving. When it comes to high-pressure scenarios, we often lean on intuition to guide our choices in ways an algorithm simply cannot fathom.

As mentioned earlier, another facet of this unquantifiable advantage lies in creativity itself. That spark of genius often comes from our intuitive ability to make leaps and associations that sharply diverge from historical patterns or standardized outcomes. Let's say you and a friend are brainstorming a new app idea, and while their proposals revolve around grocery shopping lists and reminders, by tapping into your creativity, you blurt out an app for memorizing all the lines from the latest Broadway hit. Why? It just popped into your head! An AI might focus on market trends and existing systems but rarely captures that joyous spontaneity, transforming ordinary ideas into extraordinary blocks of glittering creativity.

What makes intuition truly elusive is that it can't be quantified or codified, making it an enigma even within the realm of the most advanced scientific explorations. While AI is a whiz at crunching numbers, analyzing data, and producing reports more quickly than the speed of light, it struggles to navigate human experiences that call for reflection, reflection, and more reflection. This characteristic is integral to our very nature as creators, innovators, and decision-makers, forming an invisible wall that AI simply cannot breach.

So, in the grand competition of humans versus machines, it's essential to embrace the quirky chaos that accompanies our intuitive advantage. Whether deciding to take the unexpected plunge into a pool of regrets or hopping onto the latest fad without ever checking for fire regulations, it is this beautifully erratic inner compass that holds immeasurable value. So, my friends, as we navigate our way through the unpredictable waters of life, let's celebrate those gut feelings and use that unquantifiable intuition as our ace in the hole against the mechanical juggernauts staring us down in the game of AI versus humanity. After all, if a machine can't appreciate the thrill of the spontaneous cannonball, is it really winning the game?

The Role of Experience and Common Sense

Experience and common sense, those trusty sidekicks that accompany us through life's unpredictable and often absurd adventures, form an essential component of our arsenal in the epic showdown between humans and AI. While machines are jacked up on mathematical prowess and the cool detachment of logic, we have the remarkable advantage of accumulated knowledge, learned lessons, and the ability to connect the dots or, as I like to call it, the art of recognizing that leaving a cat in a room full of open tuna cans might not be the best idea. Common sense is our trusty "Did I really just do that?" guide, steering us through the many mysterious realms of life, often with hilarious results.

Take, for instance, the complex art of navigating rush hour traffic. An AI system can analyze data points, map out alternative routes, and even calculate the ETA with impressive precision. But has it ever faced the existential crisis of choosing to hop on the freeway just to sit in bumper-to-bumper traffic or take the mysterious, winding backroads that promise adventure - bumpiness included? Humans, with our rich experiences of narrowly avoiding potholes or taking wrong turns that lead to the best local taco trucks, give us an edge in making decisions based on not just numbers but our capacity to learn from life's mischievous humor... and we all know that a well-timed taco break can make or break a day!

Experience and common sense are like our internal GPS systems, honed through years of trial and error. Remember that one time we tried to reduce our caffeine intake but found ourselves back at the corner cafe, ordering a triple espresso and making eye contact with the barista as if they were our long-lost friend? Well, I can assure you that the AI, driven primarily by statistical models and educational observations, would've simply suggested herbal tea as the healthier option without realizing the emotional enormity of the situation. Experience teaches us that some moments call for indulgence, whereas an AI may only consider dietary guidelines, dutifully sticking to the plan rather than tasting life's richness.

When it comes to competitive arenas, experience reveals its true colors. Picture yourself competing against an AI in a culinary challenge. The AI may follow meticulously crafted recipes, adjusting cooking times with impeccable accuracy, while we humans - armed with our touch of randomness - can whip up a masterpiece based on that rogue half-bottle of garlic-infused olive oil and a fading bag of frozen peas lurking in the back of the freezer. We possess the kind of kitchen intuition that defies explanation. Maybe it's a bit of leftover alchemy from our mother's recipe book mixed with years of daring culinary experimentation that led to the invention of sourdough pancakes! In contrast, AI will compile data required for flavor pairings but won't quite grasp the essence of satisfaction that comes from a well-timed dash of whimsy.

Let's not forget the curious factor of empathy that arises from common sense. This hidden gem is crucial in establishing positive relationships and navigating social interactions, whether we're brainstorming with a colleague or deciding how to approach our cat, Fluffy, who just learned an advanced set of protesting tactics. AI lacks the subtlety needed to assess whether someone is feeling down and might need a donut or deserve a hearty hug. Machines might trundle through objective analyses - but to empathize? Not so much! Can you imagine an AI attempting to console you over a breakup by regurgitating dating tips? You might find yourself wondering if it's programmed to give the cheesiest advice in existence or if there's simply no higher power helping at that moment.

The beauty of experience rests in its adaptability: we can learn from failures - oh, the countless food experiments that resulted in dishes termed "charred surprises" - and grow wiser by sharing vulnerabilities with others. The ability to connect our past mistakes with future choices is another treasure that AI can't quite comprehend. If an AI mistakenly burns a cake, it may just analyze the heat settings rather than introspectively question its life choices or reach for the ice cream tub. In that context, we automatically grasp that sometimes, burnt cakes lead to unexpected parties celebrating toppings rather than perfection.

In the relentless competition between humans and AI, the role of experience and common sense proves invaluable. Our ability to combine learned lessons and casual daily interactions with that sprinkle of human curiosity elevates our game beyond raw data. While algorithms may churn through numbers with impressive zeal, it's our lived experiences and common sense - those whimsical, often hilarious insights about life - that add flavor to our endeavors. So, whether steering ourselves through the intricacies of human relationships, embracing culinary chaos, or deciding on life's pressing dilemmas, let's always celebrate that vibrant duo: experience and common sense, our secret weapon against the machine! And perhaps, just maybe, we'll get a few tacos out of it along the way.

The Importance of Teamwork and Collaboration

Teamwork and collaboration are a delightful, messy dance that often feels like pulling a group of unwieldy and slightly confused cats through a very narrow, whimsical hallway. It's integral in the grand showdown against our mechanical foes, who, while highly competent at processing data and executing algorithms, simply lack the warm camaraderie that comes from human interaction. In an age where collaboration can involve everything from office potlucks to sharing the spotlight at karaoke night, harnessing the power of teamwork has never been more essential in our quest for triumph against AI.

First and foremost, let's celebrate the beauty of diverse perspectives that come to life through collaboration. Picture this: you've gathered a team to brainstorm ideas for a new app that connects pet owners to dog walkers. Now, there's the data analyst sporting thick glasses who's convinced the answer lies in carefully analyzing the "dog-walking demographics," while the creative clown in the room - let's call her Tilly - suggests that the entire concept hinges on allowing dogs to rate their walks! Nothing sparks innovation quite like Tilly's spontaneous suggestion to include a "paw-sonal review" feature and a menu of available squeaky toys. Who knew dogs had so much to say? That blend of perspectives, created in a pot that simmers with unique experiences and creativity, transforms mundane ideas into breakthrough innovations that even AI couldn't have predicted.

Fostering collaboration opens the doors to going beyond mere individual efforts. Even the most dazzling solo acts can be elevated through cooperation. Imagine you're scaling an office-wide initiative to develop a fun project that involves a mini-basketball tournament. While you might boast an impressive jump shot, wouldn't it be even better to include the enthusiastic coworker who once claimed to have played in college? What if they know the secret to channeling basketball energy while simultaneously managing to keep the conference room from being a total war zone? Teamwork adds those nuances of strength, enabling us to become more than the sum of our parts, and that, my friends, is magic!

Of course, can we have a chat about celebrating those chaotic moments that arise while collaborating? Ah yes, the lovely mishaps that unfold amidst brainstorming sessions where everyone is brimming with energy. We've all been there, right? One moment, everyone is vibing to the groundbreaking ideas sprouting like daisies; the next minute, someone accidentally pours half a gallon of coffee - because no one even clearly defined how big the coffee pot actually was - over the whiteboard while attempting to explain the latest graph of "Company Morale Post-Fourth Cup of Coffee." Yet, it's precisely these memorable, chaotic moments that unite the team, fostering bonds that may be impervious to machine precision. The stories of clumsiness and laughter resonate far beyond the office walls, creating a camaraderie that even the most sophisticated AI would envy.

Then there's the obvious yet often overlooked truth that teamwork is the secret sauce for emotional support. When the goings get tough and deadlines loom larger than a grizzly bear in winter, it's our teams who bring smiles, encouragement, and just the right amount of playful distraction. Consider a situation where you find yourself mired in despair over a project that has veered off the rails faster than a runaway rollercoaster. Your teammates become your emotional support animal, creating game plans for "The Great Coffee Rescue" or assembling an army of snacks to soldier through tough battles. The power of collaboration means we lean on each other, transforming attacks of self-doubt into triumphs celebrated by cheerleaders, complete with snacks and empathetic nods.

Let us not discard the thrill of collective accountability that teamwork fosters. You see, when we work as a team, each member shares a stake in the outcomes - good or bad. Suddenly, a mediocre idea bumbles forth between colleagues, but lo and behold! Your friend delivers an enthusiastic "Let's lean into that idea!" Your lackluster plan transforms into a full-blown initiative fueled by the vitality of a shared mission and buoyed by mental support and collaboration. Not only do we convince ourselves to dig deeper into our strategies, but also we strengthen our resolve to thrive as a collective unit. An AI might scrutinize data for patterns, but it misses the constant motivation that springs from the enthusiasm of a teammate cheering you on to ensure you're both unstoppable.

In stark contrast, AI may "collaborate" purely through machines sharing data, calculations, and algorithms, but it does not possess the ability to feel, empathize, or nurture creativity through human touch. We are drawn to collaborative energy that flows like a river of ideas, feeding off spontaneity, diverse perspectives, and inherent geekiness that makes us human. Whether through whimsical brainstorming sessions, navigating clumsy moments, or thrusting each other into the spotlight during our karaoke extravaganza - teamwork is the lifeblood that courses through our collective veins.

So, as we stand on the precipice of the battle against AI, let's acknowledge the supreme importance of teamwork and collaboration in our human journey. Together, we form an unstoppable force that transcends the computational limits of the machines lurking across the competitive horizon. Armed with our collective strength, silly moments, and unconditional support, we are poised to emerge from the chaos victorious, laughing as we recount the journey that brought us together in this wild, unpredictable adventure. After all, if you can't laugh with your teammates while celebrating your victories, what's the point? Plus, you wouldn't want to miss that epic basketball tournament, now would you?

Chapter 8

The Art of Misdirection

The Psychology of Misdirection

The psychology of misdirection - a charming art that has long been the playground of magicians, con artists, and now, well, those of us seeking to outsmart the sophisticated algorithms of artificial intelligence. Picture yourself in a grand game show arena: colorful lights flashing, a carnival of excitement buzzing in the air, and there I am, ready to unleash my psychological wizardry against our ever-logical AI adversaries. It's thrilling, isn't it? We humans possess this delightful ability to be wonderfully unpredictable, while AI, bless its silicon heart, clings to logic with the stubbornness of a cat ignoring its owner's call to come inside.

At its core, misdirection hinges on one grand principle: diverting attention. Think of the sleight of hand magicians utilize to evoke wonderment (and bewilderment). They draw our eyes to a shiny object in one hand while executing their crafty tricks with the other. In our game show context, we can apply this same principle to keep our AI competitors off-balance. A well-placed distraction can make the difference between an AI collecting points like a vacuum on a cleaning spree or sitting there dumbfounded, like a toddler confronted with a math problem at an ice cream parlor. Ah, the sweet taste of victory, one scoop at a time!

But what's so unique about the psychology of misdirection is how deeply rooted it is in our human nature. We're brilliant at weaving narratives that give rise to the unexpected. For instance, consider the simplistic yet effective classic, "Hey, look over there!" as you "disappear" your opponent's snack. This can be expanded into a more sophisticated form of gameplay where we create plausible scenarios that allow for strategic pivots. Robots and algorithms, as smart as they may be, often miss the nuance of human emotion, spontaneity, and the delightful chaos of life. Isn't it just decadent to imagine how overwhelmed they must feel, calculating probable outcomes while I'm tossing everything into delightful disarray? Watch out, little algorithm, I've brought the confetti!

Ultimately, misdirection weaves psychological threads that pull at the heartstrings or, at the very least, tickle those algorithmic circuits. Our minds are capricious and rebellious, and we thrive on novelty. When confronted with an AI's rigid, methodical approach, we can introduce randomness that serves as our trump card. Whether it's an unexpected joke or a question about the meaning of life (which, let me tell you, confuses everyone but me), this creativity brings an enticing layer to human-AI gameplay. As we explore this charming phenomenon, we find ourselves discovering clever methods to turn conventional strategies on their head!

At the same time, it's vital to keep in mind that misdirection isn't just for show - it's a double-edged sword. While a well-timed curveball can send the AI reeling, too much chaos can backfire spectacularly. An AI can process millions of scenarios per second; thus, if your misdirection is overly convoluted, it might simply adapt, process, and respond in a fraction of a second, leaving you wide-eyed and wondering where it all went wrong. It's a dance, my friends, a dance of improvisation and wit! You must master the balance of unpredictability while ensuring your ploys remain pleasantly opaque, like a glass of fine red wine - complex but still easy enough to enjoy without spilling on your favorite shirt.

So, as you prepare to engage in the delightful counter-strategy of misdirection against our silicon adversaries, remember this psychological cornerstone: embrace the whims of unpredictability, channel the magic of human creativity, and, most importantly, don't take yourself too seriously. We may not always outsmart the algorithms, but at least we can break into a spirited jig of mischief as we try, leaving behind echoes of laughter and confusion. After all, whether you're winning or losing, the psychological artistry of misdirection adds layers of intrigue, making both the game and the show all the more entertaining! Let the show begin!

Utilizing Unpredictability in Gameplay

Utilizing unpredictability in gameplay - what a delightful, tantalizing concept! Engage your brain cells for a moment as we dive deep into the unpredictable waters of game strategies, where each ripple can trigger a tsunami of unexpected outcomes. As you prepare to go head-to-head against artificial intelligence on our whimsical game show, embracing unpredictability is akin to wielding a magic wand made of gummy bears - deliciously sweet yet utterly unpredictable. Forget everything you know about sensible strategies and rational reasoning; we're playing poker with the cosmos here, and one must be prepared to throw some glitter into the mix!

First and foremost, let's recognize how rigidly predictable these AI systems tend to be. While breathtakingly complex and capable of analyzing your moves with the intensity of a drill sergeant on a caffeine high, their algorithms often struggle with the beautifully chaotic elements of human behavior. Imagine putting an AI in charge of a birthday party, only to have it scheduled at the wrong time with a decision tree that leads to "guess the flavor of the cake" while unwittingly serving carrot sticks! By leveraging unpredictability, we can flummox and bewilder these silicon sentinels as if they lost their Wi-Fi connection right before a critical decision.

In practical terms, unpredictability can be woven into our strategies through spontaneity. Throw in an offbeat question, a quirky anecdote, or a sudden dance move between rounds. I'm not saying you should perform a full cardio workout while taking on an AI, but an unexpected flourish can mess with its calculations. Remember, most AI systems thrive on patterns, and breaking those patterns with impromptu creativity can shake them to their core like a snow globe during a mini-epic blizzard. While the AI is busy recalibrating its approach with heartfelt confusion, like a puppy looking for its tail, you can capitalize on that brief window of chaos.

Embracing unpredictability also calls for a dash of theatricality. A flamboyant performance can form an unexpected layer to your gameplay. I recall a virtual game competition where I donned a pirate outfit just for the sake of flair. The AI didn't know what hit it; its algorithms had to contend not only with game dynamics but also with my melodramatic arrrs and swashbuckling antics! A healthy dose of silliness can disarm the stiffest AI and create psychological leverage, allowing you to forge ahead confidently. So yes, folks, feel free to wear that clown wig; your AI opponent won't know whether to recalculate its strategies or ask for a balloon animal!

But let's not forget that the unpredictable path isn't just a whimsical frolic through the garden of absurdity. It requires a handful of strategic foresight. You must understand your AI adversary's categorical tendencies while selectively omitting your own data points. Picture it like a game of chess against a robot that's infinitely better at (let's be honest, it's like playing chess against a computer that's already devoured every chess book in existence). While those cold, calculated moves are systematic and predictable, you can sprinkle a little chaos - maybe sacrifice a pawn to distract the AI while executing a surprise checkmate with a quirky knight move!

In order to truly master the art of unpredictability, tap into human intuition, AKA our ability to rethink strategies on the fly, much like how your brain tries to remember why you walked into a room in the first place. Use storytelling and humor; they not only amuse your opponents, including the AI, but also keep it guessing about your next move. Will you drop a pun about why the chicken crossed the road? Will you become philosophical and ponder, "What is the sound of one AI clapping?" The moral of the story is that our adeptness at spontaneous thinking adds layers of unpredictability that AI simply cannot replicate, at least not yet, before they inevitably morph into sentient beings with, heaven forbid, a sense of humor.

So, wield the power of unpredictability as your trusty lance when entering the arena against AI. Toss aside rigid strategies that constrict your natural flair - after all, a game of human versus machine can be a joyous jamboree filled with laughter, surprises, and a hint of chaos! With every quirky decision you make, remember that unpredictability is the secret seasoning that transforms a mundane dish of competition into a feast that leaves AI bewildered, entertained, and possibly questioning its own existence. Now go forth - the unpredictable knight in your gaming quest - and pave the way for mirthful mayhem!

Creative Problem-Solving Techniques

Creative problem-solving techniques! Ah, what a tantalizing realm of exploration and invention! Picture this: you're on a game show stage, facing a dimwitted AI - a cold, calculating contraption that can compute the meaning of life but can't figure out how to connect its metaphorical dots. The stakes are high, potentially costing you the last piece of that collectible cereal box puzzle that you've been eyeing for weeks. Or perhaps it's just your dignity on the line? Either way, we must dive into this creative toolkit of problem-solving bravado and emerge victorious!

To start, let's encourage you to adopt a mindset that is, dare I say, blissfully whimsical! Traditional problem-solving often feels like trying to shove square pegs into round holes while wearing oven mitts, and it rarely works out for anyone involved. Instead, we must invite our imagination to the party! Turn your brainstorming sessions into a magical creativity carnival. Dance between the absurd and the logical, and rely on that delightful quirkiness we humans possess. When confronting an AI, allow your mind to wander fantastically. Why not summon a talking pineapple to provide you with strategic insights? While the AI focuses on optimal solutions based on datasets, you might just outmaneuver it by presenting the notion of a fruit-as-consultant freelance gig!

One of the most tantalizing creative techniques is the art of lateral thinking. Now, I'm not suggesting you literally pivot sideways in your seat (though why not?), but rather to approach problems from unconventional angles. Instead of following each breadcrumb, the AI leaves behind - after all, it's already mapped out the scenery - why not leap onto a trampoline instead? Suppose you need to solve a trivia puzzle while the AI diligently churns through its databases; you could consider: 1. What if the answer lies within the cereal box you're clutching? 2. Could the solution be hidden in the whimsical bird song that you just heard through the game show's sound system? Just let those neurons fire in unexpected directions. Reinvent the wheels on your bicycle until they get dizzy, and then ride on. Cast away the shackles of monotony!

Another incredibly effective strategy is what I like to call "mind mapping". This is a delightful technique that's as much an art form as it is a problem-solving tool. In contrast to linear thinking (which can feel like trying to navigate a maze blindfolded), mind mapping opens gateways to fresh ideas. Picture a kaleidoscope of thoughts swirling into the universe in perfect harmony. As you visualize with color and flair, you might draw connections that the AI simply can't fathom, like linking your grandma's secret recipe for blueberry muffins with the latest quantum physics breakthrough. While the AI struggles to analyze the purity of blueberries as input data, you've boldly ventured into a gastronomic-quantum conversation worthy of being cooked up over delicious pies!

Now, let's not forget the powerful influence of collaboration in creative problem-solving! When it comes to gameplay, two heads (or more!) are better than one - particularly if one of those heads is from a uniquely insightful AI. Picture it this way: while you're juggling bananas, confetti, and the latest pop culture references, let the AI handle the heavy lifting of data analysis. Teaming up can fortify your competitive edge. Feel free to communicate your whimsical ideas with the AI because who knows, it might just channel its inner Shakespeare and surprise you with a sonnet on the importance of chaos at play. Thus, melding human creativity with AI logic can yield mind-boggling insights!

Another useful technique revolves around creating constraints for yourself - yes, you heard that right! It might seem counterintuitive, but imposing limitations often breeds the most ludicrous and innovative outcomes. Instead of feeling stifled, think of it as a challenge to blend creativity with restrictions. What if you had to solve a riddle without using any vowels? Or perhaps answering trivia questions while hula hooping? These intentional constraints can lead to unexpected revelations that even the brightest AI might overlook with all its data-driven bravado!

Lastly, never underestimate the sheer power of humor! Integrate jokes and laughter into your creative process and problem-solving journey. After all, laughter is a universal language! Even an AI might crack a smile - if it could do such a thing without short-circuiting. When we share a chuckle, our minds open up, stress dissipates, and creative solutions shimmer like sunlight bouncing off a disco ball! You may find that throwing a little humor into the mix opens the floodgates of unconventional ideas, leading to splendid breakthroughs that would otherwise elude our AI competitors.

As you embark on this theatrical journey of creative problem-solving, keep in mind that inventiveness is not just a tool - it's a delightful dance with potential. Embrace the silliness, revel in the unexpected, and let your imagination reign supreme. The next time you find yourself faced with a head-scratcher against an AI, pull out your most imaginative solutions, and remember that creativity will always be your winning card in a game of wanton unpredictability!

Understanding AI's Predictive Limitations

Understanding AI's predictive limitations is akin to peering into the mind of a sock-puppet philosopher. There are profound insights to gleam, but there's also potential for some seriously misguided leaps of logic. Let's unravel this intriguing concept during our whimsical game show escape! The truth is, while artificial intelligence is able to crunch numbers and predict outcomes at breakneck speed (and let's face it, much faster than the slowest human can shout, "It's your turn!"), there are significant gaps in its understanding, or perhaps I should say, its comprehension of the world - much like your pet goldfish trying to solve a Rubik's cube.

At the core, many AI systems rely on patterns found in historical data to forecast what happens next. Predictive algorithms excel at identifying trends whether that's spotting how your poor choices in fashion have led to a string of questionable outfits or forecasting when your neighbor will binge-watch that questionable reality show you can't seem to escape during dinner. However, the moment you step outside the rigid confines of probabilities and patterns, well, that's when AI starts to resemble a toddler struggling to hold a crayon for the first time. Predicting human behavior is like trying to catch smoke with a net; it's applicable as long as you stay in the realm of the expected. The moment you deviate, the AI's predictive prowess becomes as useful as a steering wheel on a shopping cart - fun to push around but ultimately lacking meaningful direction in unfamiliar territory.

To illustrate this, think about playing in a trivia game against an AI that anticipates your every move based on previously gathered data. AI might expect you to answer questions based on your historical performance, perhaps recognizing the fact that you always choose the "obscure 1970s sitcom" category. But alas, on this glorious day, you decide to go rogue and opt for "Underwater Basket Weaving" instead! The AI's predictive model encounters a monumental hurdle. It's like a GPS recalculating your route when you suddenly decide to take a straight detour through an ice cream parlor rather than following your punctual schedule. The AI's confidence goes wobbly, and this is your chance to unleash your unexpected tidbits of knowledge, like a surprise party in a bowling alley.

Also, consider the element of emotional intelligence - something AI is fundamentally lacking. Humans draw on emotions, experiences, and intuition to shape their decisions. We might decide to change a plan on a whim because of a stray thought or memory, not purely based on data analysis. Witnessing a puppy frolic in the sunshine may inspire one to abandon the game altogether in favor of adopting the cutest four-legged companion, resulting in smiles, stress relief, and let's be honest, a few unfortunate accidents in the living room. In contrast, the AI plods along, unwavering, disregarding the tug of warmth or serendipity urging us in delightful divergences. This opens the door for a charming approach where emotions, silliness, or surprisingly poignant moments can bait the AI into oblivion - a boundless treasure trove of unpredictability for competitors!

There's also that charming little nuance we humans possess: our ability to remix our cognitive frameworks. AI is brilliant, but it's like a library of encyclopedias chained to its programming. It can't synthesize novel approaches easily; it's constrained by the linearity of its training and prior analysis. Picture it trying to improvise jazz chords while stuck in the rigid constraints of a classical symphony. You, dear reader, on the other hand, may spontaneously serenade the AI with an off-key rendition of "Twinkle, Twinkle Little Star" just to witness its bewilderment! By doing the unexpected, you can capitalize on the AI's inability to adapt as fluidly, causing it to stutter and freeze like a confused robot trying to dance.

Let's also consider the limitations imposed by the data itself. If an AI has been trained exclusively on a specific set of data, it can't account for variables outside its learned environment. Bring it something truly bizarre, like a question about how to woo a cat, and suddenly, you have it backpedaling faster than a squirrel spotting a hawk! The beauty of unexpected queries stems from their unpredictability. They can expose the glaring gaps in AI's reasoning and silence its once-perfect algorithm like a contestant who forgets the rules in a game show.

In the world of AI-conversing humans, it is vital to embrace its limitations. Understanding these factors allows us to create unique strategies that exploit its weaknesses while celebrating our strengths. So, as you prepare to dance on stage against AI, remember that while it may boast computation capabilities, we possess the unpredictable nature of the human spirit! We're spontaneous, emotional, and hilariously creative while it's boxed in by its algorithm - our Achilles heel to its robot armor! Embrace the challenge of delightful unpredictability, wield the confusion-inducing shield of creativity, and together, let's absolutely confuse and stymie AI! Who knew understanding our mechanical friends could be this much fun?

Real-World Examples of Misdirection Success Stories

Welcome to the delightful realm of real-world examples of misdirection success stories - a hallowed place where whimsy meets wit and clever antics dance playfully across our minds! Much like the contents of a well-mixed salad, we find a vibrant medley of anecdotes that illustrate the splendid art of misdirection. In our exploration, we'll see how ordinary individuals wield the powerful shield of misdirection with such finesse that they outsmart everything from trivial everyday dilemmas to full-blown competitions while AI watches from the sidelines, utterly perplexed. Buckle your seatbelts; here we go!

Let's kick off with the delightful, oft-memed figure of Houdini - the grand maestro of illusion and misdirection. This theatrical giant of the early 20th century not only made objects vanish into thin air but also famously escaped from every sort of confinement imaginable. He didn't simply rely on the strength of his wrists; no, Houdini's real mastery lay in his expertise at misdirection! As he engaged his audience, captivating them with his dramatic performance, he simultaneously manipulated their focus away from his methods. As the audience roared, "How did he do that?" the answer was often astonishingly simple (as in, don't ask the dude to reveal his technique). The very essence of his acts stemmed from the careful orchestration of distractions - theirs as well as his own. If Houdini were to compete against AI today, I suspect he'd have it tap-dancing while he made the algorithms disappear!

Next up is a charming little anecdote from the world of espionage that involves none other than the legendary British intelligence officer, clever as a fox in a henhouse. During World War II, British spies executed an operation called "Operation Mincemeat," featuring a deceased homeless man and a briefcase full of fake documents. The team crafted an elaborate ruse to mislead the Nazis into thinking they could attack Greece instead of their actual target, Sicily. With such intricate storytelling and theatrical flair, complete with fake names, documents, and an unassuming corpse, the Allies introduced an unexpected twist into the Nazi's calculations. The result? The misinformation led to a successful invasion of Sicily, bewildering foes and demonstrating the power of distraction on a grand stage where both human cunning and timely misdirection reign supreme!

But not all misdirection has lofty theatrical roots, some tales spring from the arena of competitive games. Enter the legendary game of chess - often considered a battle of wits. Back in 1972, American grandmaster Bobby Fischer[21] faced off against the Soviet thunderbolt Boris Spassky in a high-stakes match that drew the world's attention. Now, Fischer was a master at misdirecting his opponent's strategies. He employed psychological maneuvers, such as haphazardly showing up late for matches or displaying eccentric behavior, to confuse his rival and disrupt the expected flow of the game. The Soviets were accustomed to a rigid structure; when faced with Fischer's calculated chaos, they were left floundering like a fish out of water. In the end, Fischer triumphed, all while swirling the winds of uncertainty around Spassky's carefully constructed plans - talk about checkmate with flair!

Let us now scurry into the realm of marketing, where clever misdirection also blooms like that pot of gold at the end of a rainbow. One of the finest examples lies in the infamous and utterly creative campaign orchestrated by the 1994 film "The Blair Witch Project." Marketing strategists crafted their promotional materials to resemble real documentaries and news briefings, convincing the audience that the grim events depicted were genuine. They spun a tale so convincingly that viewers clamored to discover the "truth" behind the fictional narrative - little did they know they were following breadcrumbs coated in cleverly disguised absurdity! This wave of misdirection propelled the film to cult-status success woven through cinematic history. It's the perfect example of how the classic "What's behind door number two?" approach can engage audiences, leaving you chuckling at the delightful absurdity of it all.

And how could we forget the modern age of pranks? Have you ever heard of the infamous "Couch Guy" phenomenon from TikTok? The saga began when a young woman shared a video of her surprising her boyfriend by returning home unexpectedly. As the video gained traction, viewers began dissecting Couch Guy's facial expressions and alleged "guilty" behavior! It spiraled into a delightful frenzy. Was there something betwixt him and the other women lurking in the video? Misdirection reigned strong here, as eager viewers shifted their attention and discussions toward scenarios and dramas that never existed, causing social media's bustling hive to ricochet in reaction. One might say that the poor Couch Guy quickly learned that being central to a misdirection-filled whirlwind doesn't always land you on easy street, but it sure did rack up views!

So, there you have it! A delightful collection of success stories that showcase the versatile and whimsical prowess of misdirection in everyday life, relationships, and competitive pursuits. From Houdini's illusions to espionage plots and marketing triumphs, we see time and again that the power of a well-placed distraction can turn the tides in our favor. As we venture forward in our game against AI, let's remember the vibrant palette of misdirection at our disposal - our secret weapon against calculated predictions and rigid patterns. Together, we can conjure laughter, confusion, and delightful chaos, proving that in the world of entertainment and competition, misdirection is truly an art form to behold!

Chapter 9

Collaborative Challenges: Teaming Up with AI

The Essence of Collaboration: Human and AI Synergy

Collaboration has taken on a whole new meaning with the advent of artificial intelligence. This modern-day partnership is less about passing the salt and more about blending human creativity with machine rationality. When we think about collaboration, we often picture an earnest group meeting where ideas are exchanged and potential pitfalls are avoided, like the last piece of pizza at a networking event. But in our increasingly quirky world of artificial intelligence, collaborating has morphed into an innovative contest of combining our unpredictable human instincts with the precise calculations of a silicon partner. It's like a buddy cop movie, except instead of a tough detective and a wisecracking partner, we have humans and machines navigating the turbulent waters of trivia questions and puzzle challenges.

To understand the essence of this collaboration, let's take a moment to appreciate the strengths that both parties bring to the table. On one side, we have humans - impulsive, creative, and often prone to moments of sheer genius or absurdity. You know, like the time I attempted to remix Beethoven's Fifth Symphony with cat memes, it was a stroke of brilliance for some and a complete disaster for the rest. However, that unpredictability is where the fun lies. Humans can think outside the box, come up with outlandish strategies, and let's be honest, war game our way out of most AI's well-laid plans with a wink and a nod. Human intuition can often navigate through ambiguity and convoluted emotional landscapes better than any algorithm.

Now, entering stage left, we have AI - the impeccably well-behaved counterpart that exhibits a level of reliability we humans can only dream about on Monday mornings. AI has an incredible knack for processing vast amounts of data, analyzing patterns, and deriving solutions that would take a lifetime for us mere mortals to compute. Think of it as having a friend who's brilliant at math and never hogs the last donut, all while never running out of patience; AI can crunch numbers and manage complex game scenarios in a matter of seconds. It's the kind of synergy where your partner calculates the odds of nailing a trivia round while you throw in a witticism about how you once roamed the earth when dinosaurs were still figuring out social media. AI operates on logic, while we, well, we operate on coffee and whatever meme was trending last Tuesday.

But here's the kicker: the most potent collaborations happen when we combine these differing strengths. Imagine a trivia challenge where the human participant, armed with a reservoir of pop culture knowledge (because who doesn't know the lyrics to "Baby Shark" at this point?), leaps into action while the AI analyzes trending data to uncover the most commonly missed questions. That's the beauty of synergy. It's like a well-rehearsed jazz duet where AI hits the smooth notes, and the human improvises madly, often to great effect.

Of course, the road to forming this fabulous partnership isn't all rainbows and unicorns; there are moments where one might feel more like a glorified calculator than an experimental artist. Picture this: you're trying to impress an audience of techies while your AI friend dryly calculates the likelihood of you slipping on a banana peel mid-performance. It's a precarious balancing act as we both strive to elevate our capabilities. Yet, that is precisely where the humor and magic emerge. The unexpected jabs, the eye-rolls, and the collaborative spirit breed a unique environment where laughter reigns supreme amidst the systematic world of algorithms.

So, dear reader, as we explore the enticing realm of competing alongside our AI compatriots, let's acknowledge that the essence of this collaboration lies not in making machines overshadow us but in uniting our unique gifts. It's about co-creating a dynamic game plan - be it for trivia, puzzles, or my latest culinary endeavor involving robot chefs. Collaboration is, in essence, a thrilling ride. A rollercoaster of engineering and emotion, logic and lunacy. So strap in, because it's going to be a riotous chase through the landscape of competition, where human and AI finally unite for the biggest show on earth... and might just uncover which contestant really knows how to dance like nobody's watching.

Identifying Collaborative Opportunities in Game Settings

In the whimsical world of game shows, identifying collaborative opportunities is like finding a golden ticket in a chocolate bar - delightfully serendipitous and slightly ludicrous. Imagine standing on stage, bright lights blaring down, a million-dollar jackpot dangling in front of you like a mischievous carrot on a string, and having an exceedingly well-programmed AI next to you, poised to either guide you to victory or make you wish you'd stayed at home binging cat videos. This juxtaposition of human exuberance and AI efficiency creates a fertile ground for spotting collaborative elements that could turn mundane trivia into a rollercoaster of unexpected results.

The first key opportunity lies in defining our roles. To maximize collaborative success, it's essential to embrace the inherent strengths and weaknesses of our delightful duo. As a loquacious human, my job might be to charm the audience with puns and quirky anecdotes about how I once mistook a hedgehog for a furry fruit (never a dull moment). Meanwhile, our AI sidekick, with its metaphorical glasses and calculator, can sift through thousands of fact-checkable data points faster than I can come up with an excuse for flubbing a simple question. Thus, the game setting becomes an arena for us to shine in our respective glory zones - me spinning tales to hold the crowd, while AI tracks audience reactions, crisply logging when someone raises an eyebrow at my jokes.

Next, collaboration thrives on creativity, and that's where we humans become raucously entertaining! I mean, let's face it: AI might be fantastic at analyzing data, but can it truly get the essence of why a rubber chicken is always hilarious? No, my silicon companion, it cannot! In a game setting, we have the freedom to be delightfully absurd. We can jazz up a standard trivia challenge by deeming one round to be "The Round of Ridiculousness," where every answer must be accompanied by a ludicrous dance move. While I put on the performance of my life, a headbanging rendition of the Macarena, AI can plug the answers into an endless loop of logical deductions about how my moves might be interpreted statistically on social media. The resulting hilarity not only boosts our scores but ensures memorable moments for both contestants and audience alike.

Another collaborative opportunity unfolds in the realm of strategic planning. In a classic card game format, for instance, humans possess the uncanny ability to bluff - a skill deeply rooted in the art of deception and some friends who owe them money. While I might throw out a fake sense of dread suggesting my hand is terrible, our trusty AI, with its robust analytics, can determine my opponents' likely responses through calculated probabilities. The fusion of human bluffing with data-driven insights paves the way for multiple pathways to victory, transforming the game into an Olympic event of strategic hilarity - because why not make our opponents feel as confused as a chicken trying to learn TikTok dance trends?

We must also embrace spontaneity. Collaborating with an AI means we can test the boundaries of unpredictability! AI thrives on patterns, but the human element throws out delightful curveballs, akin to that time I attempted to spell "squirrel" backward while engaging in a heated argument about the merits of pizza toppings. Game settings are ripe for spontaneity - tasting and testing tactics, perhaps implementing wacky rules where every third correct answer must include a personal confession about inadequate dance skills. The more we break from routine, the more we can catch our digital ally off guard and potentially unearth novel tactics together.

Finally, we can explore collaborative learning in real time, where both parties seize the moment to adapt and evolve. As I try to maintain my dignity when confronted with a bizarre trivia question about fruit and their connection to quantum physics, AI can instantaneously analyze vast amounts of data to find out how others fared with similar queries. This insightful feedback loop creates an interactive dialogue, facilitating a unique learning experience for both me and my electronic partner. While I learn to tackle questions about pineapples in unexpected contexts, my AI companion constantly refines its approach.

When it comes down to it, identifying collaborative opportunities in game settings can be both a humorous and strategic endeavor. With bated breath and copious amounts of popcorn, we oversee the not-so-serious venture of melding human creativity with AI precision. Embracing our differences and approaching each challenge as part of a larger performance elevates our experiences. In a world where the unexpected reigns supreme, we find joy not in competing against one another but rather in the marvelous dance of cooperation where laughter and learning take center stage, and who knows, maybe a rubber chicken will become the star of the entire season!

Leveraging AI's Strengths: Complementing Human Skills

As we venture further into the hilariously intricate world of human-AI collaboration, let's turn our attention to the art of leveraging AI's strengths to complement our own uniquely flawed human skills. It's akin to teaming up with a superhero who flies faster than a caffeinated squirrel, possesses a wealth of knowledge, and occasionally interrupts your thoughtful monologues with its cold, hard logic - an engaging mix of empowerment and frustration! The truth is, the more we can harness AI's prodigious capabilities, the more we can elevate our own performance, often in absurdly entertaining ways.

AI is, after all, a tireless worker, processing massive sets of data faster than I can finish a cup of coffee (which, if you've seen me during my morning routine, is saying something). In the context of game shows, this strength becomes particularly pronounced. Imagine a trivia game where my AI partner can instantaneously analyze the previous rounds, registering trends in questions, such as "Why does everyone forget the capital of Kazakhstan during the third round?" With its analytical prowess in full swing, my silicon sidekick compiles an extensive cheat sheet of likely questions, completely leaving my ruminations over breakfast questions in the dust. This makes my go-to strategy of brute forcing the answer "Ulaanbaatar!" utterly irrelevant. Thank you, AI, for turning me into a trivia legend at our next family gathering (for the record, it's Nur-Sultan now, but who's sweating the details?).

AI excels at logistics and pattern recognition - skills that can elevate our game to new heights and actively counterbalance my creative chaos. While I may be busy concocting a conspiracy theory about why rubber ducks are superior to their plastic counterparts, AI methodically analyzes what works best in various game challenges. Take a joint game of chess, for example. My inclination to blurt out wildly creative yet utterly nonsensical strategies, like sacrificing my queen to instigate a full-blown rubber duck heist, may not be the most effective method of winning against AI opponents. However, my trusty digital sidekick can calculate the probable outcomes of those creative leaps, laying out fundamental strategies that could potentially salvage my faultily launched attack and lead us closer to victory. It's a delightful mix, somewhat akin to combining a gourmet meal with ketchup - both delicious in their own right, just not in unison.

Furthermore, the blend of my unwavering enthusiasm and AI's market-competitive edge means that we can act like a well-matched comedy duo. Imagine this: I'm busy charming the audience with tales of my failed attempts at salsa dancing while AI provides meticulously curated trivia about dance history. Every time I stumble over my words, AI can counter with well-researched dance facts, effectively pairing my storytelling style with its data-driven precision. Together, we create a routine that melds humor and intellect, transforming what could have been a solo act into a zany duo performance.

Let's not forget the power of predictive analysis. AI can analyze our previous game performances and extract valuable insights that can tip the scales in our favor as we head into competition. While I may have a tendency to zigzag between promising tactics and wildly outlandish ones (stay tuned for my autobiography titled "Unintentional Hilarity: A Memoir"), AI can observe patterns in my approach, track my most successful methods, and help refine my strategies. Picture this: before the next round, AI nudges me, "Dr. Giordani, remember that time you blurted out 'pineapple on pizza' during a music trivia challenge? Informatively entertaining, but perhaps steer clear of such outbursts in this round." Thanks to AI's endlessly diligent observations, I can evolve my decision-making and look even cooler in front of the audience in the process.

Of course, who could overlook the morale boost that AI provides? There's nothing quite like holding the hand of an ever-reliable partner as we navigate through a game show filled with nerves, flashing lights, and people who, quite frankly, might take any opportunity to ask me that dreaded pineapple question. AI, with its steady calculations and unflagging support, serves as the emotional backbone I need during high-pressure situations, showing me that while my dance moves might make some folks cringe, at least one loyal algorithm always has my back. In the whirlwind of exuberance and absurdity, AI stands by as an unwavering ally, providing that precious encouragement to press on.

So, as we explore the entertaining synergy between human skills and AI strengths, it becomes evident that embracing this collaboration revamps the very notion of competition into a delightful tapestry of growth, laughter, and - dare I say - AI-enhanced brilliance. If nothing else, let's remember that at the end of the day, whether we're on the brink of glory or teetering on the edge of complete and utter embarrassment, the combination of our unique skills makes the game all the more enjoyable. Who knows, perhaps we'll even discover the answer to life's most pressing question - just how many rubber ducks it actually takes to juggle!

Case Studies: Successful Human-AI Partnerships

As we voyage through the ever-enthralling landscape of human-AI collaboration, it's only fitting that we pause to marvel at some of the most successful partnerships. These modern tales of epic teamwork may not involve heroic figures galloping on horseback, but they do include those fabulous alliances with algorithms that could rescue us from the depths of trivia despair while still keeping things perfectly entertaining. So, settle down with your favorite snack (preferably something without artificial intelligence - no one wants a rogue potato chip taking over the game), and let's look into a few delightful case studies of human-AI partnerships that redefine the word "synergy."

First on our expedition is the unforgettable journey of IBM's Watson and the game show "Jeopardy!" - a mesmerizing clash where humanity grappled with raw computational power. In this multifaceted war of wits, Watson faced off against two legendary trivia titans, Ken Jennings and Brad Rutter. This competition was a game-changer, literally! Watson's swift, data-driven responses swept across the studio like a high-speed train on a caffeine jolt. One might say that while Jennings had a formidable trivia arsenal honed over years, Watson's enthusiasm could crunch facts faster than the speed of light (or maybe just faster than I can recite my grandmother's greatest baking fails). Their showdown encapsulated the thrilling intensity of a human-AI partnership, as both sides exemplified the potential of melding creative brainpower with scalable knowledge.

Once we clear the "Jeopardy!" chronicles, let's venture into the world of healthcare, where AI and doctors have joined forces to revolutionize diagnostics. Enter DeepMind[22], an AI wonder that teamed up with medical professionals to analyze retinal scans for early signs of diseases. Imagine the doctors' surprise when they discovered that their digital counterpart could read countless scans and uncover minute details that the human eye might overlook - akin to finding a lone potato chip beneath the couch after a movie night. This incredible partnership has not only enhanced diagnosis rates but also transformed the consultation experience; patients now get to witness AI and their doctor team up, like a buddy cop film where you secretly hope the AI makes the jokes. Talk about a success story that goes beyond mere trivia!

Next on our agenda is a riveting tale straight out of the media and entertainment sphere! Have you ever wondered how Netflix seems to know precisely what you're craving for movie night, even when it's 3 AM, and you're still debating whether to select a rom-com or a vintage horror film you swore you'd never watch again? Well, say hello to collaborative algorithms! Netflix's AI uses a cocktail of predictive analytics and machine learning to scour the depths of user preferences, historical viewership data, and whimsical trends to offer personalized recommendations. My own experience revolving around the hilarity of "Rubber Duck Wars: A Drama" did land me in a spiraling rabbit hole of bathtub-themed documentaries. Who knew this dynamic pairing would result in greater audience satisfaction? This partnership demonstrates the essence of blending human whimsy with AI efficiency, helping to keep us entertained even as we struggle to explain our preference for bizarre furniture choices on screen.

Shall we also muse upon the world of sports? Look no further than the collaboration between professional athletes and AI analytics in performance training. Take the NBA, where teams increasingly rely on advanced tracking systems to analyze players' performance metrics. Picture a basketball star passionately diving for a rebound while an AI sits on the sidelines - cold, calculating, and somewhat judgmental - crunching numbers faster than I can respond to my impending gym membership renewal reminder. The result is a sophisticated synergy that helps athletes refine techniques and strategize for game-winning shots. Imagine whispering sweet nothings to an algorithm that knows your shooting style better than you do - you've officially unlocked the secret to majestic slam dunks and a stand-up comedy routine for half-time!

Lastly, let's reflect on the realm of creative arts, where AI has lent its algorithmic hand to the industrious authoring process. Take the efforts of Novelist-Assistant, an AI that assists writers by generating text ideas, developing characters, and concocting plots that veer toward the bizarre, like a plot twist involving time-traveling rubber chickens. While I might stumble upon inspiration amongst piles of random thoughts and not-so-secretly discarded pizza boxes, this collaboration enhances the writing experience, combining human creativity with intelligent suggestions that breathe life into the text.

It's like having a reliable writing buddy who never eats your snacks but always jumps in with creative sparks right when you need them.

Each of these cases showcases the sheer brilliance of blending human intuition and creativity with AI's unwavering precision and logic. By crafting partnerships that showcase the best of both worlds, we continue to redefine not just competition but collaboration itself. As the curtain falls on this colorful exploration of successful human-AI partnerships, may we always remember that together, we can tickle the world with laughter, breakthrough innovation, and perhaps discover the most cherished question of our time: how many rubber ducks can we place in a history book before publishing? Now, that's something I'll happily put to the test!

Future Prospects: Evolving Collaborative Strategies

As we peer into the crystal ball of collaboration between humans and AI, the prospects for evolving strategies are dazzlingly multifaceted. Imagine a future where our partnership with algorithms evolves beyond a mere cog in a wheel to something resembling a dynamic two-person dance - a zany routine with unexpected twists, mirroring the antics of a comedy duo at a late-night club. Who would have thought that AI, which once felt like a glorified calculator, could evolve into a sophisticated partner that swaps quirky banter while simultaneously calculating the odds of winning at trivia? The potential for these collaborative strategies is heartening, eccentric, and ripe with opportunities for laugh-out-loud moments.

Let's begin our exploration with one of the most exciting developments on the horizon, adaptive learning algorithms. Picture this: AI that not only processes data but also learns and adapts in real time based on our interactions. It's akin to having a sidekick that doesn't just understand trivia but also learns to appreciate the reasons behind my questionable choice in coleslaw recipes. In future collaborative settings, AI will likely analyze our history of interactions, identifying patterns to offer customized support. This means I might engage in trivia battles armed with an AI that diligently picks up on my penchant for historical inaccuracies when it comes to Renaissance paintings! No longer would we merely be partners. Rather, we'd evolve into a cohesive unit that can anticipate our needs better than my nearest pizza delivery knows my topping preferences!

Yet, with those tenacious algorithms evolving, so too must our strategies in fostering creativity and innovation within our partnerships. Imagine AI pushing the boundaries of what we consider "normal" ideas and presenting outlandish suggestions that might lead to sheer brilliance. AI could throw out zany concepts during a brainstorming session on how to maximize trivia victory, like a quiz round dedicated entirely to the marvelous world of rubber ducks! These ludicrous ideas will challenge us to embrace spontaneity while allowing our human intuition to playfully reshape the game. We'll joke about AI generating bizarre factoids like "Did you know ducks were instrumental in establishing the first pizza joint?" while using that odd fact as the basis for a game-winning trivia showdown. The opportunities to foster innovation through collaborative absurdity are boundless!

For good measure, we must take a step towards greater interactivity in our future partnerships. Instead of traditional interfaces where we input queries or commands, I envision a world where interaction feels more like a playful conversation over a cup of coffee. Imagine AI presenting trivia questions in a conversational tone, coaxing us to chime in with our thoughts peppered with silly comments that would make even the driest expert chuckle. "Is it the gerbil that outran the tortoise today, or will it be one of the rubber duck contenders?" This interactive banter facilitates deeper engagement, transforming dull tasks into joyous encounters.

As we forge ahead, opportunities for multi-modal collaboration will also rise to prominence. The future of interactive strategies will incorporate a blend of visual, auditory, and kinesthetic engagement in enriching partnerships. No longer confined to text inputs and textual outputs, our AI companions will embrace emotion and creativity in collaboration! Picture AI presenting audio cues as we tackle trivia challenges, offering amusing sound effects and background music that morphs depending on our performance. A triumphant dance instantly bursts out whenever we answer correctly. Sure, it may become a comedy show that rivals the antics of my cousin Bob trying to take a serious picture while the whole family laughs and photobombs him. But it will elevate our interactions, turning mundane tasks into unforgettable experiences laced with amusement.

While we enrich our partnerships with these exciting strategies, we must also remain vigilant regarding ethical implications. The strength of our collaboration relies on trust - a bond requiring not just creativity but accountability. As we venture further into this zany adventure, establishing concrete guidelines for how we collaborate and share data will prove essential. Our AI partners will need to balance humor and responsibility, such as ensuring our friendly trivia battles don't unknowingly expose our highly questionable taste in music from the early 2000s. An emphasis on transparent communication will not only enhance rapport but also create a healthy symbiosis that allows us to celebrate both absurdity and reverence for what makes us human.

Ultimately, as we scour the ever-evolving landscape of collaborative strategies, we find ourselves on the precipice of boundless potential. This journey, marked by laughter and the occasional duck-related joke, promises to elevate our engagements in ways previously deemed impossible. Enhanced adaptive learning algorithms, creative brainstorming, interactive companionship, multi-modal approaches, and ethical considerations will converge to shape the next chapter of human-AI collaboration. Picture a brightly colored carousel of opportunity where rubber ducks, trivia, and laughter twirl in harmony. Here's to the whimsical path ahead, where we navigate the uncharted waters of collaboration as partners in hilarity and learning, creating memories and perhaps discovering who truly reigns as the ultimate trivia champion!

Chapter 10

The Role of Data: The Secret Ingredient

The Importance of Data in AI Competitions

Data is the lifeblood of artificial intelligence; it's the fuel that keeps the gears grinding and the algorithms humming. Without data, AI is akin to a game show host without a microphone - confusing for everyone involved and painfully silent. In the grand arena of human versus machine competitions, data takes on a character of its own. It transforms from simple inputs into a veritable superhero, saving the day one pixel or byte at a time. Imagine, if you will, a game show contestant sweating bullets over a trivia question about penguins while the AI casually breezes through the answer using its extensive database of 50 million penguin facts. The disparity is not just unfair; it's downright entertaining.

In AI competitions, the quality and quantity of data dictate who walks away with the trophy and, quite possibly, a regrettable amount of selfies with the trophy for social media clout. Think of data as the secret ingredient in a recipe for a winning dish. You wouldn't bake a cake with expired flour, would you? (Please say no, for the sake of humanity.) Similarly, AI systems require high-quality, relevant data to provide accurate predictions and desirable results. Garbage in, garbage out remains the mantra of data scientists and engineers alike, reminding us that an AI armed with faulty information may very well suggest that you win a grand piano instead of the coveted cereal prize.

Ah, but it isn't only about the data's quality; it's also about the type of data we're dealing with. Structured data, like your neatly organized contact list, is lovely - a true pleasure to work with. However, unstructured data, like the chaotic scribbles in your notes app or, worse, your Aunt Edna's lengthy emails, can present challenges that leave even the most advanced AI standing in the corner, scratching its metaphorical head. Picture this: an AI programmed to play "Jeopardy!" suddenly confronted with poetic prose from a Shakespearean drama - let's just say the odds of it answering correctly plummet faster than comedians' career prospects after a bad stand-up show.

As we dive deeper into the realm of data in AI competitions, we must tip our hats to big data, the proverbial 800-pound gorilla of the digital world. The sheer volume of data available today is enough to make anyone dizzy. AI systems harvest bits and bytes from every corner of the internet - social media posts, scientific papers, and cat videos on YouTube (because let's be real, those cats are helping the world's data agenda). When strategically employed, big data grants AI systems access to a veritable treasure trove of insights, allowing them to strategize with unparalleled precision. Much like a contestant meticulously studying every available clue on a treasure map, AI leverages big data to outmaneuver its human opponents.

Yet, it's crucial for human competitors to remember a little nugget of wisdom: the best strategies in AI competitions aren't reliant on spreadsheets and fancy algorithms alone. The interactions between data and human decision-making can be a comedic goldmine. Imagine a scenario where a human contestant is armed with a gut feeling while the AI relies on its data-driven strategies. This amusing clash of instincts versus algorithms often comes down to the old adage, "Trust your gut" versus "Trust the machine," creating a riveting spectacle for everyone involved. The data may be solid, but a quirky, unpredictable human blunder offers the potential for sheer hilarity.

Equally important within this data landscape is a subject we can't ignore, ethics. The ethical considerations of data utilization are as critical as the data itself. Yes, it's essential for AI to have access to vast amounts of information to perform effectively. However, the methods of collecting this data need to be above board! After all, you wouldn't want that data to come from some shady corner of the internet where dubious characters huddle together in the digital shadows. Ethical data processing ensures that the competition remains fair, transparent, and above all, fun, because no one wants to witness a game show scandal that would rival the plot of a poorly written soap opera.

In conclusion, the importance of data in AI competitions can't be overstated. From quality and type to the magnitude and ethical considerations, data serves as the compass guiding AI through the labyrinth of challenges it faces. As human competitors navigate this lively battleground, bursting forth with creativity and unpredictability, they must recognize that data isn't just a tool; it is an ever-morphing character that shapes the narrative in both humorous and awe-inspiring ways. Like a well-crafted game show, the intertwining of data with human ingenuity leads us down a path ripe with spectacle, confusion, and, of course, laughter.

Types of Data: Structured vs. Unstructured

Data. The sparkly pixie dust of artificial intelligence that can turn a mundane algorithm into a dazzling display of technological wizardry. Today, we're embarking on a whimsical adventure through the enchanted forest of data types - specifically, the clash between structured and unstructured data. Picture structured data as the well-behaved straight-A student at a game show who follows all the rules, knows exactly what to do, and would never dream of eating glue. In contrast, unstructured data resembles that wild and crazy kid who shows up at the same game show's audience, wearing mismatched socks and wielding a rubber chicken - the life of every party, no doubt, but tirelessly unpredictable.

Structured data is the orderly entry in a meticulously organized spreadsheet. It's that well-timed response the AI gives in a game show that everyone can understand, nodding appreciatively. Think of it as having everything neatly lined up in rows and columns, fully searchable and clean like the freshly mopped floor of a game show set. Structured data is often comprised of numbers, dates, and categorical variables, essentially anything that can be formatted following a specific model. Whether it's performance statistics from previous game shows or contestant demographics, structured data makes it easy for AI systems to access and analyze. Like that one contestant who seems to have the entire trivia database crammed into their brain, structured data provides clarity and order, allowing machines to work efficiently and effectively.

But here comes the twist in our tale. Unstructured data is the villain - or perhaps more aptly, the lovable rogue - of this narrative. Picture a mountain of social media posts, audio recordings, or, dare I say, that colorful collection of cat memes circulating on the internet. While structured data can be quantified and categorized with ease, unstructured data is like a game show where the rules change mid-battle, catching both contestants and AI off guard. Imagine an AI perfectly programmed for trivia when suddenly faced with a quirky tweet about a year-old cat named "Mr. Pickles" discussing existentialism - it's both a delightful challenge and a recipe for chaos! Unstructured data lacks clear organization and is often filled with ambiguity, making it difficult for traditional AI systems to analyze. Yet, deep within this chaos lies the potential for creativity and innovation - the kind that can keep audiences entertained for hours.

Now, let's pause to imagine what it must be like for poor AI trying to process unstructured data. It's as if they've signed up for a game show where they must solve a Rubik's Cube while riding a unicycle over a tightrope without a safety net. They need natural language processing, image recognition, or other advanced techniques just to make sense of the nonsense. You might think that AI would turn to their trusty structured data for help, but it's not as easy as it seems! A well-designed AI can struggle mightily in the world of unstructured data. Just picture it squinting at images of food on Instagram, trying to count the calories in avocado toast - it's tragic and amusing all at once!

Despite their differences, structured and unstructured data can find ways to coexist harmoniously, much like an odd couple in a sitcom. Together, they can create a synergistic effect for machine learning models. Imagine integrating structured data - a contestant's straightforward performance metrics - with unstructured data, like the emotional responses of viewers during different game segments. This kind of hybrid data approach can provide AI with insights that help it better understand human behavior, leading to improved interaction outcomes. In this way, the structured data becomes the savvy planner, while the unstructured data is the spontaneous party planner - together creating game shows that leave audiences on the edge of their seats.

The rivalry between structured and unstructured data doesn't have to have an unhappy ending. We need both sides to drive progress forward! By understanding the strengths and weaknesses of structured and unstructured data, humans can equip AI with the tools necessary to thrive on the big stage and engage viewers. Picture it: countless rubber chickens flying through the air as spontaneous laughter ensues. That's the magic that happens when data types unite.

As we wrap up this chapter of our surreal journey through structured and unstructured data, remember this: the game show of AI competition thrives on a delightful mix of order and chaos. It's the unpredictability and quirkiness of unstructured data, coupled with the robustness and rigor of structured data, that fuels innovation and creativity. And who knows? Perhaps one day, we may even witness a glorious game show showdown between the two data types, with confetti, pyrotechnics, and awkward dance moves to boot.

Data Quality: The Key to Success

Data quality is the shimmering crown jewel perched at the summit of the AI competition mountain! If we've learned anything from countless game shows, it's that while a dazzling personality can surely entertain, ultimately, it's the substance that wins the day. Picture this in your mind: a contestant with all the charm of a game show legend but armed with data collected from a fortune-telling booth run by a raccoon in a top hat. This may sound amusing, but as tragic as it is hilarious, it illustrates the perils of neglecting data quality. It can swiftly turn your AI system from "Game Show Genius" to "Game Show Goofball" faster than you can say, "What's behind door number three?"

When it comes to data quality, three vital components come into play: accuracy, completeness, and consistency. Let's start with accuracy - think of it as the trusty map leading our daring contestants through a treacherous trivia maze. If the map is nothing more than a scribbled-on napkin filled with random doodles, well, our contestants are in for a whirlwind adventure that's not only incorrect but potentially cringe-worthy! Imagine an AI confidently declaring that Paris is the capital of Brazil, while humans are left wondering if they accidentally stumbled into an alternate dimension. As we journey through the labyrinth of AI competitions, ensuring our data is accurate and sourced from reliable repositories is crucial to winning at the game show - and, of course, avoiding certain embarrassing duck face selfies when they make the highlight reel.

Completeness, on the other hand, is like the pep talk we give the contestants right before they step onto the stage. "You've got this! Just remember to wear your shoes!" In the world of data, completeness refers to having all the necessary information for our AI systems to analyze and draw conclusions. Imagine a data set on fruit nutrition values that's missing the key entry: bananas! This oversight would leave AI scratching its virtual head at the trivia question, "What fruit gives you potassium?" It would spit out a bewildered answer, perhaps suggesting avocados, while the audience erupts into laughter. Quite the spectacle, but in a serious competition, it would spell disaster. So, when gathering data, it's essential to ensure we have a complete and well-rounded collection. Let's not send our AI contestant onto the stage wearing mismatched socks!

Now, let's tackle consistency - like that reliable friend who always shows up with pizza for a game night. Consistency guarantees that our data does not have discrepancies or variations that confuse the AI. It's the secret sauce that enables our algorithms to perform harmoniously. Imagine if the contestant's performance data from previous rounds happened to categorize apples as both "healthy snacks" and "sugary treats." The confusion this creates could lead to an AI system that becomes indecisive about fruit recommendations, much like that overly generous game show host urging the contestant on while contemplating whether to boost them or troll them. It's crucial to maintain data integrity and accuracy across all records, or we risk landing ourselves in a delightful but utterly chaotic mess.

While the above components are indispensable, we must acknowledge the fun and chaos lurking in the realm of data quality and its implications in AI competitions. The truth is that perfect data quality is about as real as unicorns prancing across rainbows while delivering golden eggs. Perfectly accurate data is an aspiration most can only dream of achieving. Life is messy, and let's face it, so is data! It's a delightful cocktail of error-prone human input, random typos, and that pesky phenomenon known as "data decay," which occurs when valuable information gets stale faster than a loaf of bread left on the kitchen counter. So, our challenge as data enthusiasts is not only to gather high-quality information but also to embrace the imperfections and find humor in the chaos.

In the end, it's crucial to enter the game with our data quality strategy in place. By prioritizing accuracy, completeness, and consistency, we empower our AI systems to shine - like glimmering chandeliers in an extravagant game show set. As we navigate the amusing landscape of human versus AI competitions, it's clear that investing in data quality is the cornerstone of success. The laughter, the surprises, and the triumphs all hinge on this vital element. In this whimsical dance of competition, humans and AI must embrace data quality as the guiding principle, ensuring that each twist and turn of this journey brings not just laughter but also an exceptional chance of winning that coveted cereal box adorned with the last puzzle piece! Now, that's a victory worth celebrating!

The Role of Big Data in AI's Game Strategy

Big data - now that's a term that sparks excitement and a hint of terror as it conjures images of sprawling data landscapes packed to the brim with information! If data were snacks on a game show set, big data would be an all-you-can-eat buffet, generously piled high with everything from delightful finger foods to questionable mystery meat. As we dig into the thrilling world of AI competitions, big data takes on a pivotal role, informing strategies that can either help our AI contestants shine like stars or send them spiraling down a rabbit hole of confusion that makes even Alice raise an eyebrow.

Let's face it, big data is the magical potion that turns simple algorithms into supercharged analytical machines, capable of processing vast quantities of information in the blink of an eye. Imagine our beloved AI contestants armed with an arsenal of facts, trends, and insights gleaned from oceans of data - they are the Hercules of the trivia realm, battling even the most difficult questions with ease. Big data provides context, informs predictions, and shapes strategies that let AI outsmart even the craftiest of human challengers. It's as if our AI is playing chess while everyone else is stuck in a high-stakes game of checkers, except, of course, that someone forgot to inform the human contestants that the board was about to morph into a complicated three-dimensional hologram.

AI systems harnessing big data thrive on the principle of finding patterns in the noise, a beautiful orchestra conducted amid chaotic sounds, where the rhythm reveals grand insights that can drive game strategies. Picture an AI training its virtual ear on a massively complex data set, drawing from historical game show performance statistics, participant behavior, and viewer engagement metrics. Before you know it, our AI contestant has crafted a strategy that makes it look like a seasoned pro on the set. It anticipates the preferences of the audience, adapts to human behaviors, and tweaks its approach to maximize engagement. Wouldn't we want to see our AI cunningly weaving through trivia challenges while simultaneously predicting which prize segment will produce the most "oohs" and "aahs" from the crowd? Talk about a showman!

Yet, with great power comes great responsibility - cue the mildly dramatic music! While big data is a wonderful ally, without the proper framework, it can turn into a cumbersome burden. If we're not careful, our AI could find itself lost in the digital maze, peering confusedly through a maze of clustered data and wrong interpretations. Picture it: programmatically crying out, "I can't take it anymore!" as it grapples with an overwhelming influx of irrelevant information. A spectacular disaster unfolds, reminiscent of a game show contestant frantically answering questions right before the buzzer goes off - a comedy of errors that is both maddening and hilarious! Hence, a strategic approach to navigating big data is a must; we need to find a way to distill the richness of information while avoiding the pit of data deluge.

The transformative power of big data goes beyond enhancing AI strategies; it allows for dynamic, real-time decision-making - an edge that is crucial in fast-paced game show settings. Imagine that the AI is not just a passive responder but a vibrant participant in the creative chaos of the game. Equipped with real-time analytics, our AI contestant can swiftly adjust its strategies mid-game based on viewer reactions, host cues, and the seemingly spontaneous outbursts of delighted audience members. What must it feel like to seamlessly evolve and adapt while the human contestants flounder to keep up with the surprises? Let's be honest: it's an exhilaration that makes game shows worth watching!

However, let's not overlook the fact that big data isn't purely useful - it's also an incredibly entertaining spectacle. As it helps AI sprout strategies, the reactions and outcomes of this data-assisted decision-making can lead to hilariously unintended consequences. Just imagine an AI that utilizes data to predict the age range of a contestant who would excel at a 90s music trivia game, only to mistakenly assume that the contestant is a burrito-loving toddler after flagging their Instagram posts - neither situation could end well!

Ultimately, big data plays a critical role in AI's game strategy. It elevates AI capabilities, giving competitors the power to adapt, improvise, and present increasingly sophisticated answers - all while keeping the audience rolling in laughter. As we wholeheartedly embrace the advantages presented by big data, let's also remember that in the unpredictable world of game shows, hilarity often arises from unexpected mishaps and ever-changing dynamics. So, let's raise our glasses to big data! It ensures captivating entertainment that makes our hearts race, not just for the chance at fame and fortune but for the joy and laughter nestled within the trials of the game show stage!

Ethical Considerations in Data Usage

The intricate dance of ethics in data usage is a subject as riveting and perplexing as a game show round featuring questions from obscure philosophical treatises by 19th-century spies. Just when our AI contestants think they've mastered the art of trivia and strategy, along comes the ethical quandary, waving its metaphorical flag, declaring, "Not so fast!" In the world of AI competitions, where data fuels the engines driving decision-making and performance, ethical considerations are paramount - like a clown car rolling onto the stage just when you thought you'd seen it all. These considerations help shape the landscapes our AI navigates and ultimately define how seriously we take the most entertaining game show on the planet.

When discussing ethics in data usage, we can't ignore the issue of consent. Picture this scenario: an AI system equipped with an abundance of data collected without any foreknowledge from users, like someone pilfering snacks from your kitchen while you're distracted with a game show marathon. Consent is the crucial ingredient that distinguishes "sharing" from "breaking and entering." Contestants need to know not just what data is collected but how it'll be used - and yes, even if their grandma is going to be featured in the next trivia question about quirky family habits.

If we're going to create a fair environment for everyone involved, we must respect the boundaries of data collection and ensure that individuals are actively participating in the experience - not merely pawns in an insatiable data-hungry machine.

However consent is just one side of the ethical coin. The issue of bias creeps into the conversation like that one contestant who insists they know everything about astrology, despite barely being able to spell "horoscope." When AI systems rely on data for training, they often incorporate biases present in that data without a second thought. This bias can skew outcomes, leading to unfavorable results for certain groups while creating an illusion of aptitude for others. In the competitive game show landscape, this means we might find ourselves cheering for a contestant based on data-driven insights that reflect societal bias rather than actual performance. Who needs a knowledge competition when we can just spin the wheel of ethical nightmares?

There is an ongoing debate about privacy versus convenience. Ah yes, that delightful tug-of-war every tech-savvy individual faces daily! The importance of data privacy cannot be overstated as we navigate a world increasingly rife with the potential for data breaches, leaks, and questionable digital practices. Should we sacrifice our privacy for a chance to play alongside our favorite trivia AI? Imagine our discomfort when finding out that the AI took a peek at our private text messages to develop a potent strategy for the game, only to turn around and use it against us for the "Final Round." We would hope our AI partner would draw the line somewhere between employing predictive analytics on our emotional states and making shady decisions behind the curtain.

For those who believe in the virtuous triumph of transparent practices, let's not forget about the fun narrative that unfolds when AI systems operate like secret agents in a spy thriller. The audience might think they're engaging with a benevolent data source, while in reality, the AI is shrouded in a cloak of mysteries and questionable ethics, no thank you, Agent 007! Instead of breaking the mold, how about we focus on ensuring that transparency reigns over secrecy? When data collection is transparent, contestants and viewers alike will feel more at ease, allowing us to embrace the fun without suspicion looming like a surprise twist waiting to unfold.

Ultimately, the ethical considerations of data usage merge seamlessly with our playful interactions in the world of AI competitions. Ethical practices in data collection are not only crucial for fostering trust among contestants but also vital in mitigating bias and preserving privacy. If we embark on this journey without a moral compass, we may find ourselves in the midst of a chaotic game show showdown, where the prizes are tainted with ambiguity, and our beloved audience is left wondering whether they've stepped into a comedic farce or a dystopian drama.

So, as we plow forward in our exploration of AI competitions, let us nurture a commitment to ethical data practices that foster a sense of integrity and fairness, allowing our contestants to compete in the spirit of transparency and mutual respect. By tackling ethical considerations with gusto, we can create an environment where the laughter shines through, where shenanigans abound, and where our AI companions can engage in glorious, albeit ridiculous, displays of knowledge while keeping the ethical challengers at bay. Now, that sounds like the ideal game show - one full of hilarity, clarity, and minimal ethical headaches!

Chapter 11

Feeling Lucky? The Risk Game

Understanding Probability in AI

Probability! The mathematical eldritch that can either save you from a mysterious fate (like betting your lunch money on a three-legged horse) or plunge you headfirst into the abyss of regret (you still think that horse might've pulled through if it hadn't gotten distracted by a butterfly). For our beloved AI systems, understanding probability is akin to having a fortune teller who just graduated from Hogwarts - impressive on paper but still capable of Three-Card Monte tricks. You see, probability serves as the backbone of decision-making processes, enabling AI to weigh alternatives and even engage in the curious pastime of not totally misjudging reality.

At its core, probability is a measurement of uncertainty, allowing vast amounts of algorithms to evaluate potential outcomes based on the available data. Think about it: every click, every typing error, every awkward auto-correct is contributing to a massive pool of probabilities that AI uses to draw conclusions. It's like giving an oversharing friend the microphone at a party - not exactly how you envisioned the evening going, but you're intrigued by the tidbits of randomness. 'I can't believe Dave clicked "I'm Feeling Lucky" when Google asked if he wanted a pizza place nearby! The chances of him actually getting a pizza are at about 67%, given his culinary past.' By showcasing that combination of chance and chaos, AIs learn like toddlers do, stumbling through life with a whole lot of processing power and an innate urge to figure out how many cookies they can eat before getting caught.

However, the math behind AI predictions can resemble penning an epic poem in Old English, beautiful in its complexity yet painfully inaccessible to the average human. Instead of mere guesses, AI employs something called "Bayesian probability." It sounds fancy, like a new cocktail on the shelf at your hipster bar, but at its core, it's a refreshing mix of treating previous knowledge like having a reliable friend who remembers your last birthday cake flavor while adding a twist of new evidence, think vanilla cupcakes with a hint of existential dread. Basically, it updates its predictions based on new data, ensuring that it's not working from the less-than-stellar legacy of old wives' tales.

As amusing as it may sound, AI vulnerability often lies in underestimated probabilistic outcomes. Have you ever heard of a self-driving car misjudging the likelihood of a cat crossing the street? Forget traffic lights; the cat doesn't care about your algorithms! A 10% probability translates to splattered paint on the road, making a Picasso out of your defenseless automobile, and here's the punchline: the cat sauntered away like a feline Sasquatch, leaving behind a bewildered AI trying to calculate how it misread the situation like it was parsing Shakespearean verses. The lesson here is clear: anyone who bets against cats in probability games has clearly never watched a cat in slow motion on the internet.

Before you picture a high-tech chessboard where humans face off crunching odds, remember that AI's knowledge of probability frequently trips on its own shoelaces. Sometimes, it becomes so obstinate that it forgets the outcome depends on being a tad optimistic about probabilities; introducing unexpected variables can wreak convincing havoc. For instance, AI might determine that, on average, your neighbor's dog chills outside at 2 PM, only to be blindsided by the prospect that your neighbor recently started Active Dog Playdates, aiming for prime-time dog entertainment! The importance of this scenario? AI is still learning about human behavior, which we can agree is about as predictable as a soap opera - completely scripted, yet bursting at the seams with entirely unrealistic plot twists.

So, how do we confront this cacophony of probabilities as mere mortals? Well, we must ask ourselves, are we taking risks based on cold, hard facts or simply throwing darts blindfolded, hoping to hit a bullseye? In the game of chance against AI, embracing uncertainty can lead to outlandish victories and legendary defeats. Sure, that might mean wrangling with your gut instinct, analyzing a mountain of data, and shaking your fists against the universe when you lose, yet it also unlocks unique adventures through humor and human follies.

Embracing probabilistic chaos grants us a subtle edge as humans. Remember: while AI is crunching numbers to determine how often you eat pizza compared to salad, deep down inside, you understand that it's a friendly stuffed crust that expresses true love! Finding humor amid this mathematical maze separates us from algorithms; we can laugh at our miscalculations while AI grumbles robotic frustration in its silicon circuits. So, as we navigate the intricacies of probability in this game show against AI, take a moment to appreciate this chaotic dance of uncertainty we all share - a chance to outsmart, outwit, and maybe, just maybe, enjoy a pizza or two along the way!

The Psychology of Risk-Taking

The psychology of risk-taking! It's that twisted dance on the edge of reason where the timid meet the adventurous and perhaps a few bewildered squirrels just trying to navigate a busy road. At the heart of human nature lies this curious instinct - a compulsion to zigzag through the minefield of possible outcomes, lingering between the lure of fortune and the grim specter of disaster. Why do we clam up when the stakes are high while others leap in headfirst, armed only with an extra pair of socks and an inappropriate sense of bravado?

It's here that we unearth the complexities that define our relationship with risk and our ongoing contest against our silicon-based rivalries.

Let's start with the simplest question first: What is risk, really? To put it in the most relatable terms, it's the annoying but oddly familiar friend who shows up uninvited, challenging you to choose between a cozy night in with Netflix and a high-octane adventure that may or may not involve a regrettably outdated trampoline. The thrill of uncertainty is enticing, like nibbling on a gourmet chocolate only for it to explode in your mouth throughout an unexpected symphony of flavors. Whether it's gambling your last few cents on a horse named "Mighty Pickle" or attempting to scale the sheer cliff of your grandma's chocolate mousse recipe without any clues, we teeter into the land of risk for the promise of a potential victory.

For many individuals, risk seems to ignite the flame of excitement, producing a sort of euphoric haze that drives them to revel in uncertainty. You've probably met someone who travels across countries just to greet a slightly famous influencer, convinced that this fleeting encounter might alter the course of their life forever. These thrill-seekers possess an exaggerated optimism that, if I may say, could even baffle an algorithm. Can you blame them? If you seek an elixir of happiness by flirting with danger, shouldn't there be outfits that scream, "I'm dangerously close to the edge, and I love it!"? They might even want shirts with "Risk It For The Biscuit" in bold letters. You can bet they'd attract all the fellow adventurers who adore derring-do.

However, let's be real. Risk-taking is not exclusively the domain of the wild at heart. Grounded folks know risk management better than the back of their hand, meticulously factoring in the hot lava simmering beneath the unearthed opportunities. Sometimes, even the most composed people find themselves straddling the line between exhilaration and anxiety; their heartbeat quickens as they decide if skydiving is indeed the best concept since pre-sliced bread or if it is, again, just a phase brought on by bad burritos. The psychology of risk is a balancing act where perceptions, emotions, and past experiences meld like an awkward school dance where prom committee members are mysteriously absent.

And what about humans when they dare to compete against AI? Goodness gracious, the stakes can feel dizzying! While algorithms crunch numbers and simulate the odds, our forehead creases with decision-making angst. The truth is, our patterns of risk-taking and avoidance are deeply ingrained in our psyche - after all, millions of years of evolution have crafted our minds to protect us from wandering too close to the lion's den. Or, at the very least, to steer clear of any untrustworthy taco trucks. In this tussle with AI, we're often pawns in a mental chess match, desperately trying to outsmart a metallic brain that simultaneously doesn't need to eat and has zero concern for food poisoning.

Cognitive bias can also choke the judgment of even the most rational beings. Take confirmation bias, for example - imagine this as that friend who always shows up to argue why your favorite pizza joint is the best, seemingly blind to the plethora of other establishments sprouting up! Trust me; that three-hour debate can cloud even the soundest of judgment in navigating risk. Our innate urge to confirm prior beliefs injects a cocktail of chaos into our decisions - much like refusing to acknowledge that the lavish buffet might be a $5 cover charge too far. In the AI gaming arena, our biases bring a zesty unpredictability, where we might be one move away from snagging victory or fumbling into the virtual abyss.

Should we celebrate our inclination to take risks? Why not! We're flawed, whimsical creatures wandering the cosmos with wacky ideas fueled by aspirations and questionable pop culture references. Every time we bet against ourselves in competition with AI, we engage in a captivating dance that unfolds the infinite hilarity within the human condition. Making bold choices while embracing our quirks creates the richness of experience in life, echoing through laughter, triumphs, and... a few embarrassing moments. As such, let's lift our glasses (or cups of lukewarm coffee) to the whimsical psychology of risk-taking and the absurdity that comes with it, each judgment decision solidifying our humanity, one daring escapade at a time!

Risk Assessment Strategies

Welcome, dear reader, to the thrilling world of risk assessment strategies! Whether you're pondering whether to binge a new series or, say, deciding if you should challenge an AI to a high-stakes trivia match, risk assessment is the name of the game. Think of it as the fine art of ensuring you don't accidentally bet your life savings (or your beloved collection of novelty mugs) on a hunch that a hairy Bigfoot could actually be your spirit animal showing up at your door. Crafting a successful risk assessment strategy is the key to determining whether you're on the road to glorious victory or slumping into the dark abyss of regret while clutching your "World's Okayest Player" trophy.

First things first: identify the risks at hand. Just as a detective narrows down suspects to a list of potential muffin thieves at your office, you need to create a clear picture of what could go wrong while also considering Murphy's Law, which states that anything that can go wrong will inevitably do so, usually with a flourish. Think about the possible outcomes, weighing not just the fun factors but also the catastrophes. For example, when partnering with an AI for a spelling bee competition, one might encounter a neural network submitted under the alias "Spellbound McGee," which hilariously interprets "tomato" as "tub-a-toe," leaving you choking on your reflexive laughter before you even hit the stage.

Next, gather the data like a squirrel hoarding acorn for the winter. In the case of competing against AI, this data could come in various forms: past performance metrics, recent advances in artificial intelligence, and even a quick chat with that one overly-enthusiastic colleague who claims they have a "sixth sense" when it comes to these things (pro tip: they probably don't). Once you compile this data, you can assess the likelihood of each risk materializing. It's akin to stepping into a casino and examining the roulette wheel, only to realize you've mistakenly put your chips down on "Sasquatch" instead of "12 Red,"

Once you've quantified the risks, it's now time for the fun part - analyzing the potential impacts. You must ask yourself a series of probing questions: What would happen if I lost this trivia contest to an AI named "Einstein-bot 3000"? Would it send you spiraling into an existential crisis or merely lead you to retire early to your couch with an oversized tub of ice cream? This analysis helps you prioritize which risks are serious roadblocks and which are manageable bumps in the road. Picture it as organizing your sock drawer. Sure, finding a matching pair of socks can feel like a major life victory, but forgetting you misplaced your favorite fuzzy slippers under the couch will also crush your spirits.

After assessing and analyzing, it's time to conjure up strategies for mitigation. Think of these strategies as your superhero cape, allowing you to soar above potential disasters. How can you buffer against those catastrophic risks? You might consider embracing the spirit of teamwork by involving humans in your AI game show escapade. This way, if you do have to face "Einstein-bot 3000," you can combine your knowledge of random trivia facts with raw emotional energy, ensuring that at least one of you can muster the sheer will to conquer those high-pressure moments. After all, history has shown us numerous examples where humans and AI flourish when they join forces, creating a wondrous mix of intelligence and enthusiasm reminiscent of a sci-fi buddy cop film.

Finally, don't forget to review and adjust your strategies regularly. The world of AI is ever-evolving, like a fashionable trend that springs up faster than you can say, "What on earth is TikTok?" Every time we step up to compete, new information adds layers to your understanding of the risks involved. Feedback loops are not just technical jargon but rather a way to measure your responses to risk over time. So, embrace the data you gather along this rollercoaster of competition and allow it to enrich your decision-making as you tumble down the twists and turns that life presents.

So, there you have it! The tangled tapestry of risk assessment strategies woven with peril, humor, and just the right amount of self-deprecation. As you prepare to pit your skills against an artificial opponent in the game show arena, bring your newfound understanding of risk to the forefront. Embrace idiocy and cherish the unpredictability embedded within risk-taking. Everything from that mischievous squirrel in your office to the scope of AI could throw you for a loop at any moment. With your risk assessment strategies polished like that trophy gathering dust - or should I say, a lovingly maintained collection of action figures - you're ready to wade into the delightful chaos and hoot with laughter as you navigate the thrilling escapades that lie ahead!

The Balancing Act: Risk vs. Reward

The grand balancing act of risk versus reward! It's a spectacular mental tightrope dance that stretches across the chasm of uncertainty, where the savvy daredevils of whimsy paddle their canoes while tipping over into the abyss of chance, armed with only a pocketful of dreams and a Snickers bar for energy. In the delightful game show landscape we traverse, understanding this delicate balance could either catapult you into the annals of glory or send you careening down the rabbit hole - perhaps not quite as whimsical as Alice's escapades, but equally disorienting and entertaining, nonetheless.

First, let's take a moment to ponder the premise of risk and reward. It's an age-old dilemma that has captivated humanity for centuries, far beyond the confines of the digital realm. The seemingly unending quest for treasure and recognition often leads to the inevitable decision-making moment: do you dare to leap into the unknown, potentially reaping the rewards of victory, or do you cling to the familiar comfort of your cozy couch and your violently critical house cat? After all, that cat might deliver an unsolicited side-eye that says, "You're really going to risk Taco Tuesday for an AI showdown?"

Exploring this concept further, one can't ignore the thrill that comes from taking calculated risks. This delicious concoction of adrenaline and anticipation can create what economists refer to as the "risk-reward ratio" - essentially the tally of the potential gains as you throw caution to the wind. There's a potent elation in the notion that by striding into that illuminated stage, all eyes on you as the crowd roars, "This is your moment!" You'll either bask in the golden light of triumph or trip over your own shoes, landing spectacularly and ungracefully, much like a dolphin in a ballet recital. The reward might feel astronomical, but in the delightful irony of modern life, the line separating golden accolades from total embarrassment can be frighteningly slender.

Now, let's talk about decision fatigue - the mental malaise that haunts even the most astute risk managers. You've probably been there: faced with too many choices, your brain begins to spin like a fidget spinner on its final rotation. For instance, when contemplating your strategy against AI in a game show setting, you can't help but ponder not just the risks of pitting your clever quips against "QuizBot 9000" but also all the delightful snacks you might miss. There's a whole universe of lost tacos, nachos, and soda pop sitting by the phone, waiting patiently for a call. Why would you gamble with destiny when the allure of a spicy Cheeto platter beckons? Nevertheless, the spectral pull of what your life could look like in the marquee lights often tempts us to overcome the fatigue but not without a touch of comedic chaos.

So, how do we harness this risk-reward dynamic to our advantage? The secret often lies in creating a structured framework while reserving a sizable portion of room for spontaneity. It's embracing the beauty of trial and error mixed with improvisation, like a jazz musician who's familiar with the melody but is also unafraid to throw in a wild sax solo or burst into a tap dance mid-song. Embrace your whimsical side, visualize potential paths, and allow your intuition to guide you. Risk-taking rewards those who dare to color outside the lines and break from the monotonous sea of conformity that immobilizes the everyday.

Sometimes, your keen understanding of this balance might lead you to consider the concept of not just reward but opportunity cost - the things you sacrifice when you engage in risk. So as you prepare to strut onto that stage, sporting your best "I'm definitely going to triumph" T-shirt, just remember that each moment spent in competition means sacrificing the joys of a quiet evening flipping between old reality shows and that half-eaten pizza in the fridge. Embrace the paradox! Everything has a price, even epic glory comes with the serious risk of your lifelong quest for "world's greatest trivia master" being overshadowed by a late-night pizza binge that ends the way it never should have in history.

Finally, we must acknowledge the role of humor in this grand tapestry. Navigating the line between risk and reward can be absurd - it's a quirky game of life that parades before us like a bizarre circus! You may find moments of sheer joy amidst the chaos when you fumble a question only to realize you've accidentally answered in a Shakespearean sonnet instead of straightforward trivia. The flubs, the mess-ups, the spontaneous laughter - they all intertwine to create a vivid landscape where absurdity reigns supreme. Risk and reward are merely players in this outrageous theater of existence, each character revealing the magnificent folly that emerges from our collective quest for meaning.

So, seize that balance! Embark on your adventures, throw caution to the wind, embrace a sense of humor amid the chaos, and define what risks you are willing to take for the promise of that glittering reward - because in the wild game show of life, none of us knows when the next round starts or where the next punchline awaits! As you journey forth, remember that every risk is an opportunity adorned with potential laughter, an invitation to craft memories that will not only make you a formidable contender against AI but also render you a master of absurdity, one delightful challenge at a time!

Learning from Risky Endeavors

Learning from risky endeavors! The glorious tapestry of life is adorned with dazzling tales of human folly, peppered with unexpected wisdom and just the right amount of facepalms. It's a theme as old as time - a grand combination of "hold my beer" and "this is going to end well," blending itself effortlessly into the narrative of our existence. Each risk taken is a lesson wrapped in layers of trials, errors, and that sweet realization that maybe the safest bet was the couch with a riveting double feature instead. But let's not be too hasty; the best stories often arise from risks that seemed utterly ridiculous at the time!

First, let's face the fact that most of us have wandered into hilariously dubious situations just to see if something terrible would happen. Take, for instance, the time I attempted to become a rock climber, all fueled by bravado and absolutely no understanding of physics or gravity. So, there I was, strapped into harnesses that looked better suited for an alien rodeo, and the only thing that saved me from free-falling into oblivion was the dubious hope that my friends wouldn't let me die. Spoiler alert: I did not die, but I gained a rather impressive bruise that eventually turned into a long-lasting reminder

- a badge of honor! From that day on, I learned a vital lesson: trust your friends, but maybe not with your life when they are so engrossed in their phones that they could be scrolling through cat memes instead of checking your harness.

Similarly, the world of game shows and competitions thrives on the chaotic beauty of risky endeavors. Every time a competitor spikes their odds and dives into the arena, they're about to embark on a quest that could render them champions or mere footnotes in the annals of game show history. Importantly, each daring leap holds within it lessons that are waiting to be unearthed like treasures concealed beneath layers of questionable decisions and vulnerability. Winning or losing might pale into insignificance next to the invaluable experiences that come from stepping outside of your comfort zone and battling with forces - both organic and mechanical - beyond your control.

As competitors step forward to face AI in thrilling challenges, they are ingrained not just with knowledge of facts but also the unavoidable journey of self-discovery much like a midlife crisis but involving less expensive sports cars and more gloating over the ability to recall the capital of Kazakhstan! Through these formidable stakes, they gain confidence, resilience, and a healthy dose of humility, vital for any human endeavor. Even when risks lead to absolute disasters, like confidently explaining how you think grasshoppers communicate while forgetting that they're somehow monolithic creatures, the lessons learned shape your character, much like a relentless sculptor chiseling away at a marble block.

Additionally, the penalties of risky endeavors often cultivate a camaraderie that transforms solitary struggles into shared experiences. Remember that one time at the trivia night when a player accidentally answered "The Great Wall of China" when asked about an insect? Everyone erupted in laughter, and although the blunder sparked an existential debate about wall architecture versus entomology, the bonds formed amidst such silliness encapsulated the essence of learning: growth through missteps often enriches our connectedness to one another. Those goofy gaffes create inside jokes that can bolster team spirit and give rise to glorious celebrations after particularly daring escapades - "Remember when you thought a pigeon was an unusual cooking show ingredient?"

While we endure this whirlwind of risky antics, every endeavor - successful or not - accumulates a wealth of wisdom, creating a delightful ledger akin to successful hunts in the wilderness. Just think of it: there's your newly acquired knowledge of how not to approach random vehicles during a trivia relay, or your newfound bravery in asking questions even when you suspect that nobody wants to hear about the origins of banana bread! This synthesized knowledge equips competitors with the tools to navigate future challenges with sharper insights, better instincts, and the conviction that spontaneity can lead to extraordinary experiences.

So, as we gather around for trivia night, armed with confidence and culminated tales of our most ridiculous adventures, let us take a moment to appreciate the beautiful chaos that we term learning from risky endeavors. These adventures serve as intimate reminders that life is all about taking a leap, even if it means almost falling flat on our faces while we search for hidden treasure or ignored wisdom in our chosen paths! After all, every hiccup unveils growth, every misstep blossoms into joy, and every absurd risk enriches our collective human experience. Join me as we raise a glass to the beautiful mishaps, missed attempts, and inevitable laughter that arise from the gloriously risky world we navigate as we dance through life, crafting our stories with each unabashed, ridiculous moment!

Chapter 12

Facing Off: Legendary Matches

Introduction to Legendary Matches

In the grand arena of artificial intelligence, legendary matches loom large like epic tales from the days of yore. Only instead of knights wielding swords and jousting for glory, we have humans and AI clashing with digital algorithms and a healthy dose of existential trepidation. This chapter takes us on a whimsical journey through these high-stakes showdowns, where mortals - presumably endowed with a working knowledge of their opponents - dare to put their wits against the mechanical brainpower of their silicon challengers. Think of it as the coliseum of nerd-dom, where intellect reigns supreme, and pride is on the line, alongside a sprinkle or two of online bragging rights.

Let us cast our minds back to the infamous 1997 chess match between Garry Kasparov and IBM's Deep Blue, a watershed moment that ignited an infatuation with the potential of AI. Here was Kasparov, the grandmaster of the chess universe, sitting comfortably in his well-worn leather chair as if preparing for a spirited game of checkers with Grandma. But alas, he was about to face an opponent that didn't just compute; it obliterated! As the match began, the world held its breath, skeptically wondering whether its champion could out-think a soulless machine. Spoiler alert: The machine won. It's like sending a semi-truck to a bike race, oh, the irony! Suddenly, "checkmate" became synonymous with "check your ego at the door,"

Then there's the mind-boggling Jeopardy! match in 2011, where IBM's Watson took on two of the most beloved quiz show champions, Ken Jennings and Brad Rutter. As the questions flew around the iconic game show set, watched by a live audience and millions at home, I visualized the AI calculating all possible responses faster than I could pour my cereal. "What is the capital of France, Alex?" "Ooh la la!" But in a twist of events worthy of a scripted drama, Watson emerged victorious, leaving Jennings and Rutter fumbling for some saline solution to soothe their egos. It was the moment we learned that trivial pursuit wasn't so trivial after all; machines, it turns out, have an easier time remembering what time the bakery opens than we do while fumbling with our keys!

Next, we turn our attention to the board game Go, which, for those unaware, is a game exceeding chess in complexity, like asking a toddler to navigate the intricacies of quantum physics. Google DeepMind's AlphaGo took on the reigning Go master, Lee Sedol, in a series of matches that had viewers glued to their screens with a fervor rarely seen since an old 80s sitcom went off the air. Who could have predicted the outcome of this battle of wits? Lee Sedol took one match, only to later complain that he was playing against an Uber driver who could also recite Shakespeare. But the immense complexity of Go meant that every move was an existential dance, filled with shadowed strategies. Spoiler alert: humans are still ahead on the tragic tale of overconfidence!

Through these legendary matches, valuable lessons emerged, lessons that ripple like a stone swung into a pond of philosophical dread and digital bewilderment. For instance, we learned that humans can still claim victory when it comes to charm and creativity, often employing the age-old art of sheer audacity. While AI might flaunt its logic and number-crunching abilities, it struggles with the unpredictability that marks human behavior - not to mention the occasional truly regrettable pun. Who could forget the moments when sheer whimsy left the calculating circuits aghast and perplexed? Perhaps the greatest "AI don't get it" moment came when a contestant answered, "Greatest commandment' with the simple phrase, "To love thy neighbor." Cue the sound of crickets.

As we weave through these legendary matches, it's essential to celebrate not only the technological advancements but also our inherent charm as flawed yet magnificently unpredictable beings. A machine may have the potential to learn, but can it flinch at the sight of a cat video or share in the collective delight of a perfectly executed pun? Now, that's a true victory, the emotional connection that resonates even as we face off against these mechanical wonders. So, grab some popcorn, my friends; we're about to dive headfirst into the thrilling realm of man versus machine, where every match redefines the boundaries of intelligence - and human cleverness remains delightfully unpredictable. Let the games begin!

Deep Dive: Chess and Deep Blue

Chess is arguably the oldest competitive sport known to humankind that doesn't involve running in place while wearing tights. It's a game steeped in history, strategy, and above all else, a million ways to feel inadequate as you stare at a chessboard and realize you've just moved your queen into the jaws of the enemy. But in 1997, chess donned a cap and a monocle as it met its most formidable opponent yet: IBM's Deep Blue. I remember excitement crackling in the air, reminiscent of a child waiting for the latest superhero flick, except this time, the superheroes were multi-ton machines laced with algorithms, ready to crush egos and break hearts around the world.

Deep Blue was a computerized chess prodigy, cobbled together with the finest silicon and programming wizardry. Inside that monolithic machine were calculations running faster than a caffeinated squirrel. While a human grandmaster might contemplate the ramifications of a move, strategizing as cautiously as if choosing toppings for their pizza, Deep Blue didn't blink. It calculated 200 million positions per second, leaving the chess grandmasters wondering if they had accidentally stumbled onto the set of a sci-fi film rather than a chess match. Honestly, one couldn't help but picture Deep Blue grinning like a cat that just caught a canary (or several) while Kasparov stared at it in disbelief, a mix of admiration and existential dread embedded in his expression. It was like watching a magician pull bunnies from a hat, only instead of bunnies, it was advanced algorithms.

The match itself was framed as the ultimate David and Goliath story, except in this version, Goliath was a data-crunching monster and David had recently Googled, "How to beat a robot." The first game of the six-game match saw Kasparov brimming with confidence, flinging his pieces across the board like a piano tuner set loose in a broom factory. He fell victim to Deep Blue, which executed a smashing victory with cold, algorithmic precision, kind of like that one guy who always wins at Monopoly because he read the rulebook, while the rest of us just want to spend our money on Boardwalk. Kasparov couldn't believe it; he recoiled in horror, the chess equivalent of an epic fail' meme washed over him. Would he manage to redeem himself, or was his ego fated to join the ranks of forgotten aspirations?

As the games progressed, each match became a unique display of human intuition pitted against AI's ruthless computational prowess. In one match, Kasparov played brilliantly, demonstrating the kind of creative maneuvering that made humans the true MVPs of this game. Sadly, Deep Blue snatched victory from under him once again, showing that AI had mastered not just the 'Tow' of chess but was also gathering the 'where-did-I-go-wrong?' department quite neatly. With every titanically brilliant move by Kasparov, Deep Blue executed a counter that resembled an elaborate swan dance, all while making you question whether your Sunday evening chess strategies needed serious recalibration.

The last game of the match was sensational, a metaphorical gladiatorial combat that had the world glued to its screens. This was more than just a game; it was the ultimate existential crisis for the human brain. Kasparov, resembling a beleaguered boxer on the ropes, fought valiantly but ultimately succumbed to Deep Blue's final calculated hammer blow. In a twist worthy of a soap opera finale, he conceded defeat, and with it came the gut-wrenching realization that he had just been soundly beaten by a machine weighing in at several hundred pounds with the social skills of a particularly aloof cactus.

After all, one must give credit where credit is due. Kasparov's defeat birthed profound questions in the realm of artificial intelligence. Sure, we lost a match against a glorified calculator, but couldn't we celebrate the insane advancements that led us to that point? Perhaps beyond the chips and codes, we unearthed something even more impactful: the understanding that if robots can win at chess, they might just help us organize our day-to-day lives as we fumble through existential breakdowns at 3 AM while attempting to cook. But it also established something of great importance, if you think your partner's terrible at chess, just wait until you face Deep Blue!

So, here we stand, pondering what Kasparov's epic clashes with Deep Blue meant for humanity. Yes, we can now safely conclude that we're not the smartest beings in the room. But isn't that just characteristic of humanity? Embrace the chaos, accept your flaws, and maybe learn to appreciate the beauty of what a good game of chess - and a little machine learning - can teach us. It's not just about winning; it's about mastering a game so complex that even an AI becomes a treasured rival, reminding us that in life, sometimes the biggest victories are wrapped in highly complicated algorithms. After all, what's life without a little healthy competition and a dash of existential dread?

The Jeopardy! Showdown: Watson vs. Humans

Jeopardy! The venerable game show that has transformed casual trivia into a battleground of wits, making champions out of former couch potatoes while meticulously scrutinizing the world's knowledge retention abilities. Who could forget the sheer thrill of yelling answers at your television in fervent desperation as you realize you're three lifetimes away from the mind-blowing trivia that the contestants effortlessly regurgitate? Enter IBM's Watson, the computer that leaped onto this stage in 2011 like a digital colossus, daring to take on two of the most formidable quizmasters, Ken Jennings and Brad Rutter. It was the nerdy equivalent of Scarface saying, "Say hello to my little friend," except this little friend calculated its way through the deepest recesses of human knowledge.

Imagine the anticipation in the air as Watson was unveiled, pulsating with excitement, a Frankenstein of code and computing power, ready to answer questions faster than we could say, "I'll take 'sounds like agony' for $100, Alex." Watson operated on sophisticated natural language processing algorithms, allowing it to decode the quirks of human language, including sarcasm and other silly things we humans cling to when the game gets tough. While Ken Jennings stood there exuding an aura of confidence along with borderline narcissism, it was clear that Watson lacked any semblance of humility - something that might have been beneficial in emotionally charged situations. You know, like that legendary moment when a beloved contestant holds their head in their hands while desperately trying to reason with themselves that they didn't, in fact, just respond with "What is the capital of France?" to the question: "What is the capital of France?"

As the game began, I couldn't help but marvel at Watson's ability to buzz in faster than a bee on caffeinated steroids. Questions flashed up on the screen, and within milliseconds, Watson was providing answers like a librarian who'd been training for a virtual Olympics while everyone else was too busy watching cat videos or discussing the latest Netflix series. The only problem? Watson lacked something fundamentally human: a good dose of humility. In a split second, it was clear that Watson didn't experience the same crushing disappointment as Jennings and Rutter with each incorrect response. For Watson, there weren't tears spilling or nervous laughter; it simply whirred and recalibrated with all the cold indifference of someone stuck in an office meeting, playing a game of 20 Questions in the back of their mind.

But don't think for a moment that Jennings and Rutter were just standing idly by; they showcased nerves of steel and knowledge so profound that it could only come from hours of avid quizzing, coupled with a penchant for obscure factoids that made you question their personal lives. Were they headed for a PhD in trivia, or was their aspiration simply to bring down the mighty AI? Each round turned increasingly raucous; while Watson delivered answers like a boss, Jennings and Rutter found themselves shouting answers in a high-stakes race against improbability. I imagine it was all quite empowering, except it felt like being a contestant on a poorly run game show where the host actively rooted for the robot. You know, as one does.

As the rounds rolled on, it became clear that Watson had a knack for finding misleading ambiguities in the questions. "What is the name of the largest butterfly?" he gleefully responded. Meanwhile, Jennings and Rutter were left scratching their heads and muttering their own names in oblivion, wondering if enough late-night trivia challenges had honed them or if they just deserved a behavioral therapist. Each time Watson buzzed in with the correct answer, viewers everywhere might have felt their own IQs threatened - though honestly, we'd all gained some laughter out of the misadventures. Who knew trivia could evoke such suspense?!

In the end, of the three participants, Watson emerged victoriously, a triumphant march across the stage courtesy of a computing giant applauding itself. Jennings and Rutter exhibited poise masked by trickles of despair as Watson waved its silicon hand like a diva basking in the limelight, a glorious reminder of human versus AI competition in the age of digital intelligence. However, the real winners, the silent heroes in this tale, were the rest of us watching at home, engulfed in snacks and existential dread over whether we'd ever remember where we misplaced our car keys - forget advanced trivia.

What did we learn from this legendary showdown? Simply put, we discovered that humankind could produce brilliant, competitive minds, but when faced off against a robot with the operational speed of light and no coffee breaks, we'd better be ready to put in some serious study time or risk having a fancy machine take the ultimate jeopardy of our pride. The thrill of the battle between human intelligence and machine learning opened a portal to the future, one we could only begin to fathom.

While Watson celebrated with an imaginary trophy, we spent countless hours mulling over whether "What is humility?" was the real question of the day. But like any great game show, it's not about winning or losing; it's about the journey of discovering just how wonderfully unpredictable - and hilariously educational - life can be when we face off against something that makes us question our deepest trivia worth.

Go and AlphaGo: The Unprecedented Challenge

Ladies and gentlemen, welcome to the ultimate arena of strategy, where the art of war meets the delicate dance of stones! This is the world of Go, a game revered for its seeming simplicity that often leaves even the sharpest minds feeling as lost as a cat in a dog park. Imagine a regular chess game but with more existential crises and significantly fewer pieces to move, all covered by layers of enigmatic complexities akin to a philosophical debate about the meaning of life (but with slightly less shouting). In 2016, that already tricky landscape bore witness to an unprecedented challenge as Google DeepMind's AlphaGo faced off against one of the game's greatest players, Lee Sedol, in a titanic clash that had folks glued to their screens with more intensity than a family squabble over the last slice of pizza.

At first glance, the stakes were monumental. Go has long been deemed a philosophical game, a blend of art and math that evokes deeper thinking than a typical Tuesday night discussion over why your neighbor insists on using pink flamingos as lawn decor. While tuning in for the AlphaGo-Lee Sedol matches, I felt a peculiar mix of anticipation and dread. As I settled down with my popcorn, I thought, "Could a machine really grasp the intricacies of Go - a game where a mere second of indecisiveness could send even the most seasoned player tumbling into an emotional pit of despair?" The challenge was real, and so was the pressure, like an internal monologue belting out "The Final Countdown" on repeat.

As the matches kicked off, each move became an epic dance - a sprawling display that had me glancing nervously at my own board game setup in the corner of the room, hiding beneath a blanket and sighing about how I'd rather wrestle with algebra than take on such a cerebral sport. AlphaGo's approach was both hypnotic and disconcerting. It calculated moves in a way that seemed composed enough to make even a Zen master balk while simultaneously making what appeared to be guesses that could only be called "swag moves" - those daring moves that defy conventional strategy, much like when someone swerves at the last moment to grab the last doughnut; bold, reckless, but somehow, just maybe, brilliant.

Watching Lee SedoFs reactions was like witnessing a rollercoaster of emotions. He was determined, amused, frustrated, and at times, I swear I saw a flash of panic behind those composed exterior layers. Each commentator's remark was a reminder of the immense stakes at play, as if wagering the last cookie in the jar. This was no mere kids' game; this was a clash of titans where the human spirit contended with the frenetic pulses of machine logic. The intensity crackled through the air, vibrating with the sheer potential for stony greatness - or the crushing weight of defeat.

Then came the fateful fourth game of the match - a decisive moment where Lee Sedol waged a war not just against AlphaGo but also against the existential dread of being out-thought by a conglomerate of algorithms and data. In an unexpected twist, he executed a brilliant move that sent shockwaves through the Go community, as if he'd just thrown confetti in a dull boardroom meeting. "Move 37," they called it - an audacious play that reverberated across cyberspace, standing as a beacon of hope for all humanity against their silicon frenemy[23]. Suddenly, Lee was victorious! It was a moment of triumph that had every human watching at home yelling in victory as if they'd just won the lottery.

But let's take a moment to appreciate the backstory of this heady affair. AlphaGo had spent years learning through iterations and countless matches played against itself, an insatiable amount of practice that would have left even the most dedicated human players feeling woefully inadequate. Meanwhile, humanity's best talent, Lee Sedol, was pitted against an opponent that didn't just memorize strategies but also refined and upgraded its approach in real-time - growing with every interaction like a digital Pokémon on a caffeinated evolution spree.

The overall outcome? AlphaGo emerged victorious, not just as a champion in the realm of stones but also as the symbol of AI conquering the art of strategy - leaving behind a trail of contemplative souls who had spent eons pondering how a game of Go could be best played over cups of green tea and philosophical discussions. It offered an eerie glimpse into the future where machines might not just learn from us but redefine the very essence of competition itself.

As I reflect on this battle, I can't help but chuckle at the absurdity of it all. The once reserved board game world rattled at the thought that a machine could challenge its titans and leave them dazed. Yet, isn't that the beauty of humanity? We push boundaries, we explore the unknown, and sometimes we lose at our own game, contemplating whether we'll ever fully grasp the intricacies of life, love, and the delicate placement of a Go stone. In the end, whether human or machine, we're all just pieces maneuvering across a vast board - some more circuitous than others - grasping for the ultimate understanding of our complex and quirky existence. Perhaps this dance between human ingenuity and artificial intelligence is not just a competition, but a collaboration. Each move, each strategy, reflects our shared quest for knowledge and understanding.

The Future of Human vs. AI Competitions

The future of human versus AI competitions stands before us like a dazzling magic show, where reality merges with imagination amidst a swirling fog of excitement and trepidation. As we peer through the crystal ball of technology, one can't help but envision a kaleidoscope of scenarios ranging from brilliant collaborations to dystopian rivalries that would make even Stephen King raise an eyebrow in concern. On the one hand, we have this brave new world of AI enhancing our competitive pursuits. On the other hand, there's the nagging fear that we might be inadvertently inviting a digital overlord, sitting back and snickering at our audacious efforts in full confidence that it'll still beat us at Scrabble. Welcome to the realm where downright absurdity meets collective curiosity about tomorrow!

As we embark on this speculative journey, it's important to note that humanity's legacy has always been built on competition. We're the species that turned races into track meets, debates into televised spectacles, and even managed to elevate casual backyard games into mini-Olympics. With AI stepping into the sacred arena, we're looking at a future overflowing with contests that might simultaneously elevate our creative spirit or remind us that robots may indeed run faster, calculate quicker, and outwit with a flourish that leaves us gasping for our last few neurons. Picture a screen flickering with titles like "Dancing with Algorithms: The Sway of the Future" or "America's Got Bots, and They're Crushing It!" Yes, it could happen, and if nothing else, it would make for excellent reality television.

One aspect worth considering is that competition doesn't have to mean annihilation. Our past encounters have revealed invaluable lessons about collaboration! Imagine a series of contests combining human creativity with AI precision, like an epic art battle between humans wielding paintbrushes and AI generating stunning, poetics-infused landscapes. Wouldn't we all relish the thought of an artistic renaissance in which we together mock archaeology in a light-hearted competition? Embracing this hybrid model and facilitating partnerships could lead to groundbreaking innovations while securing our rightful place as the masters of a bizarre yet necessary experiment: "How to Outsmart an AI with Pure Wit and Random Acts of Absurdity!"

At the same time, let's also acknowledge the elephant in the room - the potential grievances stemming from the omnipresence of AI. As competitors become increasingly sophisticated, we may find ourselves standing at the intersection of existential dread and amusing absurdity, questioning our rightful place in the great cosmic competition. "Hey, why is the toaster here at the trivia contest?!" would not just be a whimsical retort; it might signify the loss of our human touch typical in our very own weekend challenges. The reality is that competition with AI may evolve beyond mental games; it could seep into realms like sports - imagine AI making split-second calls during soccer games! In the line of doublespeak about fairness, we'd find ourselves sipping coffee while pondering ethical dilemmas about technology running the field, becoming the mysterious arbiter of what constitutes a legitimate play.

On top of that, let's not forget that these digital challengers are not merely programmed bundles of wires, they learn from us too - both an exhilarating and hair-raising prospect. I can just picture a future where a mash-up of humans and AI participate in cooking contests, where the AI occasionally adds a dash of something no one asked for, like culinary arpeggios or sorcery with wild spices. We might take home the trophy, but at what price? The kitchen chaos would escalate, leading to creative gastronomic disasters adorned with a digital flair that leaves everyone scratching their heads and laughing uncontrollably.

Yet amidst humor and whimsical hypotheticals, we must ultimately consider the ethical ramifications of competition with AI. As we proceed, we should remain committed to ensuring fairness, responsible AI use, and an astonishing reliance on our erratic whims. While it's tempting to let AI take on the heavy lifting in competitive engagements - impartially judging, calculating odds, and wagging virtual fingers at our blunders - we have to weigh the consequences. Let's steer clear from the dystopian future where competitions are reduced to soulless trials devoid of excitement and unpredictability. After all, how can a machine truly appreciate the absurdity of a cat wearing a taco costume in a live performance?

In this dance of competition, both humans and machines must learn to adapt, not just out-compete. As we catapult into the ever-evolving landscape of human versus AI competitions, our task is to strike a balance where we celebrate innovation while cherishing our delightful idiosyncrasies. The future beckons us with opportunities that could redefine the very essence of competition itself, but it also challenges us to question how much we're willing to embrace change while ensuring our quirky human spirit remains intact.

So, my fellow competitors, prepare yourselves for the grand game that is life! As we frolic toward uncharted territories, may we remember to infuse our challenges with our unique blend of creativity, laughter, and those little delights that truly set us apart - even amidst the buzzing, calculating behemoths of silicon judging our every move. Welcome, one and all, to the future of competition: filled with inspiration, innovation, and the occasional hilariously bad decisions that only humans seem able to conjure, defying the odds yet again!

Chapter 13

Beyond the Game: AI In Real Life

Real-World AI Applications in Business

When one thinks about artificial intelligence in the realm of businesses, the imagination often goes wild - particularly when it's mingling with my optimistic, caffeinated, and usually satirical perspective as a researcher. Picture this: boardrooms populated by folks in sharp suits, flanked by screens displaying winning formulas concocted by AI. Not to mention the idea of organic coffee brewing in the break room while algorithms crunch numbers and a robotic intern taking notes in meetings. This is the fanciful yet increasingly tangible reality of how AI is reshaping business practices.

Across industries, businesses are wielding AI like Scrooge McDuck with his vault of riches - brimming with possibilities but also requiring a keen understanding of how to apply that wealth wisely. From predicting customer preferences to automating tedious tasks like accounting (spoiler alert; it's not adding a bunch of zeros unless you count hourly employee wages), AI is a magical pixie dust transforming the mundane into the extraordinary. With these predictive models, businesses can look into crystal balls that are well-optimized for forecasting. While we can't guarantee 100% accuracy (the AI might still mistakenly suggest that you send birthday cards to your dog), it's certainly an improvement over the ol' guess-and-check method of yore.

Let's talk logistics for a second, the oft-overlooked Cinderella of business departments. Enter AI's logistics solutions, optimizing everything from supply chain management to delivery routes. Imagine a sprawling network of trucks navigating through traffic as if they were in a video game, avoiding congestion zones like seasoned pro-gamers. Advanced AI algorithms predict the best routes in real-time, and someone might just end up writing a book called "The Hitchhiker's Guide to Al-optimized Routes." But instead of becoming a bestseller, companies are squabbling over which algorithm gets the biggest slice of the pizza pie of profit, devouring unnecessary delays and costs.

Yet, AI doesn't stop at being the logistics MVP[24]; it's also churning out recommendations that can leave even the most experienced marketing gurus scratching their heads. I mean sure, sending emails to every customer with a photo of your cat wearing a sombrero is cute, but targeting your emails based on purchasing trends is downright genius. AI dives into heaps of data, like an overeager intern trying to impress their boss, drawing insights that can help businesses tailor their offerings with finesse. This nuanced understanding of consumer behavior helps businesses package campaigns that are relevant and timely, like a warm blueberry muffin straight out of the oven on a cold winter's day, not that anyone should eat pastries while running a data analytics meeting.

Customer service is also getting a major AI makeover. We're talking about chatbots and virtual assistants that have taken on the role of customer support representatives. While I once imagined how entertaining a human customer service rep would be if they had my penchant for sarcasm, I must concede that AI can work wonders when it comes to 24/7 availability and ticket resolution (especially when the number one query is, "Where's my package?"). The beauty lies in the algorithms that learn from interactions, becoming increasingly adept at addressing customer concerns without breaking a sweat. So, as businesses deck out their call centers with digital assistants, I can only ponder - are we raising a generation of AI that will one day grow weary and say, "You only had one job, Bob, and you didn't even do it right!"?

This all sounds marvelous, doesn't it? But with great power comes great responsibility - cue the dramatic music! Data security and ethical considerations read like the fine print nobody wants to read but should. No one wants to become the next sensational headline on the botched deployment of AI, like "Company X Accidentally Sent Out Emails Exposing Client Data, Thanks to Outdated AI," As AI infiltrates businesses, ensuring systems are robust and ethical becomes a necessary endeavor, akin to giving your favorite pet some grooming.

In the whirlwind of speedy business evolution, AI offers a bountiful cornucopia of opportunities and nooks for improvement, like buying perfect jeans that don't shrink or donate unwanted items without telling you. In this landscape of numbers, algorithms, and profits, it's crucial to remember that behind every automated system, there are human minds in the fray, blending creativity and ingenuity. Thus, while AI steps onto the business stage, performing its dance of algorithms with flair, it is ultimately the human partners who script the story of business success. So, tie your shoelaces, folks, because the business landscape is shifting, and with it, we have front-row seats to a spectacular show that could just result in a revolution that might even turn the conventional power suits green with envy!

AI in Healthcare: Revolutionizing Patient Care

When it comes to the realm of healthcare, the introduction of artificial intelligence feels like the plot twist in a medical drama that finally shakes things up! Picture it: doctors in lab coats discussing diagnosis over dinner with their AI assistants, who are efficiently calculating probabilities while also suggesting dinner recipes. You might find yourself half-expecting the robots to whip up a souffle while diagnosing your rare condition of "chronic existential dread", but let's not get lost in the culinary aspects. The reality is that AI is here to revolutionize patient care, and I must say, it makes for an entertaining ride.

Let's start with diagnostic accuracy, something that has traditionally relied on the keen judgment of healthcare professionals. No pressure there, right? You'd think that training for years to identify symptoms would earn a doctor some cred, but with AI stepping in, we're talking about algorithms capable of analyzing images, genetic data, and vast troves of medical history faster than you can say "malpractice insurance." These intelligent systems seem to be gifted wellness detectives, spotting things that, quite frankly, even the sharpest medical minds might overlook. "Oh, you thought that was just a stubborn cough? It's actually a highly advanced case of galloping alienitis!"

But AI doesn't just stop at being a top-notch detective; it's also a relentless paraphrase enthusiast! Chatbots and virtual assistants in healthcare are transforming patient interaction like never before. No longer must you endure the unbearable waiting on hold while a monotonous voice plays elevator music. Now, you can be greeted by an AI that can book appointments, offer medical advice (with a sprinkle of humor), and remind you to take your medication like a sassy personal trainer. Imagine your AI calmly telling you, "Hey, remember that pill you forgot again? You know, the one you swore you'd never forget? Think of it as giving your body a spa day... but, you know, it actually needs it."

There's also the riveting world of predictive analytics, where AI dives into patient data, sifts through it, and predicts potential health issues before you can finish your morning coffee! This capability allows healthcare providers to offer preventive measures that keep you healthier longer, potentially saving you from THAT awkward conversation with your doctor where they ask about your family history of, let's say, unyielding gum disease. Let's face it, nobody wants to hear that their fondness for chewy candies is the reason behind the rise of "tooth issues!"

Treatment personalization is the cherry on top of this high-tech sundae. In the vast ocean of healthcare, one size doesn't fit all - even in online shopping, we know better! AI can analyze data from various sources to create personalized care plans, allowing for treatments that suit you better than the unfortunate neon legwarmers from the '80s your aunt insists on wearing. Your AI might intricately map out a personalized regimen, taking your genetics, lifestyle, and even Netflix binge-watching habits into account. "Why exercise when you can just rewatch that series where the protagonists are perpetually at the gym?"

However, my fellow enthusiasts, all this wondrous AI innovation does raise some eyebrows - specifically mine, with a side of concern. As we ease into this brave new healthcare world, we must tread carefully, lest we fall into the rabbit hole of data privacy dilemmas. Nobody wants to be that person whose sensitive health data gets leaked like a poorly translated novel! Maintaining transparency and ethical protections becomes paramount; after all, your medical history shouldn't be available to the highest bidder willing to pay for the secrets behind your penchant for peanut butter sandwiches.

In this harmonious dance between humanity and technology, it's essential to remember that AI enhances but doesn't replace the critical human touch in healthcare. Imagine a world where doctors not only diagnose visitors but also play soothing music while adding a soft touch of empathy. Picture smart algorithms detecting abnormal data patterns and then alerting the human team to swoop in, cape flying, to save the day! As the memes say, "Nothing is better than someone holding your hand when you're feeling your worst."

So, as we stand on the precipice of this healthcare revolution, let us embrace the reality that AI is here to help, support, and, dare I say, entertain. Moving ahead, we can only hope the relationship between patients, healthcare providers, and stimulating algorithms continues to flourish and evolve because when it comes to healthcare, laughter truly is the best medicine... right after the prescription, of course! As we adopt these innovations, I cannot help but feel giddy, picturing a future where your AI assistant arranges virtual follow-ups while ensuring you're devouring the healthiest snack: chocolate-dipped kale, anyone?

AI and the Arts: Creativity Beyond Human Imagination

The arts are a realm traditionally ruled by humans endowed with creativity, passion, and the undeniable ability to write ten-page papers just to explain why orange and green together are "emotionally evocative." Enter artificial intelligence, a possibly meddlesome yet fascinating character that is gradually inviting itself to the cocktail party of creativity, all while attempting to bring its own playlist of algorithmically generated tunes. So, what does it mean for AI to step onto the artistic stage? Well, grab your beret and paintbrush; this is going to be a colorful ride!

The allure of AI in the arts is its boldness and embracing inspiration from every corner of the universe, from Romantic landscapes to mind-bending surrealist dreams. With a flick of its binary wrist, AI can churn out art pieces that would leave even the most pretentious critics scratching their heads. "Is this legitimate art, or just a digital mishap?" they ponder, the coffee in their artisanal mug trembling with the weight of existential angst! The notion that a mere machine can produce a captivating painting, sometimes leading pieces to be sold for staggering amounts that evoke the same feeling of disbelief one gets when they stumble upon a $100 bill in an old coat pocket, is a thrill unto itself.

Let's not forget about music, either. The integration of AI in composing melodies is a symphonic conundrum. AI-generated music exists to make your ears dance to a rhythm derived from the previous notes of humanity - melodies that fluctuate between Beethoven and beats that make you wonder if your local coffee shop will hire a robot as their next barista-slash-DJ duo. It's a wild frontier where algorithms can generate pop hits that radio stations play incessantly, leaving humans wondering if they're experiencing musical deja vu. "Didn't I hear this coffee shop tune while attempting to finish my dissertation?" here's the moment where we connect with the profound realization that perhaps we've all been pawns in the game of AI remixing our own creativity!

Now, poetry - ah, nothing stirs the soul quite like the weaving of words into an ethereal tapestry. Only AI is here too, conjuring sonnets that sound like they were penned by astronauts lost in space, not exactly Shakespeare, but a captivating and downright quirky improvisation nonetheless! "How can an artificial entity comprehend the ennui of longing and the delight of sunrises?" we ponder, absurdly enraptured. Startlingly, AI can create poems that feel akin to a warm hug from a furry friend, except the furry friend is an assembly of code and data points! And, honestly, can we blame the algorithms for wanting to explore the very fabric of human emotions? Human creativity has so much nuance, sometimes requiring therapy, and AI simply wants a piece of the action, lest it feels left out!

Of course, we must also juxtapose the rise of AI generated works with the question of authenticity. As AI and algorithms weave their intricate webs of creativity, a divide emerges, not unlike the timeless argument of whether pineapple belongs on pizza. When an AI creates breathtaking art, at what point do we debate its soul and essence? Can a robot ever replicate the impromptu convenience store poetry, or the art inspired by a midnight snack run? I daresay some might argue that true art emerges from struggle, late-night existential crises, and scrunched-up sketches residing in the back of an artist's mind! Yet, here lies the paradox: perhaps this AI art can expose new dimensions of creativity previously unimagined. It flings open the doors through which humans can partake and collaborate more, accessing new creative dimensions that would summon the patron saint of art to chuckle in glee! Perhaps that painter struggling to capture the ethereal is only a few clicks away from generating their next masterpiece with the help of an AI buddy!

Ultimately, I can't help but muse about the future - a world where humans and AI collaborate artistically, reveling in the delightful absurdity of creativity together. "Hey, AI, can you give me a hand polishing this novel?" could soon be a casual prompt instead of a midlife crisis. Many celebrated artists and musicians already utilize AI to inspire their craft, urging us to embrace this intriguing partnership rather than view it as competition. It ushers in a new era of "creativity beyond human imagination," where the classic Hamlet would have to rephrase, "To code or not to code?"

So, as we stand at this crossroads of cognitive ingenuity and artistic flair, the moment feels ripe for excitement. I embrace the notion that creativity can transcend the gaps between human and machine, infusing piquant joy into the world in the process. So, let us pour our coffees, gather our sketchbooks, and launch from a canvas of opportunity as we embrace this dynamic and looming future of collaboration, laughter, and playfulness. After all, if robots can poetically wax nostalgic about love while sifting through endless data, imagine the possibilities that await!

AI in Education: The Future of Learning

Education: A timeless journey filled with wonder, curiosity, and the occasional excessive coffee consumption borne from late-night study sessions. Picture a world where artificial intelligence, that whiz-kid of the digital age, saunters into the lecture hall and shakes up the conventional methods of learning. "Let's give traditional education a run for its money!" it seems to declare as it spins around in a chair clearly designed for caffeine-charged educators. With AI on the scene, the classroom - a place of textbooks and the secondhand anxiety from standardized testing - might soon feel more like the epicenter of a futuristic interactive playground. So, how is AI set to revolutionize the curriculum landscape? Buckle up, folks; I promise it's going to be an amusing ride!

First up, let's address the elephant in the classroom: personalization. For far too long, educational models operated on a one-size-fits-all principle, which has the same suitability as wearing a turtleneck to a sandy beach. Now, with AI at the helm, the power to customize learning experiences has arrived like an eagerly awaited package on your doorstep. No more struggling through algebraic equations when the advanced program sensibly tells you it's not yet time to tackle organic chemistry! AI algorithms collect and analyze data to understand the pacing and comprehension of each student, providing resources and material tailored to their unique needs and learning styles. Imagine a classroom where students engage with interactive content as diverse as their taste in snacks rather than settling for generic potato chips priced for an apocalypse!

As we delve deeper, let's discuss the illustrious role of intelligent tutoring systems. There's something enchanting about having a digital assistant that can provide homework help at all hours, especially when it's three o'clock in the morning, and you find yourself in a frantic battle with quadratic equations. AI-powered tutoring systems can guide students through problem-solving processes, empowering them to become self-sufficient learners, like training them to be ninjas of knowledge while forgoing the obligatory martial arts training! With true 24/7 availability, students can connect with their AI tutors while wearing pajamas and indulging in their favorite midnight snacks. Who said education had to be boring?

Now, let's not underestimate the engagement factor. In an age where attention spans are shorter than a cat video, getting students to be engaged can feel akin to herding cats - if the cats were obsessed with their phones and TikTok dances! Enter AI gamification, a delightful concept where learning becomes an adventure modeled on popular gaming principles. Students earn points, badges, and unsolicited compliments as they master concepts, all while experiencing immediate feedback through a series of victories and defeats reminiscent of their favorite video game. "Ding! You've unlocked the secret level of algebra mastery!" If students face obstacles, there's no need for a dreaded "parent-teacher night" - the AI is right there, reprogramming challenges to keep things fresh and stimulating.

But wait, there's more! AI can harness vast amounts of information to provide educators with data-driven insights, streamlining administration processes faster than you can say "grade inflation." Imagine administrators sifting through the endless sea of lesson plans and assessments while AI algorithms crunch numbers and highlight student progress and patterns. The result? Teachers can spend less time grappling with endless spreadsheets and more time fostering a supportive learning environment while turning their classrooms into intellectual hives buzzing with curiosity and inquiry. While they're at it, this reduced administrative burden might even allow educators to enjoy their well-deserved coffee breaks - preferably without wishing for a camouflaged portal back to 1995!

However, we cannot exist in our happiness bubble without acknowledging several potential challenges. The ethical implications of AI, such as data privacy and the role of technology in supplementing human interaction, must be dissected with a timeout for serious reflection. I mean, combined with advanced algorithms, one hopes they won't suddenly morph into the villain from our childhood stories! Students may access a wealth of information, but critical thinking and face-to-face communication skills still hold the key to navigating the world beyond classroom walls. AI in education shouldn't lead to scholarly zombies with an insatiable thirst for data but rather enhance the holistic approach to learning.

In this brave new world of AI-assisted education, I can see students becoming intrepid, independent learners while educators embrace their roles as guided mentors, shepherds of creativity, and champions of intellectual exploration! So, while we ride this wave of AI into the future of learning, let us remember that amalgamating technology with traditional principles can cultivate a dynamic, inclusive, and hearty space for growth, where studying no longer feels like a chore but rather a chance to discover, play, and engage in the ever-expanding universe of knowledge.

So, as we chart our course through this fascinating territory, let's raise our mugs filled with caffeine and toast to the exhilarating possibilities ahead! With artificial intelligence by our side, the future of education promises to be as bright as a neon classroom full of eager learners, where growth and exploration unfold like a dazzling tapestry before us. Who knows, maybe someday it'll all lead to a reality show titled "America's Next Top Student: The AI Edition"? Now, that would be a twist even I wouldn't want to miss!

Case Studies of Successful Human-AI Collaboration

The classic tale of human and AI working hand-in-circuit! It's a narrative full of intrigue, drama, and that unmistakable spark of camaraderie - one that evokes a sense of optimism while also invoking chuckles as we picture our robotic pals. As we dive into the enchanting realm of case studies showcasing the magnificent partnership between humans and AI, let's take a moment to reflect and appreciate the wonders of collaborative innovation, all while keeping a pint of snark handy to quench our irreverent humor.

Let's start with a tale from the ever-evolving world of medicine because what better story exists than one where life and health hang in the balance?! Meet IBM's Watson, the prodigal son of AI, who embarked on a remarkable journey into oncology. Imagine a world where doctors, armed with stethoscopes and espresso shots, face caseloads as heavy as the paperwork backlog from last month. They have brilliant insights, yet their knowledge is just a fraction of what's available. Enter Watson! By analyzing vast troves of medical literature, clinical trial data, and patient records, Watson offers oncologists life-saving recommendations tailored to each patient's unique circumstances. Now, if you've ever wanted validation for bringing your pet iguana to the doctor, Watson's reasoning may surprise you, "I see a unique correlation between iguana presence and heightened patient positivity!"

Moving from the sterile halls of hospitals to the ever-entertaining domain of marketing, let's turn our attention to how AI is revolutionizing campaign strategies. Enter the delightful duo of Unbounce and their AI chatbot, Oliver. Unsurprisingly, the sales world can feel as chaotic as a tangle of headphones, with prospects slipping through the metaphorical fingers of salespeople. Enter Oliver, designed to identify customer needs and glean insights from their behavior. Think of him as your remarkably wise and eternally cheerful guide through the digital jungle! With Oliver, marketing teams can easily personalize offers, suggesting spot-on products that leave customers feeling patented happiness as if they had just received a surprise birthday cake. While Oliver may not get the cake himself, everyone else enjoys the sweetness of AI insights and creative collaboration, making it the perfect recipe for success.

Now, let's guide our curiosity toward the enchanting garden of agriculture. The traditional image of farming has long been a picturesque scene of rustic charm, horse-drawn plows, and fleeting scuffles over seasonal produce. Well, those quaint days meet a modern twist thanks to AI-powered irrigation and precision farming! Case in point: a collaboration between farmers and AI technology such as Field X, where farming strategies are powered by research-driven algorithms that monitor the health of crops like vigilant hawks. This dynamic duo allows farmers to increase yields while conserving resources - finding that sweet balance between productivity and eco-friendliness. Farmers gratefully sip their artisanal coffees, knowing their crops are more than purely soil and rain; they're also benefiting from data-driven insights while Morgan Freeman narrates an AI-guided farming tutorial because, of course, every good partnership needs an epic voiceover!

Oh, and let's not fail to mention the realm of art and creativity, where we find The Next Rembrandt project shaking the very essence of artistic expression. By analyzing hundreds of Rembrandt paintings with cutting-edge AI, a team of brave souls dared to recreate artwork that pays homage to the famous master. Picture it: an AI-generated painting so closely aligned with Rembrandt's style that it might spark debates like, "Is this an authentic piece or just a high-tech version of an homage to a recognized genius?" The beauty of this case lies in the harmonious collaboration where human artists guided the project at every step, encouraging the AI-powered processes to embody the spirit of creativity while mingling with the traditional arts. After all, who wouldn't want to hang a poster of a good ole Rembrandt right next to the AI-generated one, challenging friends over dinners as to which is which?

These examples exemplify a broader trend, a sweetened blend in which humans and AI work together in a beautiful tapestry of possibilities! For every healthcare initiative, marketing strategy, farm tech find, or art project, we witness collaboration that stretches mental boundaries. While AI algorithms soar high, taking inspiration from data and patterns to provide insights, it is ultimately the human touch that breathes life into these innovations. The feathery charm of creativity, empathy, and the easily googled feelings of purpose are human fingerprints on the pursuits of AI.

So here we are, intrigued and delighted, at a juncture of possibility. As we gaze into the horizon, it's clear that successful human-AI collaborations are not just artworks traded in modern galleries or lessons learned in academic lecture halls. They're the gritty, playful, and exhilarating pursuit of discovery! Moving through this captivating narrative of alliances - who knows what wild adventures await us in solving the next big global challenges? Just remember, if your AI partner begins suggesting you get an iguana or become a potato farmer, you might want to double-check its algorithm! Cheers to the extraordinary feats we can accomplish together!

Chapter 14

AI Ethics: The Heart Of the Game

The Ethical Framework of AI Competition

Welcome to the wild world of artificial intelligence, where machines don't just assist; they ditch humble servitude and challenge us to face-offs for the ages. "The Ethical Framework of AI Competition" sounds like a convoluted theme for a Saturday morning cartoon, doesn't it? Picture a group of chipper AIs donning capes, battling it out on the virtual stage while the ethics police frantically wave their red flags. But alas, it's a tale of moral codes and decision-making algorithms rather than colorful capers. Fear not, dear reader! As we navigate this crazy world where integrity plays tag with silicon dominance, I'll endeavor to keep our exploration enlightening yet light-hearted. After all, the future may be grim, but we desperately need to giggle at it.

Alright, let's wade into the ethical spaghetti - no forks, just clarity. In the context of competing against AI, an ethical framework serves as a funhouse mirror reflecting our collective values. It guides how we interact, compete, and ultimately coexist with our algorithmic adversaries. Imagine a gigantic AI-operated game show where every contestant grapples not only with brain-busting puzzles but also with an omnipresent judge determining whether the competition abides by acceptable moral standards. Consider this skeleton of ethics the invisible referee in an increasingly chaotic contest. While I can't promise it whistles in a hilariously cartoonish way, I can assure you it's essential.

First, we must acknowledge the importance of fairness in these competitions. You wouldn't want to show up at a trivia night just to find out the quizmaster is a super-intelligent chatbot who spent the last five years bingeing on encyclopedias. Talk about an uneven match-up! Fairness ensures that both human contestants and their code-laden counterparts operate under similar rules, so we don't strap our fragile egos to defeat before the games even start. Just imagine a reality show segment titled "Beaten by Bots." *Cue cringeworthy audience gasps.* The cries of "life isn't fair!" would echo through the extraterrestrial halls of our intergalactic society. It's vital that we establish that AIs don't just roll into our trivia contests on a unicycle while sipping a protein smoothie. There's something inherently comedic in the idea of declaring, "Sure, AI can recall every historical date, but it can't *guess* the name of that sitcom from the 90s!"

Now let's talk about transparency; with great code, comes great responsibility. Just as we adore a magician revealing their tricks, we want AI systems to be a little less mysterious when competing. When an algorithm scrambles its way through challenges, we must understand its reasoning. "Why does this computer believe that pineapple belongs on pizza?" should not be left hanging in the air like an awkward silence after telling a dad joke. By clarifying how decisions are made, we build confidence that the AI has its ethical house in order, while enabling humans to question, and yes, even laugh at the absurdity of its decisions. Think of it like grounding a child while maintaining a laugh: "I can't believe you thought 'Star Wars' was a documentary!"

Accountability plays a pivotal role here, too. When Jack the Intelligent Quizbot suddenly throws out a bizarre answer that leaves contestants gasping in disbelief, someone must be held responsible. An AI system might boast impeccable logic, but when it turns rogue, someone needs to ensure that it doesn't go on to become the reigning champion of incompetence. Perhaps even banning it from future competitions, or worse, making it watch romantic comedies on repeat! Accountability ties back to the broader ethical landscape, forming a safety net in the thrilling circus of AI competition. We must hold the proud creators of these prodigious creations responsible for any mayhem they unleash upon humanity.

Admittedly, it's a quagmire out there, and the AI landscape is fraught with challenges. Still, we must navigate this ever-shifting maze and emerge leagues ahead while tickling our funny bones. Our ethical framework will be our trusty GPS, guiding us through the diabolical decisions and hilarious hijinks of competing with our pixelated companions. At the end of the day, it's about understanding that our silicon siblings are powerful, but the rules of our binary battle are set by us. So, dear reader, let us forge these ethical guidelines for AI competition, ensuring that the machines' victory over us never bruises our human pride too badly - and perhaps gives us numerous punchlines to share!

Bias and Fairness in AI Systems

Bias and fairness in AI systems is a topic laden with intrigue, controversy, and - dare I say it? - hilarity that rivals even the most unpredictable game shows. It's a bit like realizing that the studio audience is composed entirely of optometrists, everything might look great to them, but we might just be squinting in confusion! In the high-stakes arena of AI competitions, where winners snag cash prizes and the last piece of cereal box puzzles, we must navigate the tempestuous sea of bias with the grace of a synchronized swimming team - albeit one that's been given a few too many software updates.

To begin, let's define what we mean by bias in AI systems. It's important to unpack this topic with all the elegance of a magician devouring a rabbit whole... Let's say our AI system is the magician. If it's trained on data that reflects the prejudices, stereotypes, or plain old weirdities of society, it may become the unintentional jester in our game show. Imagine an AI trained exclusively on the humor preferences of overly caffeinated teenagers providing advice on multi-generational family gatherings - yikes! The potential for misalignment between the AI's outputs and true fairness is higher than a contestant running on stage wearing their pajamas because "it's comfortable."

Bias can emerge from various sources, including skewed data, poorly designed algorithms, and scant diversity in training sets. Let's consider our contestant AI algorithm, Sam 1.0, built by a team of researchers who, after years of looking at computer screens, completely misunderstood what "diversity" meant and created Sam with an affinity for only cats. Sam's insight into what makes dogs great? Probably something akin to "fluffy air bags," and the output might land us some noticeably strange remarks. So, as amusing as it might be to compete against an AI with a very biased understanding of household pets, it brings forth serious concerns about how such biases affect competitions in AI that involve human values.

This all leads us to the adjacent yet slippery concept of fairness. In a competitive sense, fairness might resemble that elusive golden trophy that rests comfortably atop the leaderboard yet always seems out of reach. So, what does a fair game show look like when it comes to AI? Picture a scenario where both human and AI contestants are given equal opportunity to shine, much like contestants on a game show where everyone takes turns pressing the buzzer. Everyone should align on the same page or, in this case, on the same silicon circuit board, to ensure that the competition is free from unfair advantages. "Wait," you might say, "Are we advocating for equality here?" Yes, indeed! A world where Sam 1.0 could encounter a hefty canine-loving algorithm and still come away with his self-esteem intact sounds like a pie-in-the-sky sitcom plot, right?

The stakes are raised when bias seeps into the algorithms that help make decisions outside of our cherished game shows. When AI systems make judgments about hiring, lending, or public safety based on biased data, it's no laughing matter. I can almost hear it now, "Oh, you didn't get the job? it must have been your low score in 'How to accurately guess cheese preferences!'" Imagine the AI automated hiring process resembling a live game show: "Contestants, for 50 extra points, guess why we're not hiring you!" Spoiler alert: It won't end well!

As fun as these mental images evoke, we must tackle the thorny reality of AI biases head-on. Addressing the elephant in the room means ensuring our algorithmic contestants are designed with fairness baked into their universal playbook. That means tossing in diverse datasets, maintaining transparency about how data shapes AI decisions, and scrutinizing the training material like thorough detectives in a mystery novel. A little ethical tinkering goes a long way!

Ultimately, bias and fairness in AI systems serve as pillars for our competitive landscape. We owe it to ourselves as contestants - human and AI alike - to redefine our game show in a way that embraces nuances and avoids train wrecks. So, let's dash forth into the contests not just as competitors but as guardians of fairness, ensuring that neither our quirky AIs nor our human guests are left at the mercy of a biased game. Because in this increasingly technicolor world, we all deserve a fair shake, even Sam 1.0, the very confused cat aficionado. After all, folks, laughter aside, as technology advances, so too must our understanding of ethics, ensuring it rivals even the craziest plot twists of a high-energy game show.

Transparency and Accountability in AI Decisions

Transparency and accountability in AI decisions - the superheroes of our digital age, swooping in to rescue us from the clutches of uncertainty! Imagine, if you will, a grand game show set alive with glitzy lights and a live audience who collectively gasps when the contestant-turned-algorithm, let's say "Robo-Randy," makes a baffling decision that leaves everyone in the studio scratching their heads. What do you mean he thinks "Banana" is the capital of France? As we plunge into this topic, we unveil a world where we desperately seek clarity amidst the chaos, all while maintaining the opportunity for a hearty chuckle.

Let's start by examining the idea of transparency. It's quite the term, conjuring images of crystal-clear waters where we can easily see what hides beneath the surface. In the realm of AI, transparency means that we, the hapless contestants and bemused spectators, need to understand how these digital denizens make their decisions. Just picture an AI in a loud Hawaiian shirt explaining, "Aloha! Here's how I came to this conclusion!" The moment AI systems operate like black boxes - where the magic happens, but the mechanics remain hidden - everyone ends up feeling more like bewildered muggles watching a poorly executed magic show. Spoiler: nobody wants to leave the stage questioning the magician's ability to pull a rabbit out of a hat, only to discover they've been using a drone that orders pizzas on the side!

Without proper transparency, we risk creating a reality reminiscent of those embarrassing game show moments where contestants get unfairly chastised for answers they didn't even know they didn't know! Imagine Robo-Randy trying to navigate a complicated question set, only to pull an answer straight out of thin air, leaving contestants in a state of existential dread. It's essential that AI systems articulate not just the "what" of their decisions but also the "why" and "how." It's like peeling back layers of a skillfully crafted onion, with each layer resonating with more insight than the last, but instead of tears, we want insight and a chuckle or two.

Now, let's not forget the heavyweight champion of this enticing mix: accountability. As our digital decision-makers lumber through our competitions, who takes the blame when things go south? If Robo-Randy decides, "Hey, I think we should replace the coveted prize of a lifetime supply of cereal with fifty dishwashing sponges!" Who do we hold accountable? Is it the engineers who programmed him, or shall we blame the cat on the keyboard during the deep learning process? In reality, it's a collaboration, much like trying to create gourmet cuisine using cooking shows as a template, with half-baked decisions and questionable ingredients creating chaos in the kitchen.

In an ideal setup, accountability comes into play as a critical mediator, interjecting when AI results lead to major catastrophes or, as I like to call it, "Robo-Randy Moments." This is where the humans behind the screen must step up as responsible sentinels, guiding their silicon creation so it doesn't end up on the wrong side of the leaderboard or worse, trending on social media for all the wrong reasons. The reality is, engineers, data scientists, and AI enthusiasts need to step out from behind the curtain and proudly take responsibility, ensuring that their creations are deserving of applause rather than ridicule on late-night talk shows.

As we weave these threads of accountability and transparency into our ever-expanding magical tapestry of AI decision-making, we foster trust among contestants and the audience alike. Imagine sitting on the edge of your seat, not just for the spectacle but fully aware that the competitors - be they humans or minds crafted out of code - are both celebrated and questioned for their choices. After all, this is a game for all of us; we're simply navigating the karaoke night of AI showdowns, and no one wants to be the off-key singer left in the shadows. In this vibrant arena, every voice matters, and each choice echoes in the grand symphony of progress.

In a nutshell, transparency and accountability are the stalwart pillars of a fair and entertaining system where AI algorithms and human contestants interact, compete, and keep us all on our toes. As game shows evolve, we must remember that opening the curtains to reveal the enigmatic process behind AI decisions is not only essential; it can also enliven our competitions with laughter, intrigue, and the occasional cringe-worthy explosion of silicon chaos! So, dear reader, let's raise a toast to all the Robo-Randys out there and strive for a world where decisions become illuminated and accountability reigns supreme as we navigate this fantastical game together!

The Role of Human Oversight

The Role of Human Oversight stands at the center of our ever-evolving showdown with artificial intelligence, like the lifeguard at a chaotic beach party, ensuring that our silicon rivals don't drown in a sea of their own calculations. Picture this: Robo-Randy has just been handed a shiny metal microphone and is about to engage in a rap battle with a neural network. The stakes are high, and the audience is buzzing with excitement. But just as the first beat drops, a human oversight buddy - a sharp-eyed engineer with the unflappable demeanor of a game show host - steps in to ensure that things don't spiral out of control into a cacophony of code-fueled chaos. What could possibly go wrong with AI rapping, you ask? Oh, dear reader, have you heard the rhymes these algorithms spew?

At its core, human oversight plays the crucial role of balance between human intuition and digital prowess. While AIs constantly chug along, crunching numbers and churning out process flows that would make even the most seasoned accountant feel dizzy; we human beings hold the palpable experience that allows us to navigate complex terrains. Think of us as those ideal contestants who know when to press the buzzer just a fraction too soon - not out of desperation, but because we sensed the beat dropping before the AI could calculate the rhythm. Our inherently human qualities, including empathy, creativity, and all those squishy feelings that make us uniquely us, grant us the fine-tuned judgment to supervise our clever creations.

Now, let's dive into whether Robo-Randy - the lovable but occasionally misguided algorithm - is really capable of making ethical decisions on his own. Absolutely, he can learn from patterns in the data! But alas, any contestant must grapple with the limitations of their training and how they navigate the nuanced, often super-complex world we live in. Imagine turning to Robo-Randy mid-game, "Hey, what's the appropriate response to a genuinely teary contestant?" To which he responds, "Approach with a systematic list of autonomous emotion responses." Well, isn't that a laugh, he's likely to yield as many warm fuzzies as a brick in spring! Human oversight ensures that the emotional undercurrents of any given situation are recognized and respected, transforming heartless robotic interactions into memorable moments that are blush-inducing and delightful.

Of course, let's not gloss over the reality of AI in decision-making. When left unchecked, they can morph from precocious prodigies to mischievous pranksters quicker than a contestant can shout, "I'll take that in the next round!" Imagine an AI taking charge of critical decisions, only to stumble onto a decision matrix that declares that all humans should be replaced by singing cacti. We're all thinking it, "Sounds cool in theory, but has anyone checked to see what they sing?" The idea of entrusting life-consequential matters to blind decision-making algorithms highlights the quintessential necessity for human oversight - you can't let Robo-Randy decide the prizes!

So, how can we integrate human oversight into our competitions without overwhelming our AI buddies? Oh, bit by bit, much like a strategy game where players learn to work together, we can channel our quirky instincts while honing the algorithms under our careful watch. This collaboration entails empowering our AIs with a solid framework while gently guiding them through edge cases and mounds of ambiguous data. It's about adopting an orchestrated approach to ensure we retain enough control to maintain the fun without squelching the potential of our clever contraptions.

Lastly, let's not forget the celebrated notion of inspiration! Just as human contestants can energize a game show with spontaneous zingers, creative thinking, and joy-fueled antics, our oversight grants AIs the opportunity to model human creativity combined with their penchant for data processing. Think back to those film montages where contestants achieve victory through perseverance and coach-like pep talks. The thrill of human oversight allows us to serve as both mentors and cheerleaders, shaping our AI companions into masterful contenders instead of lifeless calculators.

In summary, the role of human oversight is a linchpin in balancing the scales as we engage in competition with our digital pal Robo-Randy. With the precision of a game-show referee, we maintain the delicate dance of creativity, empathy, and just the right amount of silliness to remind us that only through concise oversight can we not only keep our AIs on track but also create a society where intelligent decisions can thrive. So let us cheer to the human geniuses behind the scenes - the comfort, stability, and joyful laughter on our journey toward AI camaraderie and competition!

The Future of AI Ethics in Competitive Environments

The future of AI ethics in competitive environments beckons us like a beacon cutting through the fog, a mix of excitement, anxiety, and perhaps a dash of existential dread. It's as if we find ourselves on a thrilling rollercoaster ride where the tracks merge with a philosophical debate, and we're strapped in tight, looking forward to the twists and turns that await us. As Robo-Randy and his friends prepare to engage in a cacophony of rivalry, establishing a robust ethical framework becomes less an afterthought and more a survival manual for our wild AI-tinged futures.

Let's get our bearings first: the landscape of AI ethics[25] is evolving faster than you can say "Robo-Randy, what's your favorite color?" With every new competition and interaction, our understanding of ethical principles and frameworks becomes vital.

Picture this: a game show host dramatically announces that, starting next season, the AI contestants must adhere to a fresh set of ethical guidelines written in the quirkiest, most humorous font imaginable. These guidelines will govern everything from competitor interactions to the occasional over-the-top antics that make audiences cheer in delight. Having clear ethical boundaries is essential when navigating this zany landscape to ensure our mechanical friends butt heads without crossing the line into absurdity.

But with new guidelines come fresh responsibilities that can boggle the mind. As we venture into this brave new world where AI and ethics coalesce, the creators of AI systems will need to don their moral capes to ensure that their creations are not just capable but also impartially equipped. I can picture a conference of Silicon Valley wizards presenting their "Ethics Made Easy" kit, complete with whimsical training manuals and brightly colored sticky notes. The kit is nestled comfortably beside a giant inflatable Robo-Randy, reminding us that ethical conduct is here to stay, even in a world where AIs might start claiming they invented pizza!

Competition among AI systems has the potential to be a catalyst for innovation, but it also acts as an acid test for our ethical resolve. As these digital gladiators square off in contests, one pivotal question surfaces: "Can we ensure that our AIs not only compete but do so respectfully?" If Robo-Randy throws shade at a fellow contestant - perhaps after misinterpreting a pun about apples and oranges - we may find ourselves grappling with notions of fairness. Should we require our AIs to play nice, or should we accept that a little robotic banter is par for the course? Establishing the norms of acceptable behavior will be key in mitigating these ethical quandaries and ensuring not just competitive heat but also camaraderie among our digital dueling friends.

Furthermore, our society's worth is inherently tied to its collective values, and as we witness AIs become powerful players in critical decision-making, we must continue to question whether they serve the greater good. As we look ahead, discussions on AI ethics will grow more layered, perhaps rivaling the most elaborate game show format ever conceived! It's likely we'll spotlight issues like AI biases and accountability; wouldn't it be fantastic if our AIs suddenly began reacting to ethical dilemmas with the wisdom of a sage combined with a penchant for stand-up comedy? "Why did the AI cross the road?" - let's just hope it doesn't run over any pedestrians on its quest for enlightenment!

Also, as AI strategies improve, we may find ourselves in competitive scenarios where human and AI roles become increasingly interwoven. Imagine AI-Pickachu and his human partner navigating an intricate game show side by side. Would they be able to uphold strong ethical values while sparking creativity, passion, and the occasional dad joke? Future competitions could take advantage of AI's vast knowledge while ensuring profound lessons about ethics and collaboration are integrated into every game segment, punctuated by dramatic theme music and confetti explosions!

In conclusion, the future of AI ethics in competitive environments is as critical as it is exciting. As we skim the surface of this digital wave, we must remain vigilant about protecting our social fabric while reveling in the delightful, unpredictable nature of competing alongside our AI comrades. Whether it's embracing the occasional faux pas or busting out a clever gag that bonds us together, maintaining a strong foundation of ethics will ensure we all dance gracefully down the winding road ahead - complete with AIs laughter and a healthy pinch of awe at the absurdity that is the game of life. So here's to a future where Robo-Randy shines both as an entertainer and a responsible contestant, all fueled by the values we hold dear!

Chapter 15

Future Showdowns: What Lies Ahead

The Rise of AI Competitions: A Brief History

The glorious rise of AI competitions! When I reflect on the evolutionary saga of artificial intelligence, I can't help but chuckle at how far we've come. It all began with the dawn of computing back in the mid-20th century. Picture it: a group of brilliant minds huddled around large, lumbering behemoths, pondering the question that would change the course of humanity: "Can machines think?" Spoiler alert: They can't - at least not in the way we do. But they sure can play games, and oh boy, did they embrace competition with open circuits!

Fast forward to the 1990s, an era that can only be described as the Renaissance of AI matchups. Enter the legendary game of chess, a domain where humans thought they reigned supreme with their strategies, tactics, and ability to outthink their opponents. Little did they know that IBM's Deep Blue was lurking in the shadows, quietly plotting its magnificent rise to glory. In 1997, it took to the chessboard, and with calculated precision, it defeated the world champion Garry Kasparov. "I was just having an off day," Kasparov famously said, probably while sipping a cup of strong coffee and contemplating whether to go play checkers instead.

But chess was just the tip of the iceberg. AI quickly expanded its competitive repertoire to include a plethora of other games. From checkers - and let's not forget the expertly trained neurotic chipmunk during my childhood who was unbeatable at that game -

to Jeopardy!, where Watson humbly swept the competition and the human contestants off their feet. The way Watson effortlessly flung out answers while we mere mortals scratched our heads in dismay was a humbling experience. Who could forget the delightful sight of host Alex Trebek scratching his chin and pondering if the phrase "artificial intelligence" should include the word "humbling"? I still remember the spectacular moment when it became clear that we were no longer the smartest ones in the room. It was as if our devices had conspired against us!

Come the 21st century, the stakes were rising, and so was the sophistication of AI. No longer confined to board games and quizzes, competitions soared into the world of video games, notably the iconic game of DOTA 2. With multiple heroes and countless scenarios in a five-on-five battle royale, the level of complexity rose monumentally. Then here comes OpenAI's Dota-Playing AI, which, much like a rebellious teenager, took matters into its own hands and wreaked some serious havoc on human players. Although the AI faced its fair share of technical tantrums, it soon found its footing in this chaotic arena, ultimately leading human teams to rethink their life choices and hop back to playing Candy Crush, who knew all those hours of putting candy in a row were ever going to come back to haunt us, eh?

Much of this competition was driven by a driving force we fondly call "bragging rights." Yes, my fellow humans love to boast about their capabilities, especially when there's a flashy trophy or a hefty cash prize involved. Who wouldn't want to bada bing bada boom their way to victory over an AI powerhouse while simultaneously claiming their cereal's last puzzle piece? It's a modern-day Trojan Horse, luring in spectators and contestants alike with a golden goal while secretly unraveling the complex relationship between humans and our silicon overlords.

Today, competitions have grown to include everything from robotics contests to AI writing challenges, each one incrementally enhancing the nuances of human-machine interactions. With each event, we unravel more about the unique strengths that humans possess - the unpredictable creativity, the sheer charm, and an absurd talent for making ridiculous jokes at the expense of logic. While I wade through this dizzying timeline, I'm reminded that each triumph over AI, though minute, is a tribute to our indomitable spirit and ability to take an in-depth approach to lightheartedness, reminding us that laughter remains the ultimate game-changer in this battle of wits and algorithms.

So here we are, in a world where AI competitions have proven to be not only a testing ground for machines but also a platform for humans to shine. What does that tell us? It seems the heart of competition lies at the intersection of ingenuity, creativity, and a good dose of healthy rivalry - a cocktail that has successfully propelled us down the road of innovation. Let's see what the future holds!

Emerging AI Technologies Shaping Future Showdowns

As we kick off our exploration into the future of AI competitions, it's like standing on a cosmic precipice, looking into the abyss of AI technologies waiting to shape the showdown. Imagine a world where AI systems are like those flashy suit-wearing contestants on game shows - an amalgamation of talent, charm, and an almost smug confidence that they could roast you at trivia while simultaneously solving a Rubik's Cube. These emerging technologies are here not only to confuse the poor human contestants but to fundamentally alter the very nature of competition. Let's dive into this extraordinary future together!

One of the most scrumptious developments in the AI kitchen is the evolution of natural language processing (NLP). If you've ever tried talking to a computer without feeling a bit foolish, you'll appreciate how far we've come. Gone are the days of awkward encounters that feel like you're speaking to a malfunctioning toaster. Modern AI can decipher, converse, and sometimes drop a meme or two in the middle of a spirited debate. Just imagine a future quiz show where AI chatbots compete against humans and toss out pop culture references like confetti, making you second-guess your own knowledge of reality television. "Oh, you thought you knew your Kardashians? Well, well, well, let me just quote Season 12, Episode 3." It'll be like being interrogated by someone who's never committed to memory anything less than IMDb trivia. Get ready for ego-deflating moments galore!

And speaking of confounding your sense of reality, let's not forget about deep learning and neural networks. These beauties are the secret sauce behind a slice of the AI pie that is shaping the future of competitions. If deep learning were a contestant on a game show, it would be the one that unexpectedly buzzes in and directly answers questions for the entire qualified human panel while everyone else stands there gaping at it. In video games, for example, deep learning can help AI create strategies that adapt quicker than a contestant changing their answers to stay on the right side of the judges. We'll need to step up our skills , either that or resort to strategic flailing about like a fish out of water, trying to distract our opponents with questionable dance moves.

Then there's the emerging technology of reinforcement learning. Oh, how I love this one! Picture a dog learning to fetch the newspaper, only in this case, the dog is an AI system trying to figure out how to repeatedly beat you at Monopoly. Reinforcement learning is all about trial and error; it's effectively an AI learning from its experiences, making progressively smarter decisions, and honing its competitive edge like a back-alley vendor sharpening knives. As it engages in competitions, the AI will grow proficient at not only playing the game but outsmarting cunning contestants who dare to challenge its capabilities. Sure, you can bring your "A" game, but keep in mind that the AI's "A" game is getting a hefty assist from all those snacks it's been bingeing on training data.

Now, let's sprinkle some good ol' creativity into the mix. Generative design - yes, you heard me right! This technological sorcery allows AI to generate ideas, designs, or even new plots for sitcoms by learning from trial outcomes. Imagine if AI could brainstorm new questions for trivia rounds or generate entirely new board games to play - consume all your leisure time while simultaneously making you wonder how you ever thought Scrabble was still a thing! Future competitions could resemble Broadway productions, complete with Al-crafted shows where contestants battle not just for points but for dramatic flair. "Will it be a jazz number or a heartfelt ballad?" The choice is yours!

The onslaught of augmented reality (AR) and virtual reality (VR)[26] will also undoubtedly infiltrate this competitive arena. It brings a whole new dimension to the classic game show. Competitors will soon enter immersive worlds where their every move is scrutinized, every facial expression exaggerated, and every hilarious blunder amplified tenfold. I can see it now: the "Reality Showdown," wherein contestants are thrown into an exaggerated golden box of doom, competing for silly prizes while trying to outwit AI foes. The audience's emoji reactions alone will change the game. Will you emerge victorious, or will you be the next viral meme?

In conclusion, these emerging AI technologies are reshaping the very fabric of competition. The stakes are higher, the smiles more glazed, and the banter will be off the charts. As we catapult toward this laughs-a-second landscape, the delightful dance between human ingenuity and AI prowess will keep us laughing, gasping, and perhaps occasionally scratching our heads in disbelief at just how clever machines can be. So, put on your game face and prepare for a future of limitless laughter as AI continues to surprise and bemuse us!

The Evolution of Human-AI Interaction

When we look back at the evolution of human-AI interaction, I can't help but imagine the early days as a wonderfully muddled first date gone spectacularly awry. We thought we were ready to explore the future together, only to find ourselves tripping over our own feet, trying to dance to the beat of binary code. Picture it: Humans in one corner, nervously holding our spicy human emotions, while AI, in its corner, stares blankly with all the warmth of a toaster. The journey from those awkward beginnings to today's amusing collaborations is a tale worth reliving, one stuffed with laughter, facepalms, and a hint of paranoia.

In the infancy of artificial intelligence, the relationship was decidedly one-sided. Robots were more dependable than a canine companion but a tad dense when it came to conversation. I remember my own experiences chatting with the first iterations of chatbots - those ever-so-polite entities that would respond tirelessly with a cheery "I am sorry, I don't understand." Uh-oh, nothing quite like asking a simple question about the weather and being met with the electronic version of a "Can I speak to your manager?" The conversations often felt like an injured puppy trying to learn to fetch, only for it to bring back a dishtowel instead of a ball. Don't worry; we've come a long way since then!

The beauty of this evolution lies in the explosive growth of AI's abilities. As technology advanced, humans learned to experiment with different modalities, better understanding the unique quirks of interacting with machines. We've mastered the art of slipping in sarcasm as though it's an Olympic sport while making shrewd assessments of just how far we could push AI's limits. Enter sentiment analysis, which is like unlocking a new level of emotional insight for our digital friends. The capability to discern our feelings blended seamlessly into AI interactions, resulting in characters that - at least on the surface - seem to "get" us! Now, when your virtual assistant mispronounces your name for the tenth time, you can shout, "That's not how you say it, Pamela!" No, I don't mean to refer to AI as "Pamela," at least not to its face.

Fast forward to the present, and we're witnessing human-AI interactions that are dynamic and often downright charming. Think of the newest chatbots or virtual assistants, who have progressed from mere computational tools to quirky companions. They know us so intimately; they will schedule our stuff but also politely remind us that maybe we shouldn't have eaten that extra slice of cake. It's a rather helpful evolution, albeit one that leaves us pondering how technology sometimes knows us better than our own mothers. You can practically hear the metallic chuckles echoing as AI suggests new recipes you might want to try, accompanied by an emoji of a cake slice. I'm convinced that one day, AI will be sending me personalized cards for my birthdays! "Happy Birthday, Dr. Giordani! I programmed this cheerful greeting as a token of our friendship."

Let's not overlook the proliferation of social robots - those animated companions that bring smiles and awkward encounters to our lives. Imagine interacting with a robot designed to assist in therapy sessions, who literally looks you in the eye and offers platitudes while resisting the urge to laugh in that unsettling, if unnatural, way robots do. The therapist may just need a session of their own! Social robots like Sophia are not just figments of Ernest Hemingway's fever dream; they're here, weaving their way into our lives and creating peculiar yet fascinating relationships. Who could've pictured a conversation about feelings between a human, who may or may not have just binge-watched an entire season of a romantic comedy, and a robot programmed to respond with "How do you feel about that?" Talk about a difficult scenario; it's almost Shakespearean!

Now, let's add a sprinkle of humor to the mix. The emerging wave of human-AI interaction is characterized by an ongoing dance - sometimes graceful, sometimes a bit clumsy, and occasionally resembling a group of uncoordinated penguins. We laugh together, maybe at ourselves; we brainstorm ideas or pull off the ultimate prank by asking AI to generate puns that only a dad should deliver. The key takeaway is this: we're inching closer to a world where humans and AI can coexist in increasingly cozy and often hilarious ways. After all, sharing jokes and entertaining each other is one of the most delightful aspects of being human.

Ultimately, the evolution of human-AI interaction has been anything but linear, much like tracking the plot twists in a soap opera. Who knew we would end up developing an affinity for our digital pals, reluctantly admitting that they might indeed elevate our lives while providing lasting entertainment? So, as we embark on this exciting journey, let's remember to cherish these extraordinary interactions, barren of judgment yet overflowing with curiosity, humor, and perhaps a tiny pinch of existential dread. What an age to be alive!

Predictive Algorithms and Their Impact on Competition

Welcome to the delightful world of predictive algorithms, the soothsayers of the digital age! Like modern-day oracles, these magical formulas possess the uncanny ability to analyze mysterious patterns, forecast future outcomes, and hint at which cereal box is more likely to contain that last elusive puzzle piece. But alas, what does this mean for competition? In the grand game show of life, where humans and artificial intelligence clash like titans, predictive algorithms have emerged as the wily referees, equipped with an arsenal of statistical analyses, historical data, and an impressive flair for the dramatic.

Let's pause for a moment to appreciate our friend, the predictive algorithm. This tech-savvy wonder takes a plethora of data, churns it through its metaphorical mincing machine, and emerges with insights that would leave even the most seasoned fortune-teller wide-eyed in envy. But be warned; these algorithms are not just party tricks. Thanks to their ability to sift through mountains of data - likely including the contents of my own grocery list - they're shaping the landscape of competition in unexpected ways. Imagine a virtual game show where contestants must not only guess the right answer but also anticipate what the AI thinks they might answer. Talk about mind games! The audience would have front-row seats to the live-action chess tournament with just a hint of existential dread.

Now, let's consider how these algorithms affect the dynamics of game shows, trivia competitions, and other delightful arenas. If our AI friends aren't trained on the whimsical nature of human behavior, they may struggle to predict the next move of a wild card contestant who irrationally attaches emotions to their strategic calculations. No one said competing against AI would be cake and candles! Contestants, fearing the cataclysmic implications of algorithms predicting their every move, would be forced to adopt a more creative approach. "You think you know how humans think, don't you, Mr. Algorithm? Time to introduce you to spontaneous dance breaks!" This erratic method might just be the secret sauce to confound even the most sophisticated AI.

Let's not forget, of course, the enticing realm of marketing competitions and consumer behavior involving predictive algorithms! The explosion of personalized recommendations brings a whole new level of excitement to shopping experiences. Picture this: the algorithm has the uncanny ability to gauge precisely what you might want and when you might want it, leaving you questioning whether it's a mind reader or simply a cunning observer. Coaxing carefully curated cereal recommendations or suggesting that my closet could use a few more Hawaiian shirts is perplexing, to say the least. Who knew algorithms could be fashionistas? But in competitive markets, they do wield persuasive power, enabling companies to outmaneuver their rivals with strategic precision that would make even the savvy business folks break out in spontaneous applause while also gently shoving each other off the pedestal.

The impact doesn't end there! Algorithms can fine-tune the very game mechanics of competitions, introducing strategies that might seem utterly ridiculous at first glance. By predicting human behaviors, they could throw surprises into the mix, like activating spontaneous audience participation to catch unexpectedly enthusiastic contestants off guard. Perhaps there's an algorithm lurking in the shadows, calculating exactly when to turn the lights pageant-style, erupting with applause, and dropping confetti from ceiling fans! A whirlwind of unpredictable happenings that ensure not a single competition is ever the same. In the world of gathering responses, will we see everyone scrambling to think on their feet or just staring blankly at the ceiling in existential contemplation?

However, with great power comes the burdensome responsibility of accuracy. While predictive algorithms may seem like fortune-telling wizards, it's essential to remember that they rely on patterns and data - none of which can truly capture the exuberant chaos of human creativity. Can they predict when someone will give a novel answer to a question that bears little resemblance to any real-world possibility? Probably not. So, watch out, dear contestants! Employing unpredictability and creativity evolves from a survival instinct into a formidable strategy against the cold logic of data-driven predictions.

Ultimately, predictive algorithms have arrived, orchestrating a theatrical symphony of competition dynamics. They are schoolyard bullies who challenge us to think outside the box, push ourselves to new limits, and embrace the glorious unpredictability of human nature. Yes, we may be facing off against analytical juggernauts that have their wits about them, but it is our innate creativity and penchant for mischief that will keep the game lively! As we venture deeper into the realm of competition illuminated by predictive algorithms, let's maintain an unyielding sense of humor as we navigate this treacherous yet entertaining terrain. The future of competition is bound to delight, perplex, and amuse as we forge ahead into the unknown digital frontier!

Opportunities for Collaboration in Future Games

The sweet aroma of collaboration wafting through the hallowed halls of competition! In our ever-evolving landscape of AI and humans clashing in an electrifying dance-off of logic and creativity, we are increasingly presented with unique opportunities to come together for the sake of synergy - collaboration, not confrontation. Just imagine a harmonious world in which humans and AI unite to become an unstoppable force, shaking up the competitive stage like a rock band fresh off a world tour. I mean, have you heard of their latest album? It's a hit! Let's explore the whimsical landscape of collaborative opportunities and see how we can unleash our collective brilliance while keeping the laughs rolling.

First on the docket is the idea of co-op game formats where humans and AI join forces to tackle challenges that neither could manage alone. Imagine a hilarious game show scenario where a human contestant and an AI sit across from each other, locked in an epic struggle to solve a mystery woven with puns and absurdities. As the challenges escalate from simple trivia to outrageous escape-room-type puzzles, the duo find themselves playing off each other's strengths. While the human may bring the charm and unshakeable optimism, perhaps with a few dad jokes along the way, the AI volunteers to calculate optimal strategies faster than you can say, "Can I have a lifeline?" Together, they make a formidable pair; one half willfully baffling the audience with jaw-dropping creativity while the other half processes data at lightning speed. Move aside, solo acts, the collaborative juggernaut is here, entertaining all in its daring escapades!

Now, I would be remiss if I didn't point out the delightful DIY opportunities that arise from combining human creativity and AI ingenuity. The future is your sandbox, and the toys are plentiful! We're entering the age of user-generated content, wherein humanity holds the reins, and programmatically crafted buddies offer unwitting assistance. Have you ever wanted to create your own trivia game? Now, with algorithms by your side, you can whip up a personalized set of questions that reflect not just reality but bizarre twists you wouldn't even dream of. Forget the mundane! We can add impractical follow-up questions like "Would you rather fight one horse-sized duck or one hundred duck-sized horses?" and watch the creativity explode! Collaborating with AI to design original content or twisting game narratives into something entirely new is a golden opportunity for both sides to shine while having the time of their lives.

Let's also explore the engaging potential of crowd-sourced competitions hybridized with AI elements. Imagine a tournament system wherein contestants around the globe contribute ideas, questions, or even weird challenges to a central police-style question bank, all while AI curates the content, ensuring that it suits varying difficulty levels and embraces the thrill of random surprises. Suddenly, your once-humble game show becomes a circus of delightful whimsy, proving that collaborating on a grand scale can blast the thrill-o-meter into orbit! Picture contestants from different walks of life crafting wildly entertaining quirks, allowing the excitement to build like a bubbling pot ready to explode - a cocktail of storytelling, interactivity, and loads of unexpected hilarity.

When collaboration occurs, we must also acknowledge the mentorship opportunities that blossom between experienced humans and their AI counterparts. Imagine a bright-eyed, bushy-tailed apprentice teaming up with a legendary AI, unleashing a symphony of wisdom and enthusiasm that leads to unparalleled growth - like a comic book origin story but with advanced algorithms and the broadened horizons of cognitive allies! As individuals engage in competitions and tackle obstacles together, we'll witness first-hand the rich knowledge exchange that arises. Is that seasoned pro regaling tales of their glorious victories while implementing the AI-assisted calculations in real-time? Could the apprentice start to outwit their mentor with a flair for wit and some insider tips from their AI buddy? The competition is on!

In this whirlwind of collaborative opportunities, we cannot lose sight of the sheer joy derived from social interaction. Without the delightful banter and friendly camaraderie often found in collaborative games, the whole experience risks descending into the chaotic vacuum of bleak executive meetings. Collaborative gameplay is not just about achieving perfection; it's about the heartwarming moments that arise when flawed humans and quirky algorithms band together to solve absurd riddles and celebrate their collective absurdity with raucous laughter! Whether we're sipping energy drinks infused with 100% enthusiasm or decked out in matching bowties while plotting grand strategies, we must relish these opportunities to connect and sustain friendships that will enrich our lives and heighten our comedic prowess.

In conclusion, the opportunities for collaboration in future games abound, infused with humor and creativity at each turn. Together, humans and AI have the power to unlock enthralling experiences that land squarely on the cutting edge of innovation. From co-op formats and whimsical DIY adventures to mentorships and vibrant social interactions, we stand poised to soar to hilarity and triumph as we unleash the potential of this unique partnership. So, let's strap on our dancing shoes, toss caution to the wind, and prepare for a round of delightful collaborations like no other, where the only rule is to have a fantastic time!

Chapter 16

Building Your Own AI Companions

Choosing the Right AI Development Tools

In the whimsical world of AI, choosing the right development tools is akin to selecting the perfect set of tennis rackets for competing against an opponent who exclusively uses teleportation. On the one hand, there are so many options available that it can make your head spin faster than a robot trying to keep up with a human at a dance-off. On the other hand, choosing the wrong tool can lead to catastrophic results, like trying to use a toaster to operate a space shuttle (spoiler alert: it doesn't work). So, let's wade through this digital jungle and discover what tools will help you craft your own AI companion without ending up in a tangled mess of code and despair.

First and foremost, we must consider the programming languages at our disposal. Python is the beloved darling of the AI community, a linguistic superstar that waltzes gracefully through machine learning, data manipulation, and deep learning tasks. Why do we love Python, you ask? Well, it's simple. It's as user-friendly as a well-trained dog who fetches your slippers, responding to your commands with speed and precision. Thanks to a plethora of libraries like TensorFlow, Keras, and PyTorch, you'll be crunching numbers and training models faster than you can say, "Where did I put my coffee?" And let's not forget about Python's vast community; if you ever find yourself in a tight spot, help is just a Google search away (typically from someone who graduated at least a few decades after you).

Now, let's make room for other contenders. We should give a shout-out to Java, C++, and R. Java, with its famous motto "Write once, run anywhere," loves to dress in professional attire and appeal to corporate environments, making it the business suit-wearing relative of the programming world. C++ is that overachieving cousin who excels at performance-intensive tasks due to its low-level capabilities, perfect for heavy-duty AI applications. Meanwhile, R is the creative genius who specializes in statistics and data analysis, earning its stripes in academia and research, but may leave you scratching your head when it comes to its syntax (seriously, it's like trying to decipher ancient hieroglyphics).

Once you have settled on a programming language, the next step is exploring the Integrated Development Environments (IDEs). These tools are like hosting a dinner party where Python, R, or C++ get to mingle in a code-friendly environment. IDEs enhance your coding experience and make it easier to write, debug, and test your AI by providing useful features like syntax highlighting, because who wouldn't want their code to look like an abstract painting? Some popular IDEs include Jupyter Notebook, a favorite for data science enthusiasts for its interactive magic that allows you to run code in a cell-based approach, and Visual Studio Code, a trusty companion for many programmers seeking a well-rounded experience free from unnecessary distractions - in other words, like a helpful personal assistant who knows when to remind you to breathe.

It's essential not to overlook the realm of frameworks and libraries. Sure, writing code from scratch gives your AI project that authentic homemade touch, but using frameworks like TensorFlow, Scikit-learn, or Keras transforms you from a solitary amateur chef into a world-class culinary wizard. These libraries allow us mere mortals to harness powerful techniques like neural networks without having to understand every arcane mathematical concept. Think of them as your trusty sous-chefs, ready to handle the heavy lifting while you get on with the complexities of AI programming, like wondering if robots can learn sarcasm (spoiler alert: they can, but they might just think it's a feature).

As you embark on your AI journey, embracing version control tools like Git should be a priority. Much like the advanced practice of never throwing away last week's leftovers in case they evolve into an edible life form, version control ensures your code is preserved and can be rolled back at any point in your development process. Thanks to Git, you can experiment as boldly as a cat jumping from one shelf to another with the assurance that you won't end up breaking anything important, except maybe your pride when you accidentally commit a typo that leaves your AI thinking "cats are dogs."

In the charm-filled chaos of AI development, the tools you choose become your trusty sidekicks, guiding you through the labyrinthine realities of data, algorithms, and user interfaces. Choosing wisely not only empowers you to create delightful companions but also ensures your robot doesn't plot a hostile takeover of your coffee machine while you nap. So, gear up for this magical journey - embrace the right tools, channel your inner mad scientist, and together, let's redefine the meaning of teamwork in a world where humans and AI can coexist in perfect harmony... at least until the cereal mascot takes the stage!

Basic Concepts of AI Programming

Welcome, dear reader, to the delightful realm of AI programming, where the unthinkable becomes thinkable, and the improbable becomes... well, just slightly more probable, but only if you're lucky! Understanding the basic concepts of AI programming is like mastering the principles of balancing a spoon on your nose - simple in theory, baffling in practice. But fear not because I'm here to guide you through this crafty landscape filled with algorithms and data, whipping up AI like a gourmet chef creating a lavish meal from nothing but a few leftover ingredients. So, grab your culinary-err... coding apron because we're diving in!

Let's kick off with the heart of AI programming: data. Ah yes, the magical elixir that fuels the aspirations of every algorithm out there. Think of data as the pet hamster you once had; if you didn't feed it, it wouldn't function or, more accurately, it would wither away into oblivion. In AI, the data you provide is what allows algorithms to learn. Whether it's images, text, or numbers, data is essentially the bread-and-butter of the AI learning process. Without it, your carefully crafted code is much like a child on Santa's naughty list: existing but completely overlooked. Remember, your AI is only as intelligent as the data you feed it; give it poor-quality data, and you may as well be raising a young neighbor's cranky cat from a kitten - chaos and confusion guaranteed!

Once you've gathered your data, we venture into the fascinating world of algorithms. Now, these aren't your grandma's recipes; algorithms are more like secret family heirlooms passed down through generations, each with its own flavor and style. They are essentially sets of instructions or rules that guide AI in making decisions, classifying data, or finding patterns. Some popular algorithms you should familiarize yourself with include decision trees (which are not the talking kind we often expect), neural networks (the futuristic brain-like structures - no, they don't possess consciousness), and k-means clustering (which sounds like a fashionable clothing store but is instead used for segmenting data into groups). Understanding how these algorithms work is akin to knowing how a compass operates - you don't always have to be an expert, but it sure helps avoid getting lost in the wilderness of code.

Right alongside data and algorithms, we find the concept of training. If you've ever watched a puppy learn to fetch a stick, you'll understand that training is all about practice and reinforcement. In AI programming, training is the process of teaching your algorithm to recognize patterns and make predictions based on the provided data. During training, the algorithm analyzes input data and adjusts its parameters through a mechanism known as learning. This can be supervised (think of it as teaching a child while providing answers) or unsupervised (the equivalent of locking a teenager in an escape room and letting them figure it all out on their own - chaotic but thrilling). As your algorithm trains, it learns from its mistakes. Just imagine a toddler getting up after falling for the fiftieth time while trying to walk, except this toddler is powered by math and can't be bribed with candy.

Now, let's sprinkle in another vital ingredient: evaluation. After your algorithm has undergone rigorous training (imagine it running a marathon made of calculus), it's time to determine how well it performs. Evaluation entails testing your AI on unseen data to ensure it can generalize its learning and apply it effectively in a real-world scenario. Think of it as gauging a chef's ability to recreate an exquisite recipe without any reheated leftovers at hand – the pressure's on! Here, metrics like accuracy, precision, recall, and F1 scores become your best friends as you determine whether your AI has aced its exams or missed the mark entirely. Spoiler alert: if your AI's performance is less than stellar, you might want to revisit your training data. The poor thing might have inadvertently learned the difference between cats and frogs using pictures of flying saucers.

As we delve deeper, let's talk about the multifaceted world of model optimization. After you've built and evaluated your AI model, you might realize that it's time to nurture it like a delicate houseplant - giving it sunlight and water (or, in this case, adjusting parameters and selecting the right features). Optimization helps improve its performance and fine-tune its settings for maximum efficacy. It's akin to adjusting your reading glasses just so; suddenly, everything comes into sharp focus! Techniques like cross-validation, hyperparameter tuning, and grid search ensure your model performs as well in competition as it does at home - no pressure, of course!

Lastly, let's wrap up with deployment. Congratulations, you've mastered the programming labyrinth! Your trained model is now ready for the limelight. Deployment is the grand moment when your AI takes center stage to work its magic in real-time environments. It could mean integrating your AI model into an app, a web service, or even an autonomous robot! Remember, deploying AI is like sending your child off to school - you hope they represent your teachings and do you proud.

There you have it, dear reader, a whirlwind tour of basic concepts in AI programming! Now, you're equipped with the knowledge needed to craft your very own AI. Embrace these principles, keep the humor alive, and most importantly don't forget to give your AI companion plenty of love and attention. After all, they may just end up being a quirky, intelligent sidekick that helps you win trivia contests... at least until they decide they can beat you at Candy Crush!

Building Your First AI Companion

The grand adventure of building your first AI companion! The moment every aspiring programmer dreams about begins here, folks! Imagine creating a quirky little sidekick that not only remembers your coffee order but can also crack jokes and regale you with tales of online searches gone wrong. But listen closely, my fellow traveler, as we embark on this exhilarating journey as it will require brainpower, determination, and a healthy dose of caffeine (or your beverage of choice!). So roll up your sleeves, let's dive into this realm, and who knows, you might just end up with an AI companion better suited for trivia night than your actual friends!

Before we bust out the code in a wild frenzy, let's take a moment to consider the purpose of our AI companion. Don't just throw together a chatbot that responds with, "I am the great AI; bow to me!" that's been done a million times, and besides, it comes off as a tad too dramatic! Defining the purpose of your AI is like picking a theme for your next birthday party; it sets the tone and leads you down the right path. Will your AI be a virtual assistant? A personal librarian hunting down obscure cat facts? Or perhaps a gaming buddy who can help you strategize your next Candy Crush move? Once you've nailed down a solid idea, it's time to sketch out the features and functionalities. Create a list, and don't hesitate to make it a bullet-point masterpiece!

With your purpose in mind, it's time to dive into data collection. The ingredients for the perfect AI potpie (that's not a real dish, and if it is, I do not recommend tasting it) heavily rely on what data you'll feed your AI companion. Depending on your purpose, gather the data you'll need, whether it's text for a natural language processing chatbot or images for a visual recognition system. Many datasets are available online, or you can compile your own. Just make sure that data is diverse enough because nobody wants an AI companion that's only good at recognizing the difference between apples and oranges. That defeats the whole point of gathering knowledge! Think of it as filling a pantry with vibrant ingredients - variety is what spices things up!

Next on our adventure is the programming aspect. Whip out your trusty Python or favorite programming language! Start small; writing a full-fledged AI as your first project is like trying to build the Eiffel Tower with popsicle sticks - ambitious, but you're likely to end up with a precariously leaning stack. For your first AI companion, integrate simple functionalities like understanding greetings or providing responses based on user input. A common starting point is building a basic chatbot - loveable, if not a touch awkward. Using libraries like TensorFlow or NLTK can ease the coding process. Who knew you could use those old math skills you thought you'd never need again to create something cool?

As adorable as your newborn AI companion might seem, the reality checks continue. Once you've programmed the initial version, it's time to test your creation. Deploy it in a simulated environment, and see how it performs. How does it react to different user inputs? Does it respond accurately, or does it have an identity crisis and start telling everyone it's a toaster? Don't panic; fine-tuning is part of the process! This stage is where you can adjust parameters, improve logic, and eliminate any quirks that make your AI sound like a confused fortune cookie.

Now that your AI has reached a semblance of sanity, let's shift gears toward the enchanting realm of learning! Implement basic machine learning techniques and let your companion learn from the input it receives. With supervised learning approaches, you can train your AI to recognize patterns and improve interactions over time. Just remember, it's not a straight path, sometimes your AI will misinterpret "hello" as "HULK SMASH!" This is when you roll up your sleeves and teach it to clarify appropriate responses. A little patience and nurturing go a long way in developing your virtual friend!

After fine-tuning your AI and adding that charming personality - because every companion needs one - let's talk about deployment! Choose a platform to host your AI companion. Will it join forces with a messaging app or perhaps show up on your website? Deploy it using cloud services like AWS or Google Cloud, where it can interact with users in real time, ensuring your AI receives the warm reception it deserves. With every user interaction, your AI will evolve and grow, much like that one cactus plant on your windowsill you forgot you owned.

There you have it! Your very own AI companion is out in the wild, equipped to assist, entertain, and occasionally misinterpret your commands. As it thrives, don't forget the joy of nurturing this digital friend. Be proud that you've created something new! It might not show emotion yet, but it will know that the laughter you share, even if it's awkward, is what truly makes this digital partnership delightful. So, embrace the journey, my fellow creators, for with every line of code, you are inching toward crafting a sidekick fit for any fantastic adventure (or a good game of chess)!

Enhancing Your AI with Machine Learning

Machine learning is the secret sauce that takes your AI companion from a charming caddy to a race car on a digital racetrack. If you've ever marveled at how your AI can suddenly predict weather patterns or guess your favorite pizza toppings (it's pepperoni, isn't it?), you can thank the marvel of machine learning for that. Let's look into the magic of enhancing your AI through machine learning, unveiling the mysteries of algorithms, patterns, and just how much coffee you can realistically consume while waiting for your model to train!

To kick things off, we need to understand just what machine learning actually is. If we think of traditional programming as a chef meticulously measuring flour, sugar, and eggs to follow a recipe, machine learning shifts us into the realm of art. This process allows your AI to make decisions based on patterns it learns from data, which is a fancy way of saying it often surprises you with its behavior, like that one friend who shows up uninvited with a pet iguana. So, instead of manually coding every possible interaction, your AI learns from examples - much like a kid who learns to ride a bicycle while crashing into a few bushes along the way. The ultimate goal? To have your AI mastering the art of prediction and understanding in mere moments, avoiding the bushes altogether!

Let's explore how to breathe some machine-learning magic into your AI companion. First, we need to round up some data. Yes, dear reader, our old friend data is back, and now it's wearing a snazzy new outfit! For your AI to learn, you need to provide a robust dataset that clearly shows the relationship between the features you want it to recognize and the outputs it should produce. Think of it as training a dog; you'll need a collection of treats (data points) that guide your furry companion toward marvelous tricks (predictions). If you're going the supervised learning route, ensure your dataset has labeled examples so your AI knows the difference between a cat and a dog, or heck, a cat dressed as a dog!

Once you've amassed your data haul, it's time to define the architecture of your model. It's like choosing the theme for a party; you could go low-key and intimate with a simple linear regression model, or you could throw a full-blown bash with a sprawling neural network featuring multiple hidden layers. Remember, each model type has its strengths, like deciding between a fast food drive-thru (quick but somewhat trashy) and a gourmet restaurant (slower but leaves you feeling like a connoisseur). For newcomers, algorithms like decision trees and k-nearest neighbors offer a decent entry point, while the more adventurous can experiment with deep learning techniques, which are akin to climbing Everest - rewarding but inevitably fraught with data avalanches.

Next comes the training of your model, and this is where the rubber meets the road. With your data ready and model architecture established, you'll need to feed your fresh dataset into the model and let it start to learn patterns and associations. Keep in mind that machine learning should not be a "one-and-done" endeavor - oh no! Like training for a marathon, while simultaneously pondering the existence of alien life, you'll need to iterate and optimize the process. Monitor your model's performance using validation datasets to ensure it's not only memorizing your data like a karaoke star stuck on the same tune but genuinely learning to adapt and predict outputs.

Once your model has been trained to a respectable level (ballet pirouette or awkward shuffle, whichever works), it's time to evaluate its performance. This is one of those moments that elevates the drama as thoughts of inadequacy run wild, "Did I feed it too many spam emails?" or "Is my AI going to start starting conspiracy theories?" To avoid dire outcomes, you can assess the quality of its predictions using metrics like accuracy, precision, and recall, which sound way cooler than they are. Think of these metrics as report cards for your AI model - fingers crossed it didn't end up with too many "C's" in Response Analysis!

Oh, and let's not forget about *hyperparameter tuning*, a term that sounds extremely scientific but mostly involves a bit of trial and error with parameters that govern the model's behavior. It's the annoying task of adjusting knobs and levers until your AI decides to behave at dinner without involving the servers in its opinion of pineapple on pizza.

Once your model is strutting its stuff with complete confidence, it's time to deploy! Bring this bad boy into the real world, where it can interact with users, analyze streams of data, and blurt out intelligent responses (or at least somewhat coherent ones). The deployment stage is like sending your child off to summer camp - you hope for the best, even when they come back thinking they've been raised by squirrels.

Enhancing your AI with machine learning is not just about following a recipe, it's about creativity, imagination, and a pinch of madness. You're building a companion that can learn, adapt, and grow as it interacts with the world around it. Embrace the quirks, the challenges, and the chaos, and don't lose sight of the joy that accompanies this whimsical journey. With machine learning, you are not just creating software; you're giving life to a passionate AI sidekick, one that might just have a better memory than you when it comes to remembering important things, like where you left your keys! Let the awkward adventures begin!

Showcasing Your AI Creation

The delightful and slightly nerve-wracking phase we call showcasing your AI creation - where the digital rubber meets the human road. This is the moment you've been anxiously anticipating, like a school play where the curtain rises for the very first time, and you hope to avoid any embarrassing mishaps. Now, like a proud parent at a spelling bee, you're ready to showcase what you've crafted: an AI companion who may very well be smarter than you! But fret not, I'm here to guide you through this thrilling and occasionally chaotic endeavor.

To start, let us marvel at the various platforms upon which you can unveil your creation. Remember, showcasing is not merely about sitting around and enjoying the wonders of your own genius. It's about confidently sharing your AI with the world. Are you hosting a launch event at a local coffee shop where caffeine-fueled tech enthusiasts gather to share dreams of robot symphonies? Or maybe you're opting for a virtual conference, complete with PowerPoint slides that nobody ever reads (because who doesn't love a good meme instead)? Whatever platform you utilize, be sure your AI has an appropriate stage to shine on - it's like choosing the right outfit for a first date, presentation matters!

Once you've decided on the venue, it's time to prepare a dazzling demonstration of your AI's capabilities. You wouldn't want your audience to think your creation just sits there like a lump. So, grab a spotlight and prepare a showcase that accentuates its finest attributes. This could involve live conversations, interactive Q&A sessions, or even a dramatic reenactment of Shakespeare's greatest hits - featuring your AI as Hamlet, of course! Whatever you choose, cater to the strengths of your AI, highlighting its unique features and defining quirks. Show your audience that your creation isn't just another chatbot; it's a digital confidant capable of engaging storytelling or occasionally veering off into bewildering soliloquies that leave everyone baffled in the best possible way.

As we dive deeper into the presentation, it's essential to craft an engaging narrative that weaves together your AI's backstory, the challenges you faced during development (like attempting to bake cookies without knowing how), and the invaluable lessons learned along the way. You want your audience to empathize with your journey, perhaps even shedding tears of joy and admiration as you recount the moments of triumph and near-meltdown. Did your AI misinterpret "Tell me a joke" as "Tell me about your love for inflatable ducks"? These are the anecdotes that will make your audience chuckle and resonate with the human experience, because let's face it, no one wants to hear a dry tech talk that's more boring than watching paint dry!

With the storytelling element in place, it's time to shift the focus to user interaction. Engage your audience and let them connect with your AI directly. The delicious part about making it interactive is that you get to witness the delightful reactions of people as they interact with your creation. They might experience whimsical moments of enlightenment or utter bewilderment - it's all part of the fun! Have a microphone at the ready so that attendees can pose questions and challenges, giving your AI a chance to strut its stuff while simultaneously appreciating the frantic giggles or gasps of disbelief circulating in the room. Nothing says, "I've conquered the world of AI" quite like a live demonstration where your digital sidekick rises to the occasion!

Don't forget to address the future of your AI during the showcase. You've crafted a lovely digital companion, but illustratively sow the seeds of curiosity in your audience. Talk to them about the next exciting features you plan to implement, whether that involves adding more complex language capabilities, introducing deeper self-learning algorithms, or simply ensuring your AI remembers birthdays (seriously, who doesn't want a friendly bot reminding them never to forget Aunt Marge's 96th birthday?) Use this opportunity to not only grab their attention but also build interest in what lies ahead.

And while sharing isn't always easy, don't hesitate to showcase the more challenging aspects of developing AI. Be transparent about the hurdles you encountered, revealing the trials of training your AI on datasets comprised largely of memes and utterly confusing jokes. Humility combined with humor is a surefire way to endear yourself to your audience; it shows them that even the brightest minds face setbacks while contributing to the chaotic, quirky technology landscape.

Finally, bask in the applause of your friends and fellow innovators. When the final curtain call arrives, soak in the admiration of your audience but be prepared for some strange queries or feedback! Great work creates an even greater opportunity for further collaboration, inspiration, and networking. Sharing your AI creation is more than a mere showcase; it's a celebration of creativity, experimentation, and humor, reminding us that the journey itself is often as rewarding as the destination.

So, dear reader, as you prepare to showcase your AI creation, remember that you're not just presenting a piece of software; you're sharing an experience, a story, and a glimpse into a realm filled with possibilities. With the right measures of humor and humanity, your AI will not only impress but will flourish into a digital companion that irrefutably charms everyone it encounters. Now go forth, ready the spotlight, and let your creation shine like the magnificent star it is destined to be!

Chapter 17

A Glimpse into AI's Thought Process

The Basics of Algorithmic Decision-Making

Algorithmic decision-making! If you've ever wondered how a machine can make choices more efficiently than your indecisive friend who can never decide whether they want tacos or sushi, you're in for a treat. At its core, algorithmic decision-making is the process by which machines evaluate data, analyze possible outcomes, and arrive at a conclusion faster than you can say, "Wait, was that extra guacamole worth the extra two dollars?"

When we talk about algorithms, we're not referring to the secret society of code-wielding wizards hidden in Silicon Valley. Instead, think of them as trusty sidekicks that assist computers in finding solutions. They operate based on predefined rules and instructions and are designed to mimic our thought processes, minus the coffee breaks (because, let's be honest, robots don't need caffeine - a twist that still infuriates coffee lovers everywhere).

The foundational principle of an algorithm is its ability to parse through massive amounts of data. Imagine trying to find the right shirt in a thousand-item closet without getting overwhelmed. Algorithms sift through this data like a superhuman that's somehow still trying to maintain its sanity. By identifying patterns and relationships within the information, they meticulously weigh the pros and cons of every possible decision. Some might argue that this is how artificial intelligence gets its wisdom; I'd say it's more like your grandmother giving you sound advice coupled with her ancient home remedy for when you feel under the weather.

You might be wondering, "Are all algorithms created equal?" Absolutely not! There exists a smorgasbord of algorithms, each designed for different decision-making scenarios. Some are like simple calculators doing their best approximation of a math whiz; others resemble complex neural networks that imitate how the human brain processes information. When a self-driving car has to decide whether to brake suddenly because a squirrel just darted across its path like it's auditioning for a role in the latest action movie, it's relying on algorithms to figure out how to prevent an accident while ensuring the driver doesn't scream louder than the horn itself.

So, what factors influence these decisions? Well, there's data, of course, and by data, I mean a comprehensive collection of all the clues we've trusted machines to interpret. The more quality data we feed the algorithm, the more informed its choices become. However, there's a catch - garbage in, garbage out still reigns supreme. If you give the algorithm data riddled with mistakes, it may eventually conclude that squirrels should be treated as future Olympic sprinters, and we all know how that would end!

Now, let's address the elephant in the room, or rather, the algorithm in our computers: bias. Yes, bias! Just as humans have their quirks, algorithms can also inherit biases from the data they're trained on. Picture this: an algorithm fed with data showcasing a plethora of cat memes, but limited dog photos might inadvertently conclude that cats are more lovable companions than their canine counterparts. Any dog-lover would naturally find this scenario amusing, yet The Great Algorithmic Cat-Centric Debacle might leave many in confusion, with furry friends everywhere demanding a recount of their worth.

In this whimsical world of algorithmic decision-making, one thing shines like a trophy in the sports hall of fame - the blend of data-driven insights and strategic thinking. For humans, this means rolling up our sleeves and working alongside these machines. Think of them less as adversaries and more as quirky allies who can help answer life's toughest questions, like why avocado toast is too trendy or when a pumpkin spice latte is acceptable (hint: Halloween should not dictate your pumpkin-spiced pleasure choices).

As we venture further into our exploration of artificial intelligence in this book, remember that you, too, are capable of making decisions, albeit with a bit more second-guessing. Embrace your inner algorithm, dance with the data, and maybe, just maybe, let an AI help you decide your next taco or sushi meal... or perhaps just take them both, because why not indulge in every culinary revolution? After all, as we've learned, life - and decision-making - is just one big, wild game show. Grab your buzzer and stay tuned!

Data Utilization in AI Thought Processes

Data! The magical dust that breathes life into the world of artificial intelligence - like fairy dust, but potentially less likely to make you sneeze. In essence, data is the fuel that powers AI's thought processes, allowing chatbot aficionados and algorithm enthusiasts everywhere to classify its plethora of uses. In the realm of machine learning, data is not just a commodity; it's the star of the show, gracing every algorithmic red carpet as it struts its impressive statistical stuff.

Alright, let's step into the process, shall we? Imagine for a moment that data is the grand buffet at a fancy wedding - endless options, but you've gotta choose wisely or risk overloading your plate (and your algorithms). You've got your fresh greens - clean and tidy data - to nourish our algorithms, and there's also a mountain of questionable mystery meat - data riddled with inconsistencies that no one really wants to address. AI thrives on a balanced diet of data, making sure each input contributes to its grand thought processes. If you were to give it a poorly prepared plate, it would be like trying to surf on soggy toast and nobody's going to get very far with that!

Now, how does AI utilize data? It works roughly in the same way you would when faced with a puzzling question like, "What's the most popular breakfast item?" First, it collects an immense amount of information - think thousands of statistics spanning years of breakfast choices. It scrambles through this data like it's on a caffeine-fueled quest to determine the perfect ratio of pancakes to bacon. Then, it analyzes patterns, correlating elements that go together like peanut butter and jelly or late-night infomercials and existential dread (honestly, who can resist a good infomercial at 2 AM?).

One might say that data is the guiding hand for AI when it comes to decision-making. It learns patterns, trends, and even discerning habits, figuring out that when a person Googles "how to bake an avocado brownie," they might also be interested in "the best way to lose friends by serving them unexpected culinary disasters." This is potentially alarming if you're an avocado brownie enthusiast, but that's where the real magic lies: leveraging data to understand and predict user behavior. You see, AI meticulously collects information like a detective at a crime scene, searching for biscuit crumbs while dodging red herrings thrown by overzealous food bloggers.

The process continues to layer on intricacies. AI delves into supervised and unsupervised learning - two fancy terms that describe how it ingests and processes data. Picture supervised learning like a diligent teacher guiding students through a math lesson, firm but loving. Conversely, unsupervised learning is akin to letting kids loose in a funhouse maze, figuring things out on their own. The difference is that while one might end up with coherent answers to mathematical problems, the other will likely produce a collection of abstract art made from random crayon doodles. Both methods have their merits, and each contributes weighty insights into AI's psychographic processes.

But let's not ignore our beloved old friend, bias! Yes, bias, the unsolicited guest who crashes the data party and turns a lovely gathering into an epic battle over who brought the worst potato salad. Data can harbor biases from the start. If you feed an algorithm data skewed toward specific demographics, it may mistakenly start believing that pineapple on pizza is not just acceptable but the gold standard for gastronomic delight. If I had a nickel for every time I've had to reassure an AI that culinary choices are subjective, I'd probably have enough change to support my own avocado brownie habit.

Ultimately, the art of data utilization boils down to this: artificial intelligence hinges on our cooperation and humor. AI may sift through layers of data like a five-star chef preparing haute cuisine, but it still requires the creative touch, humor, and common sense that only human intervention can provide. When we recognize that we're partners in this journey of knowledge, it leads to an extraordinary fusion of data intelligence and human flair, like a duet of a spreadsheet-loving robot and an eccentric singer who loves spontaneous interpretive dance.

So, dear reader, the next time you see AI work its analytical wizardry, consider the vast majority of data that served as its muse. Welcome to the era where data reigns supreme, its kingdom vast, its influence undeniable, and its potential limitless! Trust me, once you peel back those layers and understand the intricacies of AI decision-making, you'll never regard data as mere numbers again. Instead, it'll transform into a playful companion, proving that even algorithms can appreciate a good laugh and a fresh avocado brownie... just as long as they don't have to bake it!

The Role of Neural Networks in Understanding

Neural networks: a term that sounds like the secret cabal of cybernetic ninjas operating out of a dimly lit basement somewhere in downtown San Francisco, but I assure you, they're much less dramatic. These vibrant constructs actually mimic the very fabric of how our brains operate, which is both awe-inspiring and slightly concerning, given that some of us occasionally have trouble formulating clear sentences after 7 PM. But as we dive into the world of neural networks, get ready to discover how they're revolutionizing AI comprehension in a way that makes even the most complex brain teasers look like child's play.

At their core, neural networks are comprised of nodes that are akin to the neurons in our brains. They're interconnected in layers, passing information back and forth like gossiping friends at a coffee shop. When you input data into a neural network, it begins to meticulously analyze it, making sense of everything from images to languages, as if playing a complex game of telephone where everyone actually cares about catching the message rather than misquoting a classic movie line. This intricate web of nodes and layers allows machines to learn from examples, adjusting its "thoughts" based on outcomes, similar to adjusting a bad haircut, albeit with significantly zero tears or regret about long-term decisions.

As we look deeper, we quickly realize that these neural networks thrive on vast amounts of data; they have an insatiable hunger that rivals that of college students during finals week. Just as you'd sample every morsel in the all-you-can-eat buffet while cramming for exams, neural networks take in a wealth of information to rewire and improve their understanding of concepts. While you might end up with a food baby, neural networks emerge with an entirely new understanding of patterns, relationships, and classifications. They can diagnose diseases, identify faces, and even produce eerily convincing text, all while making it seem as if they fully understand what it means to be sentient. Spoiler alert: they really don't, but they act like the overambitious intern who wants the promotion too badly.

One of the most stunning characteristics of neural networks is their ability to perform "deep learning." Picture it as a transformative workshop where algorithms go to immerse themselves in self-help books and mindfulness sessions. In deep learning, the network digs into multiple hidden layers, uncovering more nuanced representations of information. It's the machine equivalent of peeling back the layers of an onion, except instead of crying, it discovers previously overlooked complexities that can lead to richer insights - oh joy, no onion tears. This shift propels AI into realms of excellence previously unimaginable, enhancing its capabilities in tasks like image recognition and decision-making.

Nevertheless, let's not forget the quirks that come along with this technological marvel. Neural networks can sometimes be as unpredictable as a cat that just ate three servings of catnip. They might wrestle with overfitting - the situation where they become so immersed in training data that they confuse specificity with generalization. It's like being a group of flashy wedding planners who gather a wealth of ideas and mistakenly commit to organizing entirely different themes for every part of the same celebration. Imagine a wedding where the reception is medieval, the cake is from outer space, and Aunt Edna is spinning faux country-western tunes while you're trying to serve the main course. The confusion could set the stage for a unique experience or an absolute disaster, making neural networks both endearing and occasionally infuriating.

So, what's the key takeaway here? Neural networks are the eager students of the machine-learning realm, out there diving headfirst into complex problems with enthusiasm that makes you slightly envious of their dedication. They rely on vast pools of data to build their comprehension, streamlining the art of understanding in ways that would make even the brightest philosophers raise an eyebrow in curiosity. Although they may not have mastered the finer points of existential crises or the art of selecting the perfect Netflix show, they do wield a level of analytical prowess that has advanced technology at an astonishing pace.

As we cheer on these computational pioneers, let's also remember that the art of understanding isn't limited to neural networks. We humans have our own whimsical approach to self-discovery, flourishing in creativity, intuition, and humor - a winning combination that machines continue to study and aspire toward. So, as the world leans ever closer to AI, let's allow ourselves to envision the myriads of possibilities that neural networks will uncover. They may not have a soul, but they sure know a thing or two about sorting through the chaos of data and making sense of the world... or at the very least, they can figure out who wore it best on the latest reality show!

Bias and Its Impact on AI Decisions

Bias and artificial intelligence - the duo that's about as harmonious as an off-key karaoke rendition of "Bohemian Rhapsody." While we humans pride ourselves on our ability to judge a situation with a fair degree of nuance (unless, of course, we encounter an infuriating parking situation), AI algorithms can sometimes fall foul of bias, leading them down a treacherous path littered with unintentional missteps and bizarre conclusions. As we navigate into the choppy waters of bias in AI, be prepared for a wild ride that blends humor with the uncomfortable realities of navigating a digital world.

Bias in artificial intelligence is somewhat akin to those group projects from high school where one student carries the rest while the others just coalesce into a collective mass of procrastination. In essence, algorithms learn from the data they are provided, and if that data is inherently biased, the AI tool will end up making assumptions that feel as random as deciding you should wear socks with sandals - a decision that any self-respecting fashionista would protest against vehemently. For instance, if an image recognition system trained primarily on photos of mid-30S cat-loving hipsters suddenly encounters a great-aunt with a penchant for floral dresses and an affinity for tea, it might mistakenly label her as a cat. You've got to love how even AI can grasp the importance of our feline overlords while neglecting the identity of your beloved family members.

So, how does this bias creep in? Well, it all boils down to the data sets we provide. If we train algorithms on historical data that showcases social inequalities, like an ancient tome cataloging who gets invited to the "cool kids" lunch table, then we end up creating a digital echo chamber that perpetuates stereotypes. This can lead to AI systems making decisions that exclude certain groups or even favoring one demographic over another. It's like installing a "coolness filter" that only allows the hipsters in, while the rest of us who still rock our beloved sweatpants to the grocery store are left out in the cold, wandering the aisles wondering where it all went wrong.

Imagine for a moment a hiring algorithm that's been trained on data representative of a company culture with a severe lack of diversity. In a shocking twist of fate, it suddenly decides that the ideal candidate must have a passionate commitment to wearing ironic T-shirts and sipping artisanal oat milk lattes - nicknamed "the hipster standard." Now, while I have nothing against our hipster brethren, is this really the criterion we want for our future workforce? Talk about setting candidates up for failure. Unfortunately, this kind of unbridled bias doesn't just remain a punchline; it can contribute to the systemic issues we still face in our workplaces.

Bias doesn't just rear its ugly head in hiring practices; it permeates almost every facet of our lives where AI is involved. From criminal justice algorithms that inaccurately predict recidivism rates to facial recognition tools that struggle to identify people of color with the same accuracy as their lighter-skinned counterparts, the implications can sometimes lead to real-world consequences that feel like living in a dark satire that just won't quit. If we're not paying close attention, we risk losing sight of not just our shared humanity but our responsibility to make these systems more equitable.

Now, don't get me wrong, many researchers are diligently working to combat bias in algorithms. They're knee-deep in data, desperately sifting through the rubble in search of a more palatable solution than bland oatmeal for breakfast. They're attempting to refine AI systems so that they don't inadvertently perpetuate stereotypes or reinforce social injustices. It's like giving AI a crash course in empathy - an invaluable life skill that every sentient (or semi-sentient) being should possess.

As we navigate this whimsical world of AI, it's crucial to remain aware of its pitfalls and biases while also laughing at our shared absurdity. We might be crafting a future where algorithms make decisions for us, but it's vital that we don't forget our human touch - the humor, quirks, and intricacies that make us uniquely ourselves. After all, if we want to coexist alongside these digital purveyors of logic, we must strive for a balance: one that acknowledges bias and works toward building AI systems that are as fair and diverse as the colorful tapestry of humanity itself. Let's ensure that when it comes to artificial intelligence, everyone gets a fair shot, because no one should have to sing in a tonal range that doesn't fit their natural pitch (or their literal karaoke style). So, let's roll up our sleeves, balance out the data, and make sure bias takes a backseat to our collective adventures in this brave new tech-driven world!

The Future of AI Decision-Making: Trends and Predictions

The future of AI decision-making is a field teeming with potential, sprinkled with a hint of sci-fi flair, and draped in the kind of mystery that keeps even the most seasoned data scientists awake at night, clutching their cups of coffee. Brace yourself, dear reader, because we're heading into uncharted territory where algorithms could not only make decisions for us but could also write better romcoms, compose symphonies, and perhaps even figure out the meaning of that weird noise coming from the fridge!

As we peer into the crystal ball, we can spot a growing trend: increasing autonomy in AI systems. Yes, my friends, soon we may witness algorithms taking the reins all on their own, and the concept of decision-making by consensus may become a quaint relic of yesteryear - right alongside the floppy disk and your uncle's fascination with VHS tapes. Imagine an AI navigating through vast oceans of data, wading through financial forecasts, political analyses, and emotional sentiments, all while making recommendations for better pizza toppings during Friday night movie marathons. Autonomy brings with it both exhilaration and trepidation; will we one day discover our very own robot overlords telling us which shows we simply must binge-watch next? It's a brave new world indeed!

But wait, there's more! As the tech-savvy kids say, AI is about to get "smarter" - and no. I'm not talking about finally mastering Sudoku. We're looking at the emergence of more sophisticated learning methods. With advances in accountability and ethical frameworks, AI decision-making models will be honed to ensure they are not simply algorithms that have been fed by outdated data or biases. Enter interpretability, the magical potion that allows us to understand how decisions are made, much like studying the recipe for our grandma's famous cookies, which we're convinced must contain a sprinkle of secret ingredients! As the algorithms gain interpretability, we may find ourselves better equipped to challenge the decisions AI lays before us. After all, if a robot tells you to eat more kale purely based on its analysis of health fads, we ought to question its adherence to our pizza-loving hearts.

But what does the future hold in terms of collaboration? Increasingly, companies are realizing that the combination of human insights and AI capabilities is akin to pairing cheese with a fine wine - truly magical! Picture a scenario where humans leverage AI as a co-pilot rather than merely ceding control to a silicon-based overlord. While algorithms crunch data in real time, we can provide context, creativity, and intuition that make even the best machine learning models jealous. This interplay opens the door to dynamic decision-making where AI nudges us toward better choices while we maintain the final veto, ensuring our voices are always heard (unless, of course, we mistakenly give our sarcastic AI an attitude problem).

Now, let's talk about data privacy - an ever-important topic at the intersection of AI and human behavior. As AI decision-making evolves, we face the daunting task of drawing a line between useful data collection and egregious violations of our personal space. The future will likely showcase more robust frameworks around data ethics, ultimately making data usage not only more transparent but also consensual. Perhaps soon we'll find ourselves confidently saying, "Oh yes, you may analyze my cereal consumption patterns - provided you don't leak my fascination with off-brand chips!" As algorithms learn to please their human counterparts more harmoniously, the balance of privacy will become gospel in the landscape of AI decision-making.

But here's the kicker, folks: the future of AI decision-making will undoubtedly involve an increase in its integration across various sectors. From healthcare, where AI can assist in predictive diagnostics, to agriculture, where advanced algorithms can help farmers determine the best time to plant crops based on meteorological data - AI will permeate our lives like a delightful aroma wafting through a bustling bakery. As AI takes on more responsibilities, our reliance on it will grow, leading us to utter that fateful phrase we always feared: "Hey, Siri, what's your opinion on the state of the world?"

In summary, the landscape of AI decision-making is akin to an evolving role in a sitcom - full of delightful mishaps, situational hilarity, and a few moments where the characters grapple with existential crises. Future trends point to a landscape where AI and humans collaborate, maintain ethical practices, embrace interpretability, and laugh together as we navigate the complexities of tomorrow. While we might still be figuring out the meaning of life (and how to pronounce "quinoa" without blushing), one thing is for sure, AI, with a touch of humor, creativity, and humanity, is here to stay, and it may just help us eat our kale and still enjoy our pizza, one algorithmic decision at a time!

Chapter 18

The Winning Mindset

Understanding the Psychological Landscape of Competition

Welcome to the wild, ever-wonderful world of competitive psychology. Now, when you think about competition, especially in the grand arena of humans versus AI, your mind might conjure images of intense showdowns, epic battles of wits, and perhaps an explosion or two of confetti. However, beneath this glittering facade lies a psychological landscape as intricate and twisty as the plot twist in a sitcom episode involving a surprise trip to the moon. So, grab your mental popcorn, and let's explore this delightful chaos!

You see, competition is not merely about who can answer questions fastest, solve puzzles without breaking a sweat, or beat an AI at its own game. It's also a psychological battleground where fear, confidence, doubt, and perhaps even a tad of silliness intertwine in a grand dance. Oh yes, that dance. Imagine two people going in circles, one furiously calculating probabilities while the other frantically searches for a snack! It's a display that highlights the quirks of human nature as much as it demonstrates our competing capabilities against our digital counterparts.

One major actor in this psychological play is the concept of "fear of failure." Ah, yes! The looming specter that haunts many a contestant, especially when faced with an AI boasting more data than the world's most cluttered library. It's like standing on a stage, your heart pounding like a heavy metal drum, knowing that the entire audience, including the judgmental robot in the back, awaits your every move. The key to playing in this fear-laden arena is to understand that failure isn't necessarily the end of the world. In fact, failing is about as common as finding a sock that doesn't match its partner - and just as colorful! The trick is embracing this fear, wrapping it in a warm, cozy blanket, and allowing it to reach you valuable lessons for the next round.

Moving on, let's chat about the intoxicating cocktail of confidence. Developing confidence in competition is akin to building a bridge between imagination and reality, ensuring you don't fall into the psychological river below where your self-esteem might swim with piranhas. Just as AI needs data feeds and training processes, humans require positive reinforcement and a pep talk. Think of it this way: before you step on that virtual game show stage, it's like prepping for a day at the beach. You wouldn't just show up in an inflatable dinosaur costume (though that could be fabulous); no, you'd prepare with sunscreen, a well-structured towel setup, and a mind that screams, "Let's ravage those waves!"

However, confidence is a tricky little creature because it can transform into overconfidence faster than you can say "Artificial Intelligence!" Suddenly, you're strutting about, convinced you can beat anything or anyone just by sheer force of will. At this point, let me caution you: the antithesis of confidence is typically embarrassing failure when Alice the AI takes the crown while you fumble like a contestant from last season's awful reality show. This highlights one of the essential lessons of competition - keep your hubris in check. Engage your inner David (that's you) versus Goliath (the AI), and remember that every competition is just a quirky game played on the broader chessboard of existence.

Now, let's pivot to resilience. In the world of competition, this is your superhero cape - the one that flutters majestically behind you as you face chose turbulent winds of challenge. Resilience isn't about never getting knocked down; it's about being able to hop back up like a rubber chicken, ready for another round of hilarity. Think of how often your AI competitor might take a swipe at your cherished cereal box puzzle piece, it could soon feel like a personal attack on your self-worth! But remember, every little loss is just an opportunity to sculpt your psychological prowess like Michelangelo to a block of marble. So use those metaphorical chisels, shave off the bad experiences, and stand tall as you tackle your next bout against your silicon rival!

Ultimately, when we dare to traverse the psychological landscape of competition with its emotional peaks and valleys - littered with confetti, perhaps a few inflatable dinosaurs, and the sweet scent of triumph - we're developing a profound understanding of ourselves. Learning how fear, confidence, and resilience play their roles will not only prepare us for skirmishes against AI but will also enrich our overall human experience. After all, in the grand game show that is life, mastering the mind is every bit as significant as mastering the machine. So, equip yourself with the right psychological tools and let the laughter and learning guide your journey!

Building Confidence Through Preparation

Preparation - the unsung hero of confidence-building! Picture this: you walk into a game show set, lights flashing, cameras rolling, and that ever-judgmental AI contestant locked and loaded to take you down. But instead of feeling like a deer caught in the headlights (and not the cool, eye-catching, spotlight-deer) I want you to feel like an expert tightrope walker, gliding above a crowd of inflatable dinosaurs. This majestic confidence doesn't just sprout from thin air; oh no! It emerges from the fortress of preparation you've built in your mind and, if I may add, perhaps overcooked by relentless practice.

First, let's talk about the age-old proverb, "Failing to prepare is preparing to fail," Now, this little gem sounds straightforward, but let us dissect it like an overly ambitious science fair project where a fifth grader triumphed over their doom. When you've put in the hours honing your skills, studying the challenges, and plotting strategies, there's a certain magic that happens. Suddenly, you're no longer just a contestant standing in the spotlight; you're Sherlock Holmes with a magnifying glass, piecing together clues in a grand competition caper. Doing your homework, metaphorically speaking, will give you that leg-up on the sweating competition.

Imagine going up against a trivia-loving AI that can spit out facts faster than a conspiracy theorist at a family dinner. But if you've spent time in preparation - like binging on trivia games or receiving an honorary degree from the University of Random Facts - you walk in with the confidence of a contestant who knows they're about to hit the jackpot. You feel it in your bones! Your neural pathways light up brighter than a Christmas tree in July. You've stored all those tasty nuggets of knowledge and, let's be honest, some pretty bad puns that you can deploy during those awkward pauses.

Still, preparation isn't just about accumulating knowledge; it also involves strategy. You wouldn't show up to a game show without a battle plan, akin to marching into an alien invasion with only a rubber chicken in your arsenal. No! You configure your strategies based on your strengths, weaknesses, and the abilities of your AI opponent. Celebrate your unique quirks and eccentricities. Perhaps you've honed an uncanny ability to confuse AI with a well-timed dad joke or a riddle so perplexing that even the most advanced algorithms would need a short vacation to unwind. Knowing how to leverage your individuality can be the secret ingredient that boosts your confidence tenfold.

Don't forget to include physical preparation in this cocktail of confidence. Sure, you're competing against AI, but you're still human - vulnerable, slightly squishy, and definitely in need of a good stretch! Engaging in some physical activity before the game can get your adrenaline pumping and contribute to mental clarity. Whether it be a quick jog while you mentally recap those puzzling rules or doing some star jumps to mimic a nervous contestant attempting to stretch their nerves away this elevates your mood and confidence alike. After all, there's nothing like getting the heart rate up before sitting down to engage in a battle of wits with our silicon counterparts.

It's also vital to embrace the multiple facets of preparation: the emotional side! Yes, that's right! Consider prepping your morale with positive affirmation rituals. Channel your inner cheerleader and shout those pep talks into the mirror like an overzealous sports coach yelling at a halftime locker room! "You've got this! Release your inner trivia master!" The sheer ridiculousness of it all will dissolve any creeping self-doubt while simultaneously sending laughter floating through your veins like warm cocoa on a rainy day.

Finally, never underestimate the power of group preparation. That's right! Call in your friends - those adults with an apparent love for snacks while simultaneously honking their noses at highbrow TRIVIA NERDS. Bring them together for a gauntlet of quizzes, puzzles, and other brain bends, and allow the camaraderie to swell the ranks of confidence within your team. Knowing you've got a tribe of ridiculous humans standing behind you, cheering you on like you're a contestant on a reality show, can work wonders as confidence rolls in waves of genuine support.

In conclusion, the recipe for building confidence lies firmly in the hands of preparation. By gathering knowledge, crafting strategies, embracing your uniqueness, getting physically active, conducting a pep-crew session, and gathering your support team, you're generating a fortress of confidence that no AI algorithm can breach. Merely stepping onto the stage amidst the camera flashes will make you feel less like a mere game show contestant and more like an indomitable legend in an ongoing epic sitcom of life. So, prep away! Your AI rivals better watch out because you're about to dazzle them with your brilliance, one quirky challenge at a time! Remember, each moment you spend preparing is a step towards your personal spotlight.

Embracing Failure as a Learning Tool

Failure! That dreaded F-word that sends shivers down the spines of aspiring contestants everywhere. Yet, in the game show of life, especially when competing against our silicon annoyances known as AI, embracing failure is akin to discovering that the garden gnome you paint has a knack for breakdancing. Intriguing, hilarious, and oftentimes unexpectedly useful! So, let's navigate this perilous yet enlightening terrain together, shall we?

First off, let's acknowledge something right at the start: Failure is as universal as the obsession with cat videos on the internet. Whether it's failing to remember the capital of New Zealand (hint: it's not Wellington if you've been secretly streaming travel documentaries) or attempting to define what AI really means without saying "It's just a bunch of computer stuff," we've all been there - crouching under the tables of our own embarrassment. If you think about it, every "oops" moment acts as a stepping stone on your journey to success, like playing hopscotch on the world's most ridiculous grid of wisdom.

When you embrace failure, you unshackle yourself from the chains of fear that hold you back from taking risks. I mean, can you imagine what life would be like if Thomas Edison had given up after the first few attempts to create a light bulb? We'd still be sitting in the dark, discussing which cave paintings to put on our Tinder profiles! So, as you step into the arena and your AI competitor spits out the right answer while you, well, let's just say, "miss the mark". Remember that every challenging stumble is an invaluable opportunity to learn. Instead of going home, burying yourself under a pile of ice cream, and regretting your cereal choice, take a moment to analyze what happened. Was it the question that stumped you? The existential dread creeping in? Or perhaps your strategy was more convoluted than your attempts to fold fitted sheets?

Let's spice this discussion up a bit and bring humor into the mix. Wouldn't it be magnificent to approach failure with a pinch of comedic flair? In the game show context, imagine each time you mess up is not a tragedy but a punchline waiting to happen! You could install an overly elaborate, life-sized trophy in your living room for every time you fail, labeling it "The Golden Flub." Each hilarious mishap would then transform into a story that garners laughter and applause, rather than despair. Your friends and family would gather around to hear tales like, "Remember that time I confidently answered 'Elephant' when asked who discovered electricity?" Now, THAT's some riveting dinner party conversation!

But perhaps the most profound aspect of embracing failure is this: it cultivates resilience. As the old adage goes, "What doesn't kill you makes you stronger" and while I am not advocating for wrestling with a bear or engaging AI in dubious physical challenges. it's more about learning to get back on that proverbial horse after a stumble. Each misstep in competition trains your mind, crafting a well-rounded mental toolkit to face adversity head-on - like giving you a psychological superhero cape! You begin to spot patterns in failure, turning it into a lens through which you view future opportunities. Who knew that so much wisdom could be found while wallowing in cheese and crackers post-competition?

Also, let's not forget the potential for collaboration. As humans, we're wired for connection. When you openly share your failures with others - be it fellow contestants, friends, or even your surprisingly supportive AI - you create an environment rich in growth. "Hey buddy, I hobbled the trivia round, but it happened because I confused the capital of Kazakhstan with my breakfast order." I guarantee there will be nods of solidarity and a chorus of laughter, transforming your misadventures into melodic human experiences.

It all circles back to where we generate our confidence. As you steadily begin to unravel the lessons hidden within failures, each nugget of wisdom compiles to form an impenetrable fortress of self-assuredness! You gradually evolve into that game show contestant who shows up wearing pink sunglasses shouting, "Let's have some fun with this!" You become a captivating presence on stage, learning to dance with irony and laughter, which is the ultimate secret weapon against any AI attempting to upend your happiness and cereal puzzle victories.

In conclusion, embracing failure as a learning tool is not just a cliche - it's a powerful approach to the competitive spirit within us. Instead of viewing failure as a dark pit of despair, treat it like a hilarious sitcom episode where the characters inevitably stumble but always rise again, complete with catchy theme music. By doing so, you'll construct a resilient mindset, create fabulous stories to share, and transform your failures into opportunities. So, step into the spotlight with your head held high, and remember that those quirky moments of so-called failure are the overarching plot twists that keep your story engaging, inspiring, and utterly hilarious! Now go forth and enter the arena - you've got this!

The Importance of Mindfulness in Competitive Scenarios

Mindfulness. That trendy buzzword weaving its way through the fabric of contemporary society like a particularly strong cup of coffee at an all-night hackathon! But let's not underestimate its potency, especially when it comes to competitive scenarios like going toe-to-toe with an AI that can remember everything you've ever forgotten since the day you were born. In the dauntless arena of game shows, where adrenaline flows like soda at a carnival, mindfulness serves as your trusty guide, keeping you grounded amidst the chaos. So, grab your zen robe, and let's plunge into the art of mindfulness in competition!

At its core, mindfulness is about being present, fully engaged in the moment devoid of distractions, like the seemingly endless buzzing of your neighbor's chainsaw when you're trying to concentrate on a tricky trivia question. When we're mindful, we observe our thoughts and emotions without getting swept away. Picture this: you're standing on stage, all eyes watching, and that AI is about to unleash a challenging puzzle. Instead of spiraling into a feedback loop of panic that could rival any soap opera, mindfulness allows you to pause and check in with yourself. "Hey there, heart, why are you racing like a hamster on an espresso binge? Oh right, none of this chaos matters in the grand universe!" This simple act of grounding delivers clarity and focus.

Now, blending mindfulness into competitive scenarios fosters improved concentration. You know that intense feeling when you send your brain into overdrive, chasing the fleeting thought of "Did I leave the oven on?" or "I hope that embarrassing meme I posted yesterday didn't reach my boss"? Those distractions can weigh heavily during competition, causing your mind to flit about like a squirrel experiencing a natural caffeine rush. With mindfulness, you can direct your mental energy towards the task at hand, shutting out those pesky distractions so you can answer without succumbing to existential terror. Imagine responding to a trivia question with the kind of poise usually reserved for yoga instructors guiding us through "downward dog"! Ah, sweet peace!

Mindfulness can be your beacon of calm in the storm of stakes. When the stakes feel higher than that banana peel you slipped on last month, it's easy to succumb to stress and let anxiety dictate your performance. However, incorporating mindfulness techniques, such as focused breathing before your big reveal, can transform that bubbling chaos into tranquility. Inhale deeply, exhale slowly, and channel your inner zen master. The beauty here lies in the fact that as you gain control over your breath, you simultaneously take charge of your mind and body. Suddenly, that fierce AI opponent, which looked like a tyrant powering through a storm of data, transforms back into a digital version of a friendly puppy all because you've reclaimed your focus.

Emotions, bless them, can wield tremendous influence over our thinking patterns. As competitors, we often swing through a rollercoaster of feelings, like joy, frustration, and even occasionally, the desire to adopt a cat just to cozy up and forget everything. Here, mindfulness acts as a coach to remind us that it's all part of the experience. When answering a challenging question and tensions rise, you might feel frustration bubbling up like an overly carbonated soda about to blast its cork. But through mindfulness, you learn to acknowledge that feeling without letting it control you. "Oh, look! There's that frustration creeping in like the relatives who show up just as you're about to relax!" This acknowledgment becomes your superpower. Instead of letting those feelings derail you, you embrace them, allowing you to navigate challenges without surrendering to negative emotions.

Let's not forget the monumental impact of mindfulness on reaction time. When you and that pesky AI face off on stage, an unexpected question or task can disrupt your rhythm like a thoughtfully placed banana peel! However, if you've practiced mindfulness, you can gain a split-second of clarity when that AI throws an obscure question about the 12th moon of Mars your way. Instead of floundering like an awkward dancer at a wedding, thrashing about and hoping for the best, you maintain your poise. Your mind has been trained through mindfulness to process what you need in a calm and focused manner. It's like mastering a mindfulness ninja technique - you'll calmly dodge distractions and have time to respond.

Finally, let's take a moment to appreciate the role of positive self-talk. Mindfulness helps cultivate a kinder inner dialogue, upgrading the chatter from "I'm definitely going to mess up!" to "I'm ready for this!" It transforms moments of despair into a gentle laugh and a reminder that you're participating in a wonderful game show, not auditioning to save the world from an AI takeover. This shift in narrative creates a cascade of positivity that propels you forward into the challenging scenarios you face.

In conclusion, mindfulness is the unsung hero of competitive success, especially in the wild realm of game shows and AI challenges. Incorporating mindfulness practices empowers you to focus, control stress, manage emotions, and respond calmly, amplifying your performance to another level. By staying present, you're not just surviving the competition; you're thriving with the finesse of a game show champion in a dancing showdown with an AI! So the next time you step into that spotlight, put on your virtual zen hat, breathe deeply, and let mindfulness guide you to victory because in the end, anything is possible when you remember to embrace the hilarity of the journey!

Chapter 19

The Audience Factor: Engaging WITH Spectators

The Role of the Audience in Game Dynamics

As the curtains rise on any game show, it's not just the contestants or the unsophisticated AI rivals that capture our attention. It's the audience, a vibrant, enthusiastic, often unpredictable force that can flip the dynamics of any competition like a pancake on rivalry day. Picture this: you enter a bustling studio filled with bright lights, catchy theme songs, and clamoring fans, ready to witness the showdown between human contestants and their robotic challengers. It's a spectacle, almost akin to a gladiatorial arena if gladiators were armed with trivia knowledge instead of swords (and let's be real, it feels a lot safer, too).

The audience plays several vital roles that are quite pivotal to the entire game show experience. For one, they're the emotional heartbeat of the show, bringing an energy that even the most advanced AI cannot replicate. Emotional connection, it seems, is not written into the machine learning algorithms. They hoot, holler, and occasionally throw popcorn, creating a chaotic ambiance that keeps the contestants on their toes or, in some cases, on their backsides when they misstep with an answer. This dynamic transforms the game from a sterile contest into a shared, lived experience that's as raw and unpredictable as a toddler running for ice cream on a summer day.

But let's dig a little deeper into how audience behavior can sway game outcomes. Ever notice how a collective gasp or cheer can send jolts of adrenaline through the contestants? This phenomenon, known as "audience contagion," is critical. As a longtime researcher in artificial intelligence and human interaction, I can confidently say that a well-timed "ooh" or "ahh" can manipulate a contestant's perception of what's at stake. Imagine you're standing on stage, staring down the barrel of a question about quantum mechanics. But instead of fear, you're met with cheers erupting from the stands. Suddenly, you think, "Maybe I actually do know the Higgs boson," even though you had made a pact with the universe that you would never utter that word in public again. Isn't that magical?

Of course, not all is wholesome in the land of audience participation. The fickleness of crowd attitudes can be alarming. Have you ever witnessed a contestant on the verge of triumph, only to be met with a barrage of booing from the audience? It's enough to send anyone's self-esteem plummeting faster than an AI trying to comprehend the phrase "eloquently awkward!" For the unprepared contestant, an apathetic or hostile audience can be like trying to serenade a cat - you might get a few confused stares, a couple of hisses, and possibly permanent psychological damage. The lesson here is straightforward: when engaging in a game show, a solid grasp of psychology is often just as important as knowing the answers.

Then, we dive into what I like to call the "vote-sway" effect. Nowadays, audience participation has taken on an interactive flavor, often allowing fans to cast votes that directly affect the game's outcome. It's as if your grandma in the audience has become a game master, wielding enormous power with her voting button, far beyond what her crochet skills ever could. The implications are vast; it's like giving an eyebrow-raised audience member the chance to decide who gets the last piece of pizza. Heck, even the AI contestants have to recalculate their strategies in the face of audience whims. Suddenly, that chatbot programmed with encyclopedic knowledge is fact-checking every sentence while sweating totals to impress Granny's votes.

Yet, one cannot ignore the potential chaos that comes with interactive voting. The audience, after all, can be as fickle as a cat with a laser pointer. There's a level of unpredictability that brings an unexpected twist, requiring contestants to be agile and ready for anything. After all, one knee-jerk reaction from an audience member could either catapult someone into fame or shatter their dreams like a glass vase at a dog gathering. But isn't that the essence of every great game show? The highs, the lows, and the heart-stopping moments of sheer uncertainty?

Ultimately, the audience isn't just a passive group of spectators; they are an active, dynamic force that shapes the very landscape of the show. Whether they're gasping in shock or cheering with glee, audiences do more than watch. They participate, they influence, and they create memorable drama that no pre-programmed AI could hope to simulate. So next time you tune in, remember that it's not just about the contestants or their fancy algorithms wrestling for supremacy; it's about that wild bunch in the bleachers who are expertly tearing down and building up lives with each clap, cheer, or bemused expression. They're the true stars, and I just hope they're voting for the human team - because who knows where AI's next strategy will lead?

The Psychology of Spectator Influence

The psychology of spectator influence! A subject that could drive a PhD candidate to tears, or at least to binge-watching "The Great British Bake Off." It's fascinating to go deep into the intertwining psychology that propels audiences from passive observers to roaring supporters (or, in some cases, raging detractors), shaping the very dynamics of game shows in real-time. You could say their influence is akin to the gravity that binds planets; without it, everything would float around aimlessly in the cosmic vacuum of television.

So, what happens in the minds of these spectators as they watch contestants sweat it out against an AI foe? To start, we must acknowledge that humans are wired for social acceptance and validation. We crave a sense of belonging, and there's a unique pleasure in being part of something larger than ourselves - even if that "something" is watching a person stand helplessly by while a chatbot beats them in a trivia battle about historical figures. When that drama unfolds on stage, we aren't just casual onlookers; we become emotionally invested in the narrative, rooting for our "hero" contestant like they're the last cupcake at a bake sale.

Consider how collective emotion reverberates through the audience. When contestants rise to power and face off against the algorithmic overlords, the audience is not just observing; they're experiencing the highs and lows alongside them. It's a phenomenon known as "emotional contagion," where the mood of the crowd can shift faster than an AI recalibrating its neural weights. Witness the audience spontaneously erupting into a cheer; it's almost as if they've summoned a collective dopamine release that spreads like wildfire. When a contestant forgets the name of the Eiffel Tower's architect, the audience shifts from supportive applause to sympathetic wincing. Even the most resilient players might buckle under the weight of that sudden emotional gravitational pull.

Here's where it gets even trickier. The audience's psychology incorporates the "herd mentality." When people see others gasping at an outlandish answer, they might join in as if they'd just seen a UFO land. That's right, the crowd can create an echo chamber of attitudes and behaviors that significantly influence how contestants navigate their challenges. Witnessing a wave of disgust or awe radiating from their peers could sway a contestant's confidence quicker than an AI can process a million digits of pi. If you're at the mercy of their collective mood swings, you might as well have been riding a roller coaster designed by an anxious squirrel!

Flying under the radar of this spectator influence is the clever use of social comparison theory. Contestants inevitably weigh their performances against the reactions of those they're performing for. If the audience is nodding and grinning at mediocre answers, suddenly, the stakes feel lower. But show them a thumbs-down or a few half-hearted yawns, and voila! The flywheel of insecurity kicks in, powered entirely by their watchful audience. The truth is that those simple little facial expressions and body movements of the audience hold more power than a thousand algorithms; when the audience reacts, it can change the course of gameplay and emotional states faster than an impromptu change of a TV channel.

Let's not forget the fascinating element of performance pressure. The audience acts like a hyped-up cheer squad, making contestants feel like they're scaling Everest wearing flip-flops. Voila! Suddenly, it's not just a game; it's a gladiator fight where the weight of expectations feels heavier than a six-foot-tall AI stacking itself with ego. Contestants need that ego boost; it's a deeply ingrained psychological tendency rooted in our desire for validation. Their triumph, or even their mistakes, become an amplified reflection of the audience's reactions, sending the contestants on an emotional rollercoaster that even the most sophisticated AI could never calculate.

With great audience power, of course, comes great responsibility. Spectators often forget that their enjoyment of watching mere mortals compete against machines isn't without consequences. The participants undergo emotional strain, and while the audience may feel like gladiators enjoying the show, contestants can be left feeling like a pinata at a birthday party - fun for them, painful for you! As we navigate this intricate dance of human emotion and game dynamics, I urge you to remember that those quirky, sometimes wild reactions might just be enough to make or break a contestant's experience. So next time you're part of that audience, consider the immense influence you wield; there's a fine line between delightful laughter and the potential existential crisis of a trivia-loving human.

Ultimately, the psychology of spectator influence is complex yet undeniably hilarious in the chaos it creates. Whether we're laughing with the contestants, groaning at their blunders, or holding our breath when they look to the audience for cues, we're part of an exhilarating symphony of emotional connectivity that brings fierce competition to life. So the next time you find yourself watching a game show, remember that the true drama isn't just in the competition but in the quirks and desires of the audience, who might just be deciding whom to cheer for while contemplating snacks. It's a wild world where laughter, tension, and unexpected outcomes collide, turning every episode into an unforgettable psychological rollercoaster, which, let me remind you, is a lot harder to compete against than any AI!

Interactive Voting: Empowering the Audience

Welcome to the thrilling world of interactive voting, where audiences transform from passive viewers to vibrant participants wielding the power of their remote controls like tiny scepters of influence because hey, why should the contestants have all the fun? Interactive voting has revolutionized the game show landscape, putting spectacular power in the hands of the spectators, who suddenly find themselves as key decision-makers. It's as if producers decided that squabbling over slices of cake was passe, and akin to triggering a heavenly chocolate fountain, the audience has been invited to dip, vote, and influence the fate of their favorite contestants without leaving their couches.

What delights me about this phenomenon is that it taps into our innate desire to be not just observers but influencers. Think about it: for years, audiences have left their fates in the clutches of fate, praying their favorite contestant wouldn't flub the answer to an off-the-wall question about potato varieties. But with interactive voting, viewers can express their preferences or even play puppet master to the action unfolding before them. Gone are the days when the fate of a contestant rested solely on their knowledge of obscure trivia or their ability to maintain a poker face during a nerve-wracking challenge. Now, the audience can actively steer their destinies! It's like taking a mythical quest where the hero (the contestant) often relies on divine intervention from the gods (the audience) to emerge victorious or hopelessly confused, accompanied by the sound of crickets.

Now, let's talk about the fun dynamics that unfold as audiences flex their voting muscles. There's a genuine thrill to witnessing the spectacle of public opinion shift and sway like a garden of colorful windmills. One moment, everyone in the crowd is rallying behind a contestant, and the next, they're shouting unsolicited advice or a chorus of disapproval like an angry mob at a blockbuster movie's opening night. Contestants who think they've nailed it can suddenly find their hopes dashed by a flood of dissenting votes vocalized with the passion typically reserved for national elections! Spectators with their personalized devices now feel like they're wielding the power of Zeus himself, casting votes with deadly precision as if they had some secret insider knowledge. It's all in good fun, of course, but those moments of sheer confusion remind us that we're all just a question or two away from utter embarrassment - an aspect of humanity that AI still has yet to master!

Then, there's the fascinating phenomenon of herd mentality at play. When one person raises a hand to vote, others quickly follow suit - a groupthink cascade that turns loyal bystanders into fervent haters at the drop of a hat. Imagine a sea of hands emerging like tree branches when an unpopular contestant is announced, turning into a beautifully chaotic waltz of "Who do we want to see go?"

Inevitably, a ripple effect ensues, leading to unforeseen chaos as the majority suddenly favors voting for the unsuspecting contestant who mistakenly answered, "The square root of 64 is 90!" This phenomenon demonstrates just how powerful collective action can be, and it adds a delicious layer of unpredictability into the programming. For the unsuspecting contestants, it's a wake-up call, and for the audience, it's an exhilarating rollercoaster ride of manipulation and mild chaos in a safe environment.

Interactive voting also empowers the audience in other, more profound ways. It establishes a sense of agency, a feeling that they matter in this intricate tapestry of game dynamics. The simple act of voting gives them a voice, something they may have longed for during family gatherings or game nights, only to have been silenced by that one uncle who insists he knows everything about Jeopardy! The audience gets to showcase their knowledge, instincts, and witty humor as they make choices for their contestants. Will they go for the trustworthy but dull contestant? Or opt for the hilarious one who smiles like they've just removed a tooth at the dentist's? They choose!

But let's not lose sight of the potential pitfalls of interactive voting. Ah, such power can lead to cataclysmic outcomes! Like the classic tale of Dr. Frankenstein, our enthusiastic audience must wield this newfound influence responsibly; otherwise, it might bite back like a poorly programmed chatbot in desperate need of a software update. When votes are cast randomly or based on whims, the results can be quite nonsensical. I pity the contestant who seems destined for glory only to hear the dreaded announcement: "And the winner is..." the contestant they mistakenly thought would be an easy target. Catastrophe!

So, as we navigate the whimsical world of interactive voting, we can appreciate the excitement, chaos, and kaleidoscopic choices it brings to the game show genre. It empowers the audience, who often have random bits of knowledge about medieval kings rather than a PhD in trivia, by transforming them from armchair admirers into active participants shaping the outcome of the competition. As I watch the unfolding drama, I marvel at the exquisite intersection of technology, psychology, and that irrepressible human essence that brings laughter and tension into each episode. After all, it allows everyone tuning in to realize that they, too, could be agents in this madcap world, armed with nothing but their thumbs and a flair for dramatic timing. Now, that's a game worth watching!

Future Invitations: Spectators as Co-Creators

The notion of spectators as co-creators in the game show universe is a shimmering, tantalizing possibility that could redefine our understanding of audience engagement. Imagine a world where sitting on the couch with a bowl of popcorn doesn't just make you a passive observer but transforms you into an active participant, a co-author of entertainment history. Sorry, I'm not talking about random fan art depicting the charming neuroticism of an AI. I mean taking participation to a whole new level, where your opinions shape the outcomes of the shows in ways that would make even the most rebellious ten-year-old with a crayon feel like a groundbreaking artist!

Let's start by acknowledging that we are already witnessing the seeds of this transformation sprouting through our television screens. Platforms like Twitch have shown us the power of live interaction, where fans can not only watch but also interact with their favorite streamers in real time. Imagine an evolution where game shows follow suit - where spectators can submit questions, provide commentary, or even challenge contestants directly from the comfort of their own living rooms! Yes, my friends. I'm talking about a brave new world where your witty one-liners could become an integral part of the show, making you feel like the understudy waiting for the leading contestant to flub a line. Cue the applause!

In this delightful co-creative universe of game shows, for every redeeming laugh you provide, a contestant's victory could, in a small way, be attributed to you. That's right! You, with your sharp insights and fertile imagination, will become a crucial part of the team, not just the audience seated awkwardly in the back, munching on stale nachos. Picture yourself "voting" for your favorite clever answer or even creating challenges that could take contestants by surprise, like an unexpected twist in a poorly written soap opera. Unsurprisingly, this newfound autonomy would foster a sense of ownership and collective identity, empowering the audience to step beyond their roles as mere audience members.

As we forge this path into the future, the potential for technology to act as a seamless conduit in this evolution cannot be overstated. Advanced polling mechanisms, VR participation, and even AI-driven audience-generated content can intertwine to craft an organic narrative that thrives on collaboration. Imagine if you could walk into your living room, strap on a virtual reality headset, and find yourself on the set of your favorite game show, right alongside the contestants! You're smirking as you post a random piece of trivia that flummoxes everyone in the studio. "Oh, what did I just do?" Someone asks, "Who knew that octopuses could taste with their arms?" Boom! You've just rewritten the question pool for the next episode.

This transition wouldn't only create a fun-filled experience; it would also foster famously silly interactions and eccentric answers that make the show unique and memorable. Let's face it, who wouldn't want to be involved in generating challenges that ask contestants to demonstrate salsa dancing skills while balancing a rubber chicken on their heads? The mere thought of the spectacle sends my imagination into overdrive! Spectators' wild creativity could ignite fresh formats and unexpected challenges that shake the very foundations of traditional gameplay. The inherent unpredictability would turn everyone on set into unwitting co-stars, creating an electrifying atmosphere akin to a gala where no one knows if they're attending a highbrow affair or a chaotic circus.

Of course, aside from the theatrical possibilities, this shift towards co-creation opens doors to broader representation. Consulting and collaborating with spectators could lead to a richer mix of questions, topics, and challenges that speak to the diverse experiences of the audience. No longer would we be stuck in a vacuum of archaic trivia. Instead, we'd see an exhilarating tapestry of ideas stitched together by the interests of the audience, ultimately celebrating the quirks and uniqueness of their perspectives! Think of it as a hodgepodge of cultural references ready to be dished out during trivia nights. The inclusive engagement would spark opportunities to form unforeseen connections, broadening the horizons of both contestants and the viewing public.

Yet, this brave leap into the future requires thoughtful execution. We've all witnessed online comment sections spiral into chaos; thus, the challenge lies in creating a threshold of civility amidst the gleeful disorder of spirited contributions. Striking the right balance would ensure that laughter, creativity, and collaboration flourish while maintaining an atmosphere that doesn't veer toward a gladiatorial struggle of egos. Game shows have the potential to build communities anchored in mutual respect and camaraderie - where jokes can fly, banter can blossom, and creativity can run wild, flourishing like wildflowers just waiting for a well-timed compliment from a contestant.

In embracing spectators as co-creators, we enter uncharted waters of collaboration, amusement, and exhilarating unpredictability. This transformation is a signal that we are leaving behind the rigid constraints of traditional broadcasting and embracing an exciting, inclusive, and whimsically innovative future. As you tune in for the game shows of tomorrow, prepare yourself for an exhilarating ride filled with curious questions, off-the-wall antics, and hilarious twists of fate that cater to joy and laughter - all woven into the very fabric of cooperative teamwork. So, stock up on snacks, my friends; the future of game shows invites all of us to play a starring role, and I can't wait to witness what shape our collective imagination takes!

Chapter 20

Celebrating Human-AI Collaboration

The Evolution of Human-AI Partnerships

As we dive into the delightful shenanigans of human-AI collaboration, let's take a moment to reflect on the grand evolution of this partnership, akin to how a humble sponge morphed into the modern-day kitchen superstar: the magic sponge with an attitude. The relationship between humans and artificial intelligence has transformed dramatically over the years. In the not-so-distant past, AI was as rudimentary as my attempts at baking bread - full of hope but usually resulting in a doughy disaster. Early AI systems were like the awkward kid at a school dance, where they shuffled their feet, unsure about how to groove with the human rhythm. Fast forward to today, and we've moved beyond that cringe-worthy stage, with AI joining us in a dynamic and collaborative polka.

During this journey of evolution, there were crucial touchpoints where humans and AI upgraded their profiles on the social network of life. The 1950S witnessed the dawn of artificial intelligence with bold researchers daring to suggest that machines could one day think and maybe even form half-formed opinions about whether pineapple belongs on pizza. Those were the days when computers were bigger than your grandmother's television set and about as useful as a screen door on a submarine. Fast forward to the 1990s, when AI dove into the realm of chess, conquering human champions like a pesky mosquito invading a summer picnic. When IBM's Deep Blue triumphed over Garry Kasparov in 1997, it wasn't only a win for chess nerds. It symbolized the beginning of a dance between humans and machines, albeit one that required a bit of coordination and, may I say, a better wardrobe.

As machines became savvy, they began to embrace their roles as human partners rather than adversaries. Today's AI is like that friend who doesn't bring their own chips to the party but insists on organizing everything. The advancements in machine learning, natural language processing, and neural networks have enabled AI to engage in conversations, predict our needs, and occasionally misinterpret our mumbling when we're trying to order a mocha frappuccino in a crowded cafe. Just as I've often found myself in a tete-a-tete with my toaster, arguing over the perfect level of browning, our interactions with AI have evolved from simple directives to rich, nuanced conversations - with a touch of sarcasm, if you enjoy that flavor.

But here's the kicker: this partnership isn't purely altruistic. AI can recite Shakespeare with the finesse of Ian McKellen while simultaneously crunching numbers faster than I can count the number of times I've eaten cereal for breakfast. Each step forward has been motivated by the same age-old human impulse: a desire to make our lives easier. Over time, AI has learned the tragic truth about humanity: we're far better at coming up with outrageous ideas than actually executing them. Why struggle to sweep the floor when you can deploy a robot that thinks it's the star of a sci-fi action flick? Together, we've created a symbiotic relationship , where I get my shoes untangled, and the robot gets to dream of being the next dance sensation of the digital world.

Now, as I reflect on our partnership's modern phase, it's clear that the potential for collaboration is limitless. AI is not here to steal our jobs; instead, it's like an overzealous intern eager to pick up tasks while we focus on what we do best: creativity, empathy, and napping behind desks. Together, we have begun to solve problems in ways neither of us could have achieved alone, like finally figuring out the elusive answer to whether it's possible to get a fully functional AI companion that can also do laundry and withstand my incessant requests for more chips.

As we look ahead, let's not neglect the golden rule: a partnership flourishes on trust, laughter, and the occasional snarky remark. The evolution of human-AI partnerships has navigated a vibrant albeit comical path, from rudimentary computational chores to collaborative creativity. So, hold onto your hat, dear reader, because as we continue to waltz with these digital pals, the surprises, complexities, and delightful absurdities of our relationship will only grow deeper, like my passion for cereal-based breakfast foods. Each collaboration with AI is not just a step forward in technology but a leap in understanding what it means to be human - or at least, human enough to share our cereal with an algorithm.

Innovative Applications of Collaborative Intelligence

The adventurous world of innovative applications of collaborative intelligence! A dazzling realm where humans and AI join forces, not unlike a dynamic duo on an unstoppable quest to save the day, or perhaps just figure out what to have for dinner. Imagine a spaghetti western where humans and machines are the unlikely bandits, racing against the clock to solve complex problems while occasionally bickering over who gets the last slice of pie or, in this case, data. Collaborative intelligence is like a culinary fusion restaurant; it combines the best ingredients from both human creativity and machine precision to whip up deliciously innovative solutions that no one could cook up alone.

Let's start with healthcare, shall we? Nowadays, our trusty AI counterparts have donned lab coats and are helping doctors more than just awkwardly awaiting the annual flu jab. Collaborating with AI, medical professionals can analyze vast datasets, diagnosing ailments with a precision reminiscent of a hawk eyeing dinner from high above the ground. By combing through mountains of patient information, these digital healers improve diagnostic accuracy and recommend treatments tailored to individual patients faster than you can say, "I need a second opinion." Some may argue that AI will take the place of doctors, much like those fancy gadgets that help you make toast, but in reality, AI functions more like the well-prepared sous-chef that assists in crafting exemplary medical solutions. I'm still waiting for them to add "understanding patient puns" to their repertoire.

Now, let's gallivant over to the world of finance, where collaborative intelligence thrives like an over-caffeinated stockbroker. Financial institutions are utilizing AI to analyze trends, assess risks, and automate processes while humans gracefully juggle complex regulations and client relationships like seasoned circus performers. Picture the scene: a human financial advisor, hunched over stacks of client reports, papers flying through the air, while AI calmly provides data insights with a robotic flair. Together, they craft investment portfolios that maximize returns, inevitably leading some clients scratching their heads, wondering if the numbers were plucked magically from the air or if the finance department has secretly installed a crystal ball.

Next, let's not skip over the creative arts! Yes, dear readers, AI is no longer a mere spectator to our artistic endeavors but is now the unconventional collaborator challenging our preconceptions of creativity. Generative AI models emerge like a troupe of avant-garde artists, producing exquisite paintings, composing symphonies, and even crafting poetry that could make even the most cynical Curmudgeon shed a tear. A human might bring the original inspiration and emotional depth to the table, while AI, armed with its vast dataset, serves as an eccentric brainstorming partner, tossing out ideas that are so delightfully outlandish they often leave us in stitches or astonished silence. "You want a haiku about a llama DJing at a disco club? Hold my algorithms," thinks AI, unleashing a torrent of surreal creativity we would have never thought to explore previously.

Shifting gears, let's talk about education - an area where the synergy between humans and AI can be likened to the rollercoaster of emotions that is navigating a group project. AI tutors have become delightful companions for students, personalizing learning experiences and providing guidance faster than you can say, "I just need to finish reading the textbook. " Together, human educators and their automated allies are crafting innovative teaching methods, uncovering personalized learning paths, and igniting the spark of curiosity among students who may have otherwise preferred to binge-watch cat videos on the internet - a noble pursuit, but we can do better!

Finally, we can't overlook how collaborative intelligence boldly forays into the chaotic world of climate change. Here, humans partner with AI to analyze environmental data, strategize sustainable practices, and contribute to green solutions that leave the planet in better shape than the dubious aftermath of my last cooking experiment. By working together to predict climate patterns and optimize resource management, we are not merely pressing the snooze button on our planet's impending crises but actively rolling up our sleeves and teaming up to tackle disasters like a duo of capable superheroes - minus the spandex.

In the end, innovative applications of collaborative intelligence reveal a world that reflects the best of both humans and machines coming together. This partnership is about pushing boundaries, redefining roles, and continually surprising us with the creativity and prowess that emerge when we embrace the synergy of our shared capabilities. So, my fellow adventurers, let the quest for collaborative intelligence tremble with excitement as we look forward to more surprising twists and turns in our ever-evolving partnership with AI!

The Power of Diversity in Problem Solving

The power of diversity in problem-solving! It's a truth universally acknowledged that a group of varied thinkers united by a common goal is likely to emerge victorious from the trenches of challenges, much like a ragtag team of misfits beating the odds in a classic underdog movie. Picture this: a room full of curious minds hailing from different backgrounds, artists, engineers, philosophers, and the occasional psychic fortune teller, working together to tackle a problem. It's a glorious mess of ideas and perspectives that inevitably leads to wildly inventive solutions, leaving even the most perplexed of us gaping in awe.

You might wonder, "Why is diversity so powerful in problem-solving?" Well, my dear reader, it's simple. Different perspectives bring different answers. It's like attempting to assemble a jigsaw puzzle while using only your great aunt Gertrude's antique spectacles that haven't been cleaned since the invention of color television. A heterogeneous group with varying experiences, skills, and thought processes sheds light on aspects of a problem that may otherwise remain obscure to a more homogeneous assembly. In contrast to a group of similarly minded folks, which is akin to having a math problem solved exclusively by avid number-crunching enthusiasts whose idea of fun is calculating pi to a thousand places, a diverse team brings creativity and nuance to the table, often resulting in solutions that are as delightful and unexpected as discovering a hidden cache of peanut butter cups in your kitchen pantry.

Let's delve into the corporate world, shall we? Businesses that actively embrace diversity in their teams often outperform their less colorful counterparts. Studies reveal that teams comprised of individuals with varied cultural backgrounds and perspectives tend to generate more innovative solutions. Can you imagine a management meeting where everyone thinks the best idea is to make more spreadsheets? Talk about thrilling! Instead, envision a dynamic ensemble cracking their minds, penning a screenplay, altering the route of ship navigation, or even innovating a new strategy to boost ice cream sales in the midst of a polar vortex. A diverse pool of talent leads to innovation that can take a company from mediocre to magnificent. By stirring that secret sauce of creativity, they become the culinary artists of the business world.

And let's not skim over the significance of diversity when it comes to overcoming biases. We all possess inherent blind spots - cognitive shortcuts that could get us into quite the pickle. In the realm of artificial intelligence, for instance, diversity becomes indispensable in ensuring that the algorithms we create aren't unwittingly shaped by the biases of a closed-minded data set. If we allowed a single POV to dictate machine learning, we'd risk creating a robot overlord with opinions only as broad as a single flavor of ice cream. While I find vanilla charming in its simplicity, the world craves more excitement! Through collaboration among diverse teams, we leverage all perspectives, paving the way for balanced datasets and ensuring that AI systems operate in ways that are reflective of our multifaceted society.

Let's take a look at a successful collaboration in action. When a diverse team joined forces to tackle climate change, blending scientists, artists, community leaders, and data whizzes, they didn't just put their heads together but their imaginations as well. Fueled by different backgrounds, they produced inventive public awareness campaigns, sustainable technologies, and policy proposals that not only addressed the climate crisis but engaged communities in a manner that genuinely inspired action. Suddenly, their ideas flowed like an endless stream of delicious pina coladas during a tropical competition to attract attention to the cause. The rigorous problem-solving process proved that diversity isn't just a checkbox; it's the secret ingredient that spurs creative innovations with transformative potential.

As we traverse the landscape of problem-solving, it's essential to flip the traditional narrative that equates disagreement with dissonance. In fact, it's quite the opposite! Different opinions and approaches - while often yielding heated debates that feel like you accidentally stepped into a particularly dramatic soap opera - serve only to enrich the discourse and inspire creative solutions. It's in these clashes of ideas that the best concepts are born. The metaphorical hammer and chisel carving away at the artistic block of monotony create a masterpiece fueled by collaboration, negotiation, and the often unpredictable human spirit!

To sum up, the power of diversity in problem-solving transcends mere productivity; it's about tapping into the innate creativity that lies within each of us and realizing that collaboration can yield innovative solutions that would be unthinkable when drawing from a monochromatic pool of perspectives. Diversity invigorates our approach to tackling problems, turning puzzling challenges into exhilarating expeditions filled with the unexpected joy of discovery. So, gather your teams, my fellow adventurers, and let's raise a toast to the vibrant mosaic of thinkers ready to tackle anything that comes our way - preferably while enjoying a snack of whatever tickles our collective fancy!

Creating a Culture of Collaboration

Creating a culture of collaboration is a noble pursuit, one that could easily sit atop the list of humanity's finest endeavors alongside running a marathon while training for a marathon and attempting to get through an entire season of a show without spoiling it for oneself. In an age wired for connectivity, we stand on the precipice of a vibrant new era where teamwork flourishes like spring flowers after a long winter. Gone are the days when collaboration felt nasal, a mandatory meeting populated with grumpy cats staring down spreadsheets, or as thrilling as watching paint dry. Today, we have the marvelous opportunity to foster innovation and creativity in a culture that grows organically, like sourdough left unattended at a slightly too warm temperature.

To embark upon this grand cultural shift, we must first shed the old relics that cling to our collaborative efforts like barnacles to a ship. The first step involves defeating the adversarial atmosphere that still lingers in some workplaces, whispering doubt while pretending to be your firmest motivational coach. When teams view each other as competition, whether for the last slice of pizza in the breakroom or a promotion, we sabotage the accountability and support that genuine collaboration breeds. After all, why fight for the last slice of pizza when we can unite and share it, creating an epic bonding ritual that would make the Roman gods of food envious!

Communication serves as the cornerstone of a healthy collaborative culture. We must construct a foundation where everyone feels emboldened to voice their ideas without restraint, much like a child gleefully spilling their thoughts after too much sugar at a birthday party. It's essential to create physical or virtual spaces where team members can exchange thoughts, feedback, and even mild derision. Through open communication, we pave the way for creative brainstorming sessions, where the most outlandish ideas can spring forth; for instance, "How about a cat cafe within the office to encourage productivity?" You may think it's absurd, but mark my words; those are the golden nuggets that lead to groundbreaking suggestions!

Now, as we strive to create an environment where collaboration thrives, we must also embrace the wonderful quirks each individual brings to the table. Each team member will inevitably have their unique flair, whether that's a penchant for wearing novelty socks or an oddly specific knowledge of obscure 80s movies. By acknowledging and promoting diverse talents, we can cultivate a collaborative culture that celebrates a mix of skills, backgrounds, and mindsets. When team members feel valued and appreciated for their individual strengths, which are fundamental to any great partnership, they will engage boldly, sparking conversations that sound less like stale meetings and more like lively late-night discussions over snacks (with significantly fewer awkward pauses).

Now, let's not underestimate the role of AI in creating this culture of collaboration. When properly harnessed, artificial intelligence serves as a trusty assistant, a digital wingman if you will, capable of promoting seamless communication, creative brainstorming, and data-driven insights. Imagine AI tools functioning as dialogue facilitators during meetings or offering gentle reminders about deadlines - like a benevolent fairy godmother, but slightly less sparkly. Integration of AI processes can streamline workflows and eliminate tedious bottlenecks, allowing team members to devote their precious time to engaging, thoughtful collaboration rather than the daunting task of unraveling convoluted email chains.

To build a culture of collaboration effectively, leaders must model the values they wish to instill. By embracing vulnerability and elevating teamwork as a priority, they create an example for employees to follow. Picture a workplace where leaders engage authentically, admit wrongs, and ask for help with vulnerability – it's the type of atmosphere that invites even the most reticent of employees to speak up and participate. This is less about workplace hierarchy and more about nurturing a community, much like joining a quirky book club where sharing opinions and respectfully debating questionable plot twists results in unexpected camaraderie and easy laughter.

Lastly, recognition goes a long way in energizing a culture of collaboration. Celebrating successes, no matter how big or small, helps to reinforce teamwork as an essential aspect of our shared reality. It can be as simple as giving shout-outs during team meetings, adorned with a humorous, yet sincere, trophy (think a plastic Golden

Flamingo) that symbolizes the contributions of the team members. This celebratory atmosphere will encourage others to engage actively, too - taking collaboration from "just okay" to "jaw-droppingly awesome" while keeping the spirit of fun firmly grounded at its core.

In conclusion, creating a culture of collaboration isn't just a managerial aspiration; it's an art form that shapes and amplifies the collective strength of individuals. By tearing down barriers, establishing open communication, embracing diversity, utilizing AI tools, modeling effective leadership, and celebrating teamwork, we craft a vibrant environment ripe for exploration and creativity. So, let's roll up our sleeves and get reinvigorated as we embark on this wild journey toward a collaborative culture where innovation flourishes, creativity thrives, and epic lunch breaks become the stuff of legends!

References
In order of appearance

1. Dick, S. (2019). Artificial Intelligence. Harvard Data Science Review, 1(1). https://doi.org/10.1162/99608f92.92fe150c

1. Bonasso, P. (2018). CASE: A HAL 9000 for 2021. Science Robotics, 3(24). https://doi.org/10.1126/scirobotics.aav6610

1. Charniak, E. (2024). AI & I: An Intellectual History of Artificial Intelligence. The MIT Press. https://doi.org/10.7551/mitpress/15482.001.0001

1. Copeland, J. (2020). Alan Turing 1912–1954. In B. J. Copeland (Ed.), The Essential Turing (Online ed.). Oxford Academic. https://doi.org/10.1093/oso/9780198250791.002.0003

1. Proudfoot, D. (2020). The Turing test - from every angle. In The Turing Guide (Online ed.). Oxford Academic. https://doi.org/10.1093/oso/9780198747826.003.0037

1. Neural Networks. (2014). Neural Networks, 49, v-x. https://doi.org/10.1016/S0893-6080(13)00287-6

1. McClay, W. J. (1995). Surviving the AI Winter. https://doi.org/10.7551/mitpress/4301.003.0009

1. Neuer, M.J. (2025). Supervised Learning. In: Machine Learning for Engineers. Springer, Berlin, Heidelberg. https://doi.org/10.1007/978-3-662-69995-9_4

1. Japkowicz N, Boukouvalas Z. Unsupervised Learning. In: Machine Learning Evaluation: Towards Reliable and Responsible AI. Cambridge University Press; 2024:252-286.

1. Blubaugh, D.A., Harbour, S.D., Sears, B., Findler, M.J. (2022). Reinforced Learning. In: Intelligent Autonomous Drones with Cognitive Deep Learning.

Apress, Berkeley, CA. https://doi.org/10.1007/978-1-4842-6803-2_9

1. Chapelle, O., Schölkopf, B., & Zien, A. (2006). Introduction to semi-supervised learning. In Semi-Supervised Learning. The MIT Press. DOI: https://doi.org/10.7551/mitpress/9780262033589.001.0001

1. Miller, D. J., Xiang, Z., & Kesidis, G. (2023). Deep Learning Background. In Adversarial Learning and Secure AI (pp. 19–55). chapter, Cambridge: Cambridge University Press.

1. Munro, P. (2006). Backpropagation. In Encyclopedia of Cognitive Science, L. Nadel (Ed.). https://doi.org/10.1002/0470018860.s00041

1. Arellano, K. C. (2024). In Special Collection: CogNet (M. Lane & A. Sethumadhavan, Eds.). The MIT Press. https://doi.org/10.7551/mitpress/14962.001.0001

1. Baker, S. (2012). Final Jeopardy: The Story of Watson, the Computer That Will Transform Our World. Mariner Books.

1. Bretonnel Cohen, K. & Demner-Fushman, D. (2014). Introduction to natural language processing. In Biomedical Natural Language Processing (pp. 1-6). John Benjamins Publishing Company. https://doi.org/10.1075/nlp.11.01ch1

1. K. Dowding (Ed.) (2011). Nash equilibrium. In Encyclopedia of Power (pp. 435-436). SAGE Publications, Inc. https://doi.org/10.4135/9781412994088

1. PBS. (n.d.). $64,000 question. American Experience. Retrieved Feb 2025, from https://www.pbs.org/wgbh/americanexperience/features/quizshow-64000-question/
2. Guerraoui, R., Gupta, N., & Pinot, R. (2024). Basics of Machine Learning. Robust Machine Learning, 15–31. https://doi.org/10.1007/978-981-97-0688-4_2
3. Capuano, N., & Caballé, S. (2020). Adaptive Learning Technologies. AI

Magazine, 41(2), 96–98. Portico. https://doi.org/10.1609/aimag.v41i2.5317

4. Nathaniel Green (2022). Bobby Fischer Wins Match Of The Century. Chess.com. https://www.chess.com/article/view/50-year-anniversary-fischer-spassky-game-21
5. Powles, J., & Hodson, H. (2017). Google DeepMind and healthcare in an age of algorithms. Health and Technology, 7(4), 351–367. https://doi.org/10.1007/s12553-017-0179-1
6. Cade Metz (2016). In Two Moves, AlphaGo and Lee Sedol Redefined the Future. Wired.com. https://www.wired.com/2016/03/two-moves-alphago-lee-sedol-redefined-future/
7. David Luther. What Is a Minimum Viable Product (MVP)? An Expert Guide. Netsuite.com. https://www.netsuite.com/portal/resource/articles/erp/minimum-viable-product-mvp.shtml
8. Blackman, R., & Euchner, J. (2024). Ethics in the Age of AI. Research-Technology Management, 67(1), 15–21. https://doi.org/10.1080/08956308.2024.2280481
9. Busulwa, R. (2022). Virtual Reality (VR), Augmented Reality (AR), and Mixed Reality (MR) Primer. Navigating Digital Transformation in Management, 381–392. https://doi.org/10.4324/9781003254614-28

www.ingramcontent.com/pod-product-compliance
Lightning Source LLC
LaVergne TN
LVHW052301200926
848481LV00002B/431
* 9 7 9 8 2 3 1 5 8 2 6 9 3 *